Art of Dealing With Two Faced People

FLIPPING THE SCRIPT ON FRIENDS, FAMILY AND CO-WORKERS

LARRY JAY LEVINE

Art of Dealing With Two Faced People
Copyright © 2025 Larry Jay Levine
All rights reserved.

This book is a work of nonfiction based on the author's opinions, research, and personal experiences. The content herein is intended for informational purposes only and should not be construed as legal advice. While the author and publisher have made every effort to ensure the accuracy and completeness of the information presented, they make no guarantees and disclaim all liability for any errors, omissions, or outcomes resulting from the use of this book.

Legal Disclaimer:
The author and publisher are not lawyers. The strategies, insights, and opinions presented in this book are for informational purposes only and are not a substitute for professional legal advice. Readers are strongly advised to consult a licensed attorney for any legal concerns or questions related to their specific circumstances. By using the information in this book, you agree that the author and publisher will not be held liable for any outcomes resulting from its application.

First Edition
Printed in the United States of America

Publisher Information:
World Crime Media
New York, NY
For inquiries contact worldcrimemedia@pactel.net

ISBN: 979-8-9921484-3-5

Additional Notes:
All names, dates, and specific details in any examples or case studies presented have been altered to protect the identities of those involved. Any resemblance to actual persons, living or dead, is purely coincidental unless otherwise stated.

Books by Larry Levine

Released Titles

- **Crimes That Never Happened: Beating Federal Conspiracies**
  A sharp and strategic guide to dismantling the myths and manipulations behind federal conspiracy charges.
- **Prison Politics 101**
  An unfiltered exposé of the hidden power structures, manipulation tactics, and survival strategies inside America's prison system.
- **Cookinn in the Clink**
  A bold and entertaining journey through the culinary creativity of inmates who turned the worst prison food into something worth remembering.
- **The Art of Dealing with Two-Faced People** –
  You're holding it. If you didn't learn something from this book, you weren't paying attention.

Coming Soon

- **Lies My Lawyer Told Me: Volume One – Prelude to Justice**
  (Coming March 2025)
  The first in a two-part series exposing the lies, failures, and backroom deals that define the justice system.
- **Lies My Lawyer Told Me: Volume Two – The Courtroom Conspiracy**
  The sequel that digs deeper into the systemic corruption from trial to sentencing.

- **Mind Over Machine: A Rebel's Guide to Beating the Poly**
  A fearless and practical handbook for mastering and outsmarting the polygraph test.
- **The Art of Perjury: Mastering the Witness Stand**
  Courtroom strategies how to weaponize testimony and win the battle on the witness stand.

Acknowledgments & Dedications

Dedication

To every lying, backstabbing, manipulative bastard I've ever met—

Thank you.

Without your bullshit, this book wouldn't exist. Without your betrayals, I wouldn't have learned to see through people like you in under five seconds. And without your attempts to drag me down, I wouldn't have climbed higher just to spite you.

You tried to take me out, but all you did was make me sharper.

So this one's for you—enjoy reading about yourselves.

Acknowledgments

A normal author would use this space to thank their loved ones and supporters. But let's be honest, this isn't a normal book.

So instead, I'll acknowledge:

- **The Fake Friends** who showed me exactly how two-faced people operate in the wild. Without your insincere smiles and behind-the-scenes betrayal, I wouldn't be an expert at sniffing out bullshit from a mile away.

- **The Business Partners Who Turned Into Snakes**—your greed, jealousy, and lack of integrity turned out to be the best business lesson I ever got (for free).
- **The Ex-Wife Who Played the Victim Like a Professional**—I learned more about manipulation from watching you twist reality than I ever did from studying actual con artists.
- **The Family Members Who Proved Blood Doesn't Mean Loyalty**—your backstabbing was impressive, but your predictability was pathetic. Thanks for reinforcing that trust is earned, not given.
- **The Federal Prison System**—for providing a decade-long crash course in human deception, manipulation, and survival. You housed some of the best manipulators in the game, and I took notes.
- **And finally, my readers**—if you're reading this, chances are you've dealt with your fair share of two-faced assholes too. Consider this book your weapon of choice. Use it well.

And to the manipulators who think they're slick—**I see you.**

My Daily Writing Companion Hazel

"Crazy Hazy" is a purebred purple tongue Chow Chow that my wife Letecia and I rescued when she was a puppy just before Covid. If she's not busying playing or destroying her toys, she's constantly busting my balls banging on the door demanding to be let in or out, and can be found nearby as I write, trying to charm more nummies from me!

Introduction

Mastering Dealing with Two-Faced Bastards

Hi, it's Larry Levine, your favorite no-bullshit, sarcastic author. This is my fourth book, and let me tell you, this one's been simmering for two decades. I started writing it back in 2003, during my ten-year stint in federal prison, surrounded by every type of **manipulative** asshole you can imagine. Since my release in 2007, I've made it my mission to pull back the curtain on lies and the general bullshit people pull. You might've seen me on CNN, Fox News, or maybe even flipping through Court TV or Inside Edition. I've been featured in newspapers and magazines around the world, and if you know me, you know I don't pull punches.

My first three books—*Crimes That Never Happened*, *Prison Politics 101*, and *Cookinn in the Clink*—focused on my time in the criminal justice system. They're raw, real, and unapologetically in-your-face. But this book? *The Art of Dealing with Two-Faced People*? This one's personal. It's not just about surviving the shitshow that is life—it's about thriving despite the deceptive bastards that infest it.

Why This Book Exists

Life isn't some fairytale where everyone plays nice and the good guys always win. Life's a brutal, no-rules game, and if you don't know how to play it, someone else will make damn sure you're the pawn they sacrifice to get ahead. I've seen it all. I spent ten years in federal prison, where lies, and betrayal were as common as ramen noodles. I watched people sell each other out for a cigarette, for ego, for nothing at all. And trust me, the staff were just as shady as the inmates—sometimes worse.

But **manipulation** isn't confined to prison walls. It's everywhere. It's in the "friend" who pretends to have your back while they're whispering your secrets to everyone else. It's in the coworker who steals your ideas and spins them as their own. It's in the business partner who smiles at you while they're quietly cutting you out of the deal. And don't even get me started on family. Blood ties don't mean shit when people are lying through their teeth to cover their asses. Aunts, uncles, cousins—they're just as likely to screw you over as a stranger, and they'll smile while they're doing it.

This Book Is Your Survival Guide

I'm not here to hold your hand or tell you to "find your inner peace." Fuck that. This book isn't about meditation or forgiveness—it's about survival. This is a masterclass in emotional warfare, written for people who are tired of being played. It's about understanding exactly how these two-faced bastards work, dismantling their tactics, and turning yourself into someone they can't touch.

By the time you're done with this book, you'll have the tools to:

- Recognize **manipulators** before they can do real damage.
- Outsmart their games and make sure they know they've lost.
- Take control of your emotions so they can't use them against you.
- Set boundaries so ironclad that even the most persistent asshole can't break through.

Why You Should Listen to Me

I'm not writing this from some comfy office in an ivory tower. I've lived through the trenches, dealt with every type of piece of shit you can imagine, and come out sharper on the other side. I've had ex-wives who made victimhood their full-time job while stabbing me in the back. I've had business partners who shook my hand one day and screwed me over the next. I've had "friends" who were all smiles until they needed someone to blame. And I've had jealous siblings who couldn't handle my success and decided to turn on me.

Then there's prison. A decade of liars, con artists, and snitches who would sell you out for a pack of smokes. I saw deceptive people exploit each other for nothing more than their own personal jollies. And let's not forget the staff—half of them were just as corrupt as the inmates they were supposed to be watching. That environment forces you to adapt. You either learn how to protect yourself, or you become someone else's pawn.

What You'll Get Out of This Book

If you've ever been lied to or screwed over—and who the fuck hasn't?—this book is for you. It's not a fluffy self-help guide filled with feel-good platitudes. It's a blueprint for spotting, confronting, and outmaneuvering the two-faced assholes in your life. Whether it's a fake friend, a shady coworker, a conniving ex, or a backstabbing family member, you'll learn exactly how to handle them.

Here's what's coming:

- **The Art of Recognition**: Learn how to spot the liars and manipulators in your life before they can do any damage. They rely on being underestimated, so let's rip that advantage away.
- **Emotional Mastery**: **Manipulators** thrive on triggering your emotions. This book will teach you how to control your reactions so they can't use your feelings as a weapon against you.
- **The Power of Boundaries**: You'll learn how to set—and enforce—boundaries that even the most persistent asshole can't cross.
- **SWOT Analysis for People**: Treat every relationship

like a business deal. You'll learn to analyze the strengths, weaknesses, opportunities, and threats of the people around you so you can decide who stays and who goes.

This isn't just a book—it's a goddamn survival guide for dealing with the backstabbing **manipulators** that infest your life. So buckle up, because by the time you're done reading, you'll have everything you need to take control and shut these bastards down for good.

Let's get to work.

CHEAT SHEET

Identifying & Shutting Down Two-Faced People

Two-faced people are the ultimate predators, and you're their prey—unless you're smart enough to see them coming. They thrive on deception, manipulation, and turning your blind spots into their advantage. That's where the **Assessment**, **Analysis**, and **Action Plan** come in. Here's why these tools aren't just helpful—they're absolutely critical:

- **The SWOT Analysis**: This breaks down their strengths, weaknesses, and the opportunities you have to expose them. You'll also uncover the potential threats they pose to your reputation, peace, or relationships.
  - *Why It Matters*: Manipulators rely on their ability to stay hidden. The analysis pulls back the curtain and gives you a clear view of their game.
- **The Intelligence Assessment**: This shows you exactly who you're dealing with. Are they sloppy manipulators or calculated operators? Knowing their level of skill determines how much of a threat they really are.
  - *Why It Matters*: You can't fight what you don't understand. The assessment lets you size them up before they strike.
- **The Action Plan**: This is your roadmap for shutting them down. It equips you with specific strategies to cut

off their influence, expose their lies, and reclaim control of your life.

- ○ *Why It Matters*: Without a plan, you're just reacting to their chaos. The action plan puts you in the driver's seat, ensuring they can't fuck with you again.

This isn't just a toolkit—it's your survival kit. These steps aren't optional if you want to protect your sanity, reputation, and peace. Use them like weapons to dismantle their manipulation before it even starts. Trust me, these manipulative pieces of shit are banking on your ignorance. Let's make sure they lose that bet.

SWOT Analysis: Dissecting Two-Faced People

Use this framework to understand exactly how these people operate, where they're vulnerable, and how to protect yourself. Treat this like a forensic tool for relationships.

Strengths

- **Fake Charm**: They know how to butter you up. Their smiles, compliments, and "support" are weapons designed to lower your defenses.
- **Manipulative Tactics**: They're pros at guilt-tripping, gaslighting, and playing the victim. They use these tactics to control you and shift blame when caught.
- **Networking Skills**: Two-faced people are often social butterflies. They collect contacts like trophies and use them to build a web of influence.

Weaknesses

- **Insecurity**: Deep down, they're scared little cowards.

They manipulate because they're too weak to succeed honestly.
- **Predictable Patterns**: Once you recognize their tactics—lying, spreading rumors, or twisting facts—you can anticipate their moves.
- **Dependence on Others**: Their entire game hinges on people trusting them. Once their mask slips, they're screwed.

Opportunities

- **Expose Them**: Keep a record of their lies, inconsistencies, and betrayals. Confront them publicly or within the right circles to destroy their credibility.
- **Cut Them Off**: They can't manipulate you if they don't have access to your life.
- **Redirect Their Tactics**: Use their need for control against them. Stay calm, refuse to react, and let them self-destruct.

Threats

- **Social Damage**: Two-faced people often operate in your social or professional circles. If unchecked, they can tarnish your reputation.
- **Emotional Manipulation**: They're skilled at making you doubt yourself, which can derail your confidence and decision-making.
- **Collateral Damage**: Their lies can hurt not just you, but also those around you—coworkers, family, or mutual friends.

Intelligence Assessment Factor: Rating Their Manipulative Game

Not all two-faced people are created equal. Use this assessment to figure out just how dangerous a particular manipulator is—and how much effort they deserve from you.

1. Deceptive Intelligence

- Are they subtle or obvious? A low-IQ manipulator will get sloppy, while a high-IQ one covers their tracks and plays the long game.
- *Example*: A sloppy manipulator might spread easily debunked rumors, while a calculated one slowly builds a network of lies that's harder to untangle.

Rating Scale:

- 1–3: Amateur (easy to catch, full of contradictions)
- 4–6: Competent (they're sneaky but slip under pressure)
- 7–10: Expert (they play the long game and are dangerously convincing)

2. Emotional Control

- How good are they at keeping their cool? A manipulator who panics under pressure is easier to expose.
- *Example*: If you confront them, do they lash out immediately, or do they try to redirect the blame calmly?

Rating Scale:

- 1–3: Hothead (falls apart when challenged)

- 4–6: Steady (holds it together but shows cracks)
- 7–10: Stone-cold (keeps the act going even when cornered)

3. Social Influence

- How many people believe their bullshit? A manipulator with influence can cause more damage, especially in shared networks.
- *Example*: A coworker who manipulates your boss is a bigger problem than one who just gossips in the break room.

Rating Scale:

- 1–3: Isolated (no one takes them seriously)
- 4–6: Moderate (a few people fall for their act)
- 7–10: High (they've built a loyal following of suckers)

4. Desperation Level

- How badly do they need to manipulate you? The more desperate they are, the more erratic and dangerous they become.
- *Example*: An ex who can't let go might escalate their tactics, while a casual manipulator moves on to an easier target.

Rating Scale:

- 1–3: Low (they'll give up if ignored)
- 4–6: Moderate (persistent but manageable)
- 7–10: High (obsessive, will stop at nothing)

The Action Plan: How to Shut Them Down

1. Expose Their Lies

- *What to Do*: Document everything. Keep a paper trail of texts, emails, and interactions. When the time is right, confront them with the facts in a calm, controlled manner.
- *Why It Works*: Two-faced people hate being caught. Exposing their lies shatters their credibility and weakens their grip on others.

2. Cut Off Their Access

- *What to Do*: Limit what they know about you. Stop sharing personal details or future plans. If possible, reduce direct contact altogether.
- *Why It Works*: They can't manipulate you if they don't know what buttons to push.

3. Flip the Script

- *What to Do*: Use their tactics against them. Stay calm, play dumb, and let them dig their own grave. Ask leading questions that expose their contradictions.
- *Why It Works*: It forces them to reveal their hand while keeping you in control.

4. Strengthen Your Network

- *What to Do*: Build strong, trustworthy relationships with others in your circle. Share your concerns about the manipulator carefully with people you trust.
- *Why It Works*: A manipulator can't survive in a group

that's united against them.

Closing Thoughts: The Power of Knowing Their Game

Two-faced people rely on your ignorance and emotional reactions. But now? You've got the tools to see through their facade, dismantle their tactics, and protect yourself from their bullshit. With a SWOT analysis and an intelligence assessment in your back pocket, you're not just ready to deal with them—you're ready to dominate. Let them play their games; you're already ten steps ahead.

Now go out there, expose their lies, cut them off, and reclaim your peace. They'll hate it, but who the hell cares?

TABLE OF CONTENTS

CHAPTER ONE 1

How to Spot Two Faced Assholes ....

CHAPTER TWO...28

NO MORE BULLSHIT ....

CHAPTER THREE 48

Exposing Lies and Bullshit...

CHAPTER FOUR 68

Turning Manipulation Against Them...

CHAPTER FIVE 89

Outsmarting the Manipulators ....

CHAPTER SIX 109

Cleaning up the Shit Storm...

CHAPTER SEVEN 129

Living Two-Faced Free...

CHAPTER EIGHT 150

Toxic Two-Faced Friends & Family...

CHAPTER NINE...192

Jealousy and Manipulation...

CHAPTER TEN 237

Psychological Warfare Strategies ....

CHAPTER ELEVEN...287

Thriving in Chaos: Outsmarting Manipulators ....

Types of Two Faced People You Will Meet...........................341

Betrayal, Lies, & Two-Faced Parasites....................................372

Final Words: Stay Sharp, Stay Unbreakable...........................380

CHAPTER ONE

How to Spot Two Faced Assholes

Let's cut the bullshit: the world is crawling with two-faced assholes who thrive on manipulation, backstabbing, and stirring up drama. They smile to your face while they're plotting behind your back, and if you're not paying attention, you'll fall right into their toxic trap. These aren't just annoying people—they're professional chaos creators who weaponize trust and kindness for their own gain.

Spotting them isn't just a skill—it's survival. This chapter is your crash course in recognizing these sneaky douchebags before they can wreck your peace, your relationships, or your sanity. Pay attention—because the bastards already are.

Lesson 1.1: Red Flags to Watch For

1.1.1 The Overly Charming Act: Why Excessive Flattery Often Masks Hidden Motives

Let's get something straight: charm isn't inherently bad. It's not illegal to be likable, smooth, or charismatic. But when someone lays it on so thick you could drown in their compliments, you need to take a step back and ask yourself: *What's their fucking angle?* Because trust me, no one is that charming without an agenda. Excessive flattery isn't kindness—it's a weapon. And if you don't spot it early, you'll be halfway down a manipulation rabbit hole before you even realize you're falling.

Why Over-the-Top Charm Is a Red Flag

The overly charming act isn't about making you feel good—it's about disarming you. They want to lower your defenses, make you feel special, and get you to let them in. But here's the kicker: it's not about you. It's about what they can get from you. Here's why charm is their favorite weapon:

- **It Creates a False Sense of Trust**: "Wow, you're so amazing! I've never met anyone like you." Bullshit. They barely know you, but now you're flattered enough to overlook the red flags.
- **It Distracts You from Reality**: While you're busy soaking up their compliments, they're quietly steering the conversation—or your life—in a direction that benefits them.
- **It's a Set-Up for Favors**: "You're so good at [insert skill here]! Could you help me with something?" And just like that, you've been roped into their agenda.

How to Spot the Overly Charming Assholes

Not everyone who's nice to you is a manipulator, but if their charm feels like it's on steroids, pay attention. Here's what to look for:

- **Compliments That Feel Too Polished**: If it sounds like they rehearsed their praise in front of a mirror, it's because they probably did.
- **Instant Best-Friend Energy**: They've known you for five minutes, and suddenly, you're their "favorite person ever." Red fucking flag.
- **Flattery That's Clearly Self-Serving**: "You're so good at organizing—could you handle this for me?" They're not complimenting you; they're buttering you up to use you.

What to Do When You Spot the Act

Once you see through their charm, it's time to shut their shit down. Here's how to handle it like the badass you are:

1. **Call It Out**
   "That's nice, but why are you laying it on so thick?" Watch their face as they scramble for an excuse.
2. **Stop Giving Them the Reaction They Want**
   If they're fishing for validation, refuse to bite. "Thanks," said with zero enthusiasm, will shut down their flattery faster than a brick wall.
3. **Keep Your Guard Up**
   Don't let their compliments cloud your judgment. Pay attention to their actions, not their words. If their behavior doesn't match their charm, you've got your answer.

The overly charming act is manipulation wrapped in a sugar-coated package. It's not about you—it's about them and whatever the hell they're trying to get out of you. Spot it, call it out, and don't fall for the flattery. Let them play their charm games with someone else while you keep your head on straight. You're too smart, too sharp, and too experienced to let a little sweet talk screw you over.

1.1.2 The Eternal Victim: How Perpetual Sob Stories Are Their Favorite Manipulation Tool

The eternal victim is the person who can turn a sunny day into a goddamn tragedy. Nothing is ever their fault. Ever. Life is just *so unfair* to them, and you're supposed to feel bad about it. They're masters of guilt, spinning every interaction into a sob story. "My boss hates me. My friends are fake. My family doesn't understand me." Translation: *I'm a manipulative pain in the ass, and everyone's figured it out except you.*

Here's their move: they bait you with their sad little tales to pull you into their orbit. Suddenly, you're the unpaid therapist, problem-solver, and cheerleader for someone who doesn't actually want help. Why? Because solving their problems means they lose their favorite weapon—your guilt.

Example: Taylor Monroe, your "bestie," calls you crying about how her coworkers are so toxic. Meanwhile, she's the one bad-mouthing everyone and stirring the pot. But sure, Taylor, you're the victim here.

How They Operate

- They always have a villain, and surprise, it's never them.
- Solutions are "too complicated." They want your sympathy, not your advice.
- They'll gaslight you into thinking you're heartless if you set boundaries.

The Rule:

If their sob story sounds like a soap opera, it probably is. Cut the guilt and step back. Eternal victims don't want your help—they want your energy. Don't give them a damn thing. Let them wallow in their misery without dragging you into the quicksand.

1.1.3 The Rule Bender: Spotting The Ones Who Always Have An Excuse For Bad Behavior

The Rule Bender is the sneakiest bastard in the game. They don't break the rules outright—oh no, that would be too obvious. Instead, they twist them, bend them, and contort them into shapes so unrecognizable you'll feel like you're the crazy one for calling them out. Their motto? *"Rules are for suckers—unless I can use them to screw someone else over."*

How They Operate

Rule Benders are professional excuse-makers. They miss deadlines? *"Oh, I thought it was next week."* They "forget" to tell you something important? *"Oops, must've slipped my mind!"* They screw up and somehow blame you? *"Well, you didn't remind me, did you?"* They're always the victim of "misunderstandings" while you're left cleaning up the mess.

Example: Jake Rivers from your office "accidentally" forgets to add you to an important email chain about your project. When you confront him, he smirks and says, *"Oh, I didn't think it mattered."* Yeah, Jake, because stealing credit definitely doesn't matter.

How to Spot Them

- They always have a perfectly rehearsed excuse for everything.
- They gaslight you into thinking you're overreacting.
- They're suspiciously consistent in their "mistakes."

Don't let them wiggle out of accountability. Keep receipts, call out their bullshit with facts, and don't buy into their charm. Rule Benders think they're clever, but when you expose their tactics, they crumble. No excuses, no second chances. Shut them down.

1.1.4 The Gossip Factory: People Who Spill Secrets Will Eventually Spill Yours

If someone can't shut the fuck up about other people's business, here's a newsflash: they're not keeping your secrets either. The Gossip Factory lives for drama. They thrive on the chaos of whispered half-truths and shady "did you hear about so-and-so?" moments. Their goal? To stay relevant by stirring the pot and keeping everyone just suspicious enough to avoid trusting anyone—including you.

How They Operate

Gossip isn't just their hobby—it's their currency. They dish out dirt like they're Oprah handing out cars, but the price is your trust and reputation.

- **Baiting You**: They share something juicy to test if you'll share something back.
- **Twisting Words**: What starts as a harmless observation ends up a full-blown scandal by the time they're done spinning it.
- **Creating Drama**: They love pitting people against each other and then sitting back to watch the fireworks.

Example: Aunt Lydia casually drops, *"Did you know Taylor skipped work to go shopping? I only mention it because I care about her, of course."* Fast forward, and now Taylor's boss is giving her the side-eye thanks to Aunt Lydia's "concern."

How to Shut Them Down

- **Don't Take the Bait**: When they try to rope you into gossip, respond with, *"Oh, I don't really get into that."* Boring them is the fastest way to escape.
- **Call Them Out**: Hit them with, *"Wow, you seem to know everyone's business. Do you ever talk about me like this?"* and watch them backpedal.
- **Keep Your Secrets Tight**: The less they know, the less they can weaponize.

If they gossip to you, they'll gossip about you. Starve their drama machine, keep your distance, and let them implode without you in the blast zone. You're not here to be anyone's headline.

1.1.5 The Too-Good-To-Be-True Vibe: Why Perfection Is Usually A Red Flag In Disguise

Nobody's perfect, and anyone who tries to convince you otherwise is full of shit. The "too-good-to-be-true" type isn't just putting on a show—they're building a fortress of lies and hoping you're too distracted by the glitter to notice. They're the ones who always say the right thing, always look like they have their life together, and somehow never have a single flaw. Spoiler alert: their perfection is just a mask, and underneath it? A manipulative mess waiting to blow up in your face.

These people use their polished act as a weapon. They want you to think they're better than you, smarter than you, more trustworthy than anyone you've ever met. Why? So you'll let your guard down. Once you buy into the illusion, they've got you. You'll start doubting yourself while they quietly plot how to use you to their advantage. It's not admiration they're looking for—it's control.

Derek Collins is the poster child for this. He's the perfect partner who brings flowers to your mom, tells your friends how "lucky" he is to have you, and volunteers to handle everything. But behind the scenes, he's keeping secrets, twisting narratives, and setting you up to look like the bad guy when it all falls apart.

Perfection isn't real—it's a trap. The shinier someone seems, the more you should question what they're hiding. Stop being dazzled by their act and start looking for the cracks. They're there, and once you see them, you'll never unsee them.

Lesson 1.2: Behavior Patterns and Manipulation Tactics

1.2.1 Gaslighting 101: Making You Question Reality is Their Bread and Butter

Gaslighting isn't just a manipulation tactic—it's a goddamn art form for toxic assholes. These people don't want to argue with facts or logic; they want to rewrite your reality so they can control the narrative and make you feel like you've lost your mind. It's not just cruel—it's calculated. And if you don't learn how to spot it, you'll end up questioning your own shadow while they sit back and laugh at how easy it was to fuck with you.

How Gaslighting Works: The Ultimate Mindfuck

Gaslighting isn't about convincing you—it's about confusing you. These manipulative bastards don't need you to believe them; they just need you to doubt yourself. Here's how they pull off this mental circus act:

- **The Denial Game**: "I never said that." Oh, but they did, and you remember it clearly. Too bad they're hoping you'll second-guess your memory instead of calling out their blatant lies.
- **Twisting Your Words**: They'll take something you said, distort it beyond recognition, and throw it back at you like a grenade. "You said you didn't care about that." No,
- **You said:** about *your* opinion, which is not the same damn thing."
- **Blaming You for Everything**: "You're just being too sensitive." Translation? "Let me dismiss your feelings so I don't have to take accountability for my toxic bullshit."
- **Rewriting History**: "That's not what happened." Funny, because your receipts say otherwise. They'll try to edit the past like it's their own personal documentary, conveniently omitting all the incriminating parts.

Why Gaslighting Works (If You Let It)

Gaslighting is a manipulator's wet dream because it fucks with the very thing that keeps you grounded: your sense of reality. Here's why it works—until you wise up, that is:

- **It Creates Doubt**: When someone makes you question your own memory, instincts, and judgment, you start relying on *their* version of events.
- **It Shifts the Power Dynamic**: By keeping you off-balance, they stay in control. The more confused you are, the easier it is for them to steer the ship.

- **It's Emotional Poison**: Gaslighting isn't just about winning an argument—it's about breaking you down so they can build you back up the way they want.

How to Spot a Gaslighting Bastard

Gaslighters aren't as sneaky as they think. If you know the signs, you can see through their manipulative shitstorm before it takes hold:

- **You're Constantly Second-Guessing Yourself**: Did you really say that? Did you overreact? Are you the crazy one? Spoiler: no, you're not. They're just fucking with your head.
- **Conversations Feel Like a Maze**: Talking to them is like being in a psychological funhouse—nothing makes sense, and you always leave feeling worse than when you started.
- **They Play the Victim**: "I can't believe you're accusing me of that!" Oh, please. Their fake outrage is just a cover for their manipulative bullshit.

How to Shut Down a Gaslighter

Once you recognize the game, it's time to flip the script. Here's how to shut their shit down:

1. **Keep Receipts**
   Gaslighters hate evidence. Save texts, emails, and any other proof of their behavior. When they try to deny reality, hit them with the facts.
   - **Example**: "Really? Because here's the text where you said exactly that."
2. **Stick to the Facts**
   Don't let them drag you into their emotional spiral. Keep the conversation grounded in reality.
   - **Example**: "We're not discussing feelings—I'm sticking to what actually happened."

3. **Call Out the Manipulation**
Name their behavior for what it is. Gaslighters hate being exposed.
   - **Example**: "You're trying to make me doubt myself, and it's not going to work."
4. **Refuse to Engage**
Sometimes the best response is no response. Walk away and let them stew in their own toxic mess.

Gaslighting is their favorite tactic because it's easy, effective, and destructive as hell. But once you see through the smoke and mirrors, their power evaporates. Call out the lies, stick to the facts, and don't give them the reaction they're fishing for. Let them spiral in their own chaos while you walk away with your sanity—and your reality—intact. You're smarter, sharper, and way too badass to let a manipulative bastard fuck with your head.

1.2.2 *The Divide-And-Conquer Strategy: Pitting People Against Each Other To Stay On Top*

Two-faced manipulators love to stir shit up, and their favorite tactic is the divide-and-conquer strategy. Why deal with one person at a time when you can turn everyone against each other and sit back to enjoy the chaos? These bastards live for it. They create drama not because they're bored, but because it gives them control. If everyone's too busy fighting each other, no one has time to notice they're the common denominator screwing everything up.

Here's how it works: they plant seeds of doubt, whispering things like, "You know, Jake didn't seem too impressed with your presentation," or "Karen mentioned she doesn't think you're pulling your weight." The best part? They say the exact same thing to Jake about *you*. Now you're both side-eyeing each other while they're over there, stirring their coffee, acting innocent.

They don't stop at just planting doubts—they'll escalate things at the perfect moment. Maybe they "accidentally" let it slip in front of a group, or they twist your words into something juicier than reality. Either way, the room explodes, and they quietly step back, pretending to be the peacemaker. *"Let's all just calm down, guys."* Oh, how noble of them.

The next time someone starts "sharing concerns" about another person, remember: they're not your confidant; they're your manipulator. Don't take the bait. Call them out or, better yet, cut them off. Let them conquer their own damn self-destruction. You've got better things to do.

1.2.3 The Lies That Bind: Identifying Habitual Liars And Their Techniques

Habitual liars don't just bend the truth—they break it, shatter it, and glue it back together into a warped version of reality where they're always the hero. These are the people who lie so casually, so effortlessly, you almost have to respect the sheer audacity. Almost. But here's the thing: their lies aren't harmless—they're calculated, toxic, and designed to screw you over while they walk away looking squeaky clean.

You can spot a habitual liar by their greatest hits:

- *"That's not what I said!"* (It is.)
- *"I never agreed to that."* (They did.)
- *"You must've misunderstood."* (You didn't.)

These assholes don't just lie to cover their own mistakes—they lie to manipulate you into questioning yourself. And the best part? They don't even have to remember their lies because they know you'll twist yourself into knots trying to make sense of their nonsense.

Example? Jake Rivers tells you he's got your back in a meeting, but when the time comes, he conveniently "forgets" what you agreed on. Suddenly, you're the one explaining why the project's off track while Jake sits there nodding like a damn bobblehead.

The trick to dealing with habitual liars? Stop assuming they'll tell the truth. Fact-check everything. Keep records like you're preparing for a court case. And don't waste your energy trying to catch them in the act—they're already ten lies ahead. Call out the pattern, not the individual lies. Let them choke on their web of bullshit. You've got receipts; they've got excuses. Guess who wins? You. Every time.

1.2.4 The Puppet Master Move: Pulling Strings While Pretending To Be Innocent

The Puppet Master is the most dangerous type of two-faced bastard. They don't just cause chaos—they *orchestrate* it, sitting quietly in the background while everyone else dances to their manipulative tune. They don't need the spotlight; they're too busy pulling strings, twisting narratives, and making sure every move benefits them. The best part? They always play innocent. *"What? Me? I had no idea this would happen!"* Sure, buddy, and the fire started itself.

These people don't fight their battles directly—they're too clever for that. Instead, they pit others against each other, spread subtle misinformation, and make sure someone else takes the fall when it all blows up. They're the ones whispering, *"I just thought you should know,"* or, *"I didn't want to say anything, but I think Karen's been talking about you behind your back."* They don't want resolution—they want a goddamn war.

Example? Sophia Lane tells you Jake's been undermining your work in meetings. Meanwhile, she's the one planting doubts about your competence to the boss. By the time you and Jake are at each other's throats, Sophia's sitting pretty, looking like the reasonable one.

The only way to deal with a Puppet Master is to stop being their puppet. Cut the strings. Don't react to their bait, don't take their whispers at face value, and, for the love of all that's holy, don't let them stir shit up in your life. Expose their game with facts and receipts, then watch them squirm when their web of manipulation comes crashing down. They're not as clever as they think—they're just assholes with good timing.

1.2.5 Passive-Aggressive Warfare: The Subtle Digs And Guilt Trips You Shouldn't Ignore

Passive-aggressive people are the worst kind of cowards. They don't have the guts to confront you directly, so they weaponize snide comments, guilt trips, and those irritating "I'm just joking!" remarks that make you question whether you're being too sensitive. Spoiler: you're not. They're being assholes—they're just doing it with a fake smile plastered on their face.

These people specialize in the art of plausible deniability. They'll say something shitty and then immediately follow it up with, *"Don't take it personally,"* or, *"I didn't mean it like that."* Bullshit. They meant every word—they just don't want to deal with the fallout. And guilt? Oh, they wield that like a damn lightsaber. *"I guess I'll just handle it myself since you're too busy,"* they'll sigh, hoping you'll feel bad enough to jump in and fix their mess.

Example? Karen from accounting emails you, cc'ing half the office, with, *"Just a gentle reminder that the deadline was yesterday. I'm sure you're doing your best!"* Translation: *"You screwed up, and now I'm making sure everyone knows it."*

The worst part? Passive-aggressive people are experts at making *you* look like the bad guy if you call them out. That's their whole game: undermine, guilt, and needle until you snap, so they can say, *"Wow, you're so dramatic."*

How do you deal with them? Kill them with directness. *"If you have an issue, let's address it directly instead of hinting around it."* They hate when you strip away their plausible deniability. No more digs, no more games. Just cold, hard accountability. Watch them crumble.

Lesson 1.3: The Emotional Fallout

1.3.1 Recognizing the Emotional Drain: How These Bastards Suck the Life Out of You

Let's cut the crap: dealing with manipulative assholes isn't just annoying—it's *exhausting*. These people don't just take up space in your life; they drain your energy like emotional vampires. You start the day feeling fine, and by the time they're done with you, you're ready to crawl into a hole and never come out. Why? Because these toxic bastards thrive on turning your mental bandwidth into their personal playground, leaving you with nothing but stress, doubt, and a headache.

Why Emotional Drainers Are the Worst

These people aren't content with being shitty—they need to drag you down with them. Here's how they suck the life out of you:

- **Constant Drama**: Everything is a crisis with them. Their problems become your problems, whether you signed up for it or not.
  - **Example**: "I can't believe this happened! What should I do?" Translation? "Let me dump all my problems on you while I do absolutely nothing to fix them."
- **Endless Complaining**: Nothing is ever good enough for these people, and they love to let you know about it.
  - **Example**: "I hate my job, my friends, my life…" Cool. Then *do something about it* instead of sucking the joy out of everyone else's day.
- **Attention Black Holes**: They can't let a single conversation happen without making it about them.
  - **Example**: "Oh, you're going through something? That reminds me of this one time when *I* had it worse."

The Signs They're Draining You Dry

Not sure if someone's an emotional vampire? Here's how to tell:

- **You Feel Drained After Every Interaction**: If you feel more tired after spending time with them than before, congratulations—you've been emotionally mugged.
- **You're Always on Edge Around Them**: You're constantly waiting for the next outburst, complaint, or guilt trip.
- **Your Problems Take a Back Seat**: Whenever you try to bring up your own issues, they hijack the conversation and make it about them.

How to Stop the Emotional Drain

1. **Set Hard Boundaries**
   These people thrive on access. Cut them off at the source by limiting how much time, energy, or attention you give them.
   - **What to Say**: "I'm not available to talk about this right now." End of story.
2. **Refuse to Be Their Emotional Dumping Ground**
   It's not your job to solve their problems—or even listen to them if it's draining you.
   - **What to Say**: "I understand you're struggling, but I can't help you with this."
3. **Keep Conversations Surface-Level**
   Don't give them the chance to pull you into their drama. Keep things light and redirect when they try to unload.
   - **Example**: "That's tough. Anyway, did you see the game last night?"
4. **Walk Away When Necessary**
   If someone refuses to respect your boundaries, it's time to cut them loose. Your peace is worth more than their endless bullshit.
   - **What to Say**: "I need to take a step back from this relationship."

Why Cutting Them Off Feels So Damn Good

The second you stop letting these emotional leeches drain you, you'll feel lighter, freer, and more in control of your life. Your energy is yours, and you'll finally have enough of it to focus on the things—and people—that actually matter.

- **You'll Sleep Better**: No more lying awake at night replaying their latest tantrum.
- **You'll Reclaim Your Time**: Without them hogging your attention, you'll have more space for yourself.
- **You'll Feel Stronger**: Setting boundaries and cutting them off proves you're not here to be anyone's doormat,

Recognizing emotional drainers is the first step to taking your life back. These people don't care about your peace—they care about feeding their own drama addiction. Spot them, call them out, and cut off their access to your energy. Let them find someone else to leech off while you thrive without their bullshit weighing you down.

1.3.2 The Self-Doubt Spiral: Why You Start To Question Your Own Instincts

Two-faced manipulators are experts at planting seeds of doubt, and before you know it, those seeds have grown into a full-blown forest of self-doubt. You'll walk into a situation feeling confident, but after dealing with them, you're left questioning everything: *Was I too harsh? Did I get it wrong? Am I the problem?* Spoiler alert: you're not. They are.

Here's the thing—they don't just lie to you; they make you doubt your ability to trust your own damn judgment. It's not an accident. It's a strategy. They'll twist the truth, rewrite history, and hit you with lines like, *"I never said that,"* or, *"I think you're reading into this too much."* Translation: *"Let me gaslight you into shutting up."*

It works because most people don't like conflict. You want to believe the best in people, so you second-guess yourself instead of questioning them. And guess what? That's exactly how they win. The more you doubt yourself, the more they control the narrative.

Here's the fix: trust your instincts. If something feels off, it probably is. Start keeping track of conversations, even if it's just a mental note, so when they try to twist things, you can shut them down with confidence. Stop giving them the benefit of the doubt, and start giving it to yourself. Remember, their whole game depends on making you feel small. Don't give them the satisfaction. Take back your power—and your gut instinct—before they destroy both.

1.3.3 The Anger Trap: Learning How They Provoke You To Derail Your Focus

Two-faced people are like arsonists—they don't just start fires; they sit back and watch you burn while pretending to be the firefighter. Their favorite weapon? Your anger. They know exactly which buttons to push to make you lose your cool, and when you do, they get to play the innocent victim. *"Wow, I didn't mean to upset you. Why are you so sensitive?"* Sound familiar? That's their game.

Here's how it works: they'll drop a snide comment, twist your words, or conveniently "forget" something important. When you call them out, they double down with passive-aggressive bullshit, all while keeping a calm, smug demeanor. The goal is simple: make you explode so they can turn the spotlight onto your reaction instead of their behavior. Now *you're* the one who looks unhinged, and they're just "trying to help."

Example? Karen from accounting "innocently" emails the team about a missed deadline and adds, *"I'm sure you did your best."* Cue your blood boiling. But the second you fire back, you're the one who looks unprofessional.

The fix? Don't take the bait. Their power lies in your reaction, so starve them of it. Stay calm, stay factual, and refuse to let them drag you into their petty little circus. Hit them with, *"I'd be happy to clarify if there's confusion,"* and watch their smirk fade. You win when you stay composed—because nothing pisses off a manipulator more than someone they can't manipulate.

1.3.4 The Guilt Gambit: Their Favorite Weapon To Keep You Feeling Responsible

Manipulators love guilt like it's their secret sauce, and trust me, they pour that shit on thick. They'll twist every situation until you're the one apologizing—even when they're the ones who screwed up. Guilt is their go-to move because it's easy, effective, and lets them avoid accountability while you're too busy feeling like a villain in their pity party.

Here's how it works: they frame everything to make it seem like you're the problem. They'll drop lines like, *"I thought I could count on you,"* or, *"After everything I've done for you, this is how you treat me?"* Suddenly, you're bending over backward to make it up to them, even though you didn't do a damn thing wrong. It's a guilt trip with no destination except their benefit.

Example? Aunt Lydia asks why you didn't help her with something you didn't even know about, then sighs dramatically: *"Well, I guess I'll just handle it myself... like I always do."* Now you're feeling like an ungrateful jerk for not reading her mind.

Here's the truth: their guilt trips aren't about fixing a problem— they're about control. The fix? Stop buying the ticket. If someone's trying to make you feel bad for setting boundaries or putting yourself first, that's *their* issue, not yours. Hit them with, *"I'm sorry you feel that way, but that's your choice,"* and let their guilt boomerang right back. You don't owe them your guilt—you owe yourself your peace.

1.3.5 Breaking Free From The Cycle: Understanding Their Triggers And Taking Control

Breaking free from a manipulator's grip isn't just about walking away—it's about burning the goddamn bridge so they can't follow you. These two-faced bastards thrive on keeping you stuck in their endless cycle of guilt, anger, and self-doubt. They poke, prod, and provoke until you're so tangled in their web that you forget you can cut the damn thing down. But here's the kicker: their power only works if you let it.

The first step to breaking free? Figure out what triggers them. Manipulators have specific weak spots—control, attention, validation—that they can't live without. Once you know what feeds their toxic behavior, you can starve them of it. If they crave drama, stop reacting. If they thrive on guilt, refuse to play along. You're not just taking control; you're flipping the script.

Example? Taylor Monroe always gets her way by dropping passive-aggressive guilt bombs like, *"I guess I'll just handle it myself."* Next time? Smile, say, *"That sounds like a great plan,"* and watch her flounder when her usual tricks fall flat.

The second step? Set boundaries and enforce them like your peace depends on it—because it does. They'll test you, push back, and try every dirty trick to keep their hold, but stay firm. Let them squirm. The beauty of breaking free isn't just getting rid of them—it's realizing they were never as powerful as they pretended to be. Take the control they stole, and leave them in the dust.

Lesson 1.4: Building Your Bullshit Detection Toolkit

1.4.1 Trust Your Gut: How Intuition Is Your Best Early-Warning System

Here's the thing about your gut—it doesn't lie. That little voice in the back of your head that says, *"Something's off"*? It's your early-warning system screaming at you to pay attention. And yet, how many times have you ignored it because you didn't want to seem paranoid or overreacting? **Spoiler alert:** every time you ignored it, you ended up kicking yourself later when the manipulative bastard you gave the benefit of the doubt **proved your gut right.**

Trusting your gut isn't paranoia—it's **self-preservation**. And if you're going to survive in a world full of two-faced assholes, you better learn to listen to it.

Why Your Gut Is Smarter Than Your Brain

Your gut doesn't waste time with excuses, overthinking, or "seeing the best in people." It's **direct, raw, and brutally honest**—and it can **spot even the most polished faker** long before they slip up.

It Picks Up on Subtle Bullshit

Your gut notices the little things your brain ignores: **tone of voice, microexpressions, calculated charm.** It also spots people who **try too hard to look impressive but never deliver.** Ever meet someone who talks big, name-drops, and claims expertise in everything—but **never actually backs it up**? That's your gut saying, *"This person is full of shit."*

It Cuts Through the Noise

While your brain is busy rationalizing, your gut is like, *"Nah, something's not right here."* This is especially true when dealing with **image-obsessed manipulators**—people who survive on perception, not competence.

It's Built on Experience

Every red flag you've ever missed? Your gut **logged it**. Now it's trying to save your ass from making the same mistake twice. When someone **sounds too perfect**, **looks too polished**, or **avoids** specifics, your gut **remembers past encounters with similar fakers** and waves a big red flag. **Pay attention.**

What Ignoring Your Gut Looks Like

We've all been there: you get a weird vibe from someone, but you **brush it off** because you don't want to "jump to conclusions." Then, **surprise!** They turn out to be **exactly as shady as your gut told you they were.**

- **You Get Burned:** That coworker who was "just being friendly" is now **taking credit for your work.** Good job ignoring the warning signs.
- **You Waste Time:** Instead of trusting your gut, you **spend weeks (or months) analyzing their behavior** while they keep **screwing you over.**
- **You Doubt Yourself More:** Every time you override your intuition, you **teach yourself not to trust your instincts.** Stop doing that.

How to Start Trusting Your Gut Again

Listen to the First Ping

The moment something **feels off**, pay attention. Don't rationalize it away or try to give them the benefit of the doubt.

What to Ask Yourself: *"Why does this feel wrong?"* If you **can't pinpoint it, that's your answer**—it's instinct.

Keep a Mental Receipt

Your gut's not perfect, but **it's usually right**. When you get a bad vibe about someone, make a note of their behavior and **watch how it plays out.**

What to Do: Start connecting the dots. Over time, you'll see that your gut **was onto something.**

Stop Apologizing for Being Cautious

Trusting your gut **doesn't make you paranoid**—it makes you **smart.** You're not here to give everyone a free pass to screw you over.

What to Say: *"I'm getting a weird vibe, so I'm keeping my distance."* No need to explain yourself further.

Act Quickly

The longer you wait to act on your gut, **the more time they have to sink their claws into you.** If something feels wrong, **nip it in the bud before it becomes a problem.**

Why Manipulators Hate Your Guts

Manipulators rely on **their ability to bullshit you into submission.** Your gut **ruins that plan.** It sees through their charm, their excuses, and their **carefully crafted personas.** Here's why they hate it:

- **It Exposes Their Lies:** Your gut doesn't need proof—it just knows **they're full of shit.**
- **It Makes You Harder to Manipulate:** If you're listening to your gut, you're not **falling for their games.**
- **It Protects You from Their Drama:** By trusting your instincts, you can **cut them off before they wreak havoc** in your life.

Your gut is your **best friend** in a world full of two-faced manipulators. It's not here to make you feel warm and fuzzy—it's here to **keep you safe.** Trust it, act on it, and don't waste time second-guessing yourself.

Let the manipulators play their games with **someone else** while you stay one step ahead, guided by the one thing **they can't outsmart**: **your instinct.**

1.4.2 The Test Drive: Setting Traps To Reveal Their True Colors.

If you want to know whether someone's two-faced, don't wait for them to slip up—give them the damn opportunity. The "test drive" is how you figure out who they really are without letting them know they're under the microscope. Think of it as a little social experiment with you in the driver's seat and them unknowingly strapped into the crash test dummy role.

Start small. Drop a piece of harmless information—something trivial but slightly sensitive. Then, sit back and wait. If it comes back to you through someone else's mouth or gets twisted into a drama-filled soap opera, congratulations: you've just confirmed you're dealing with a manipulative bastard. Two-faced people can't help themselves; they love turning minor details into major problems.

Example? Tell Taylor Monroe that you're considering a big career move but haven't told anyone yet. When your boss starts hinting about "loyalty" the next day, you'll know exactly who's been running their mouth.

This isn't about being paranoid—it's about protecting yourself. Testing someone's loyalty or honesty isn't manipulative; it's survival. The world is full of snakes, and sometimes you need to poke the grass to see what slithers out.

Here's the deal: two-faced people don't know how to play it straight, even when they try. Give them a chance to reveal themselves, and they will—every damn time. And when they do? Cut them loose before they turn your life into their next reality TV episode.

1.4.3 Fact-Checking Frenzy: Cross-Checking Their Stories And Finding Cracks.

Two-faced people have one major weakness: their lies are about as sturdy as a house of cards in a hurricane. They love spinning stories, twisting the truth, and playing every side of the field, but here's the thing—they can't keep it all straight. That's where you come in, armed with the power of fact-checking to dismantle their bullshit one crack at a time.

Start by listening carefully. Pay attention to what they say to you versus what they tell others. Two-faced manipulators can't resist tailoring their narrative depending on the audience. *"Wait, didn't you tell Karen last week that you agreed with the new plan? So why are you telling me it's a bad idea now?"* Boom. Lie exposed.

Example? Aunt Lydia casually mentions that she's "worried about you" because *"your priorities seem a little off lately."* Funny—last week, she told your cousin you were the only one in the family who had their shit together. What changed, Lydia? Oh, that's right—she's full of crap.

The trick is to cross-check. Gossip about you? Verify it with the source. "Conflicting" information? Pull up the receipts. Whether it's a conversation, an email, or a meeting, two-faced people hate being fact-checked because it shatters their carefully constructed web of lies.

Here's the rule: if their story doesn't add up, it's because they're bullshitting. Don't assume. Don't excuse. Just hit them with the facts and watch their whole game fall apart. Receipts don't lie, but they sure do.

1.4.4 Eyes Wide Open: Staying Vigilant Without Becoming Paranoid.

Dealing with two-faced people is a balancing act. You need to keep your guard up without turning into a conspiracy theorist with a corkboard full of red string and "suspects." The goal? Stay sharp, stay alert, and keep your eyes wide open—but don't let their bullshit take over your brain.

Here's the truth: two-faced manipulators thrive on subtlety. They don't come at you like a wrecking ball; they chip away at your trust, bit by bit, hoping you're too distracted or naive to notice. Your job is to notice. Start watching patterns, not one-off moments. If Karen from accounting "accidentally" forgets to CC you on an important email once, it's an oversight. Twice? It's a habit. Three times? She's a snake.

Example? Sophia Lane compliments you in public—"You're so talented!"—but privately tells your coworkers you're "a little full of yourself." Sound familiar? That's the kind of two-faced move you catch when you're paying attention to what's said behind the scenes.

Staying vigilant isn't about paranoia; it's about being observant. Listen to what people say *and* how they say it. Watch how they treat others. Notice when their words and actions don't line up.

Here's the rule: stay alert, but don't let them live rent-free in your head. Two-faced people count on you not noticing their patterns. Spot them early, and you'll never be blindsided by their bullshit again. Keep your eyes open, and keep your power.

1.4.5 The Bastard Radar: Creating A Mental Checklist For Spotting Two-Faced People.

If you want to avoid getting blindsided by manipulators, you need a Bastard Radar—a mental checklist to sniff out the two-faced assholes before they get too close. Think of it as your personal defense system, one that lights up the second someone's actions don't match their words. Trust me, once you have it, you'll wonder how you ever lived without it.

Here's how to build it:

1. **Watch the Consistency**: Do they act differently around you versus other people? If they're sweet to your face but throw you under the bus when you're not around, that's a big, flashing red light.
2. **Track the Gossip**: If they're constantly spilling everyone else's dirt, guess what? They're spilling yours too.
3. **Note the Patterns**: One lie might be a mistake. Two is a habit. Three? You're dealing with a full-blown manipulator. Pay attention to repeated behavior.
4. **Listen for Fake Support**: Over-the-top compliments, constant "helpful" advice, or endless concern? They're setting you up to trust them so they can screw you later.

Example? Jake Rivers keeps praising your work in team meetings, but every time something goes wrong, he's the first to point fingers in private. Bastard Radar activated.

Here's the deal: your checklist isn't about being paranoid; it's about protecting your peace. Spot the bastards before they cause damage, and you'll save yourself the headache of cleaning up their mess later. Your gut plus this radar? Unstoppable. Let them try— just once. You'll see them coming a mile away.

Know the Enemy Now Crush Them

So, now you know how to spot these two-faced bastards before they sink their claws into your life. You've seen the red flags, you've mapped out their manipulative patterns, and you're officially done falling for their bullshit. But knowing who they are is only step one.

Because here's the ugly truth: these snakes don't slither away just because you recognize them. No, they double down. They adapt. They twist the game in ways you never saw coming. And if you're not ready, you'll find yourself right back in their web, wondering how the hell it happened *again*.

That's why Chapter Two exists—to make sure that never happens. It's time to stop playing defense and start building an offense so ruthless, so impenetrable, that no manipulative liar will ever get past your gates again. You're not just spotting the problem anymore— you're shutting it down before it can even start.

Welcome to No More Bullshit: Building a Defense Against Manipulative Liars. Get ready to bulletproof yourself against every dirty trick in their playbook.

CHAPTER TWO

NO MORE BULLSHIT

The world is a goddamn minefield of manipulators, liars, and drama-fueled chaos agents, and if you're not ready, you'll end up as their favorite target practice. These toxic assholes don't care about your boundaries, your peace, or your sanity—they're here to break you, use you, and leave you questioning your entire existence. But not after this.

Bulletproofing yourself isn't about playing nice or "rising above"—it's about building a defense so impenetrable, so ruthless, that no amount of their manipulative bullshit can get through. By the time you're done with this chapter, you'll have the tools to spot their games, shut them down, and walk away untouchable. They'll try to knock you down, but guess what? They'll fail. Every. Fucking. Time.

Lesson 2.1: Sharpen Your Awareness

2.1.1 Patterns Don't Lie: Recognizing Recurring Red Flags

Here's the brutal truth: people will show you exactly who they are if you bother to pay attention. Manipulators, two-faced bastards, and drama-hungry assholes aren't nearly as clever as they think—they operate in patterns. The problem? Most people are too busy making excuses for their bullshit to notice the glaring red flags waving in their faces. But not you. You're about to become the master of spotting patterns because once you do, these toxic idiots will never get the chance to fuck with you again.

Why Patterns Are the Ultimate Truth

Talk is cheap, but behavior? That shit doesn't lie. If someone's actions consistently scream "toxic," believe them. Here's why patterns are the key to decoding their manipulative games:

- **Consistency Exposes Their Bullshit**: They'll deny, deflect, and spin their actions like a goddamn politician, but patterns don't lie. If they've screwed over three people before you, guess what? You're next.
- **They Can't Fake It Forever**: Even the most skilled manipulators can only keep up the act for so long. Their true nature always comes out in the patterns of their behavior.
- **It Removes the Guesswork**: Instead of overthinking every little thing they say, you can step back and look at the bigger picture. Patterns turn chaos into clarity.

The Red Flags You Can't Ignore

If someone's behavior sets off your alarm bells, don't silence them. Here's what to watch for:

- **The Chronic Excuse Maker**: They've got a justification for everything. Late to work? "Traffic." Forgot your birthday? "I've been so busy." Cheated on their last partner? "It wasn't serious." Spoiler: the problem isn't their circumstances—it's them.
- **The Perpetual Victim**: Every story they tell ends with them being the innocent party. "Everyone's out to get me!" No, Karen, maybe you're just an asshole.
- **The Emotional Rollercoaster**: One day, they're your best friend; the next, they're ghosting you. If their mood swings faster than a toddler denied candy, it's a pattern worth noting.
- **The Gossip Machine**: They're always whispering about someone else's drama. Newsflash: if they're constantly trashing others, they're trashing you too.

How to Spot Patterns Like a Pro

1. **Keep a Mental Log**
   You don't need to go full FBI, but start keeping track of their behavior. If you notice the same shit happening over and over, it's not a coincidence—it's who they are.
   - **What to Ask**: "Is this a one-time mistake, or is this their MO?"
2. **Trust the Red Flags**
   Don't make excuses for their actions. If something feels off, trust your gut. Your intuition is smarter than their fake apologies.
   - **What to Remember**: One red flag is bad; three is a goddamn parade.
3. **Stop Believing Their Words**
   Manipulators are pros at saying the right things to smooth things over. Ignore their words and watch their actions instead.
   - **What to Say**: "I'm not interested in what you're saying—I'm looking at what you're doing."

Why Spotting Patterns Makes You Untouchable

The second you start recognizing patterns, you take away their power. Manipulators rely on you being too distracted or forgiving to notice their bullshit. Once you see through the act, they're exposed—and there's nothing scarier to a toxic person than being seen for who they really are.

The Bottom Line

Patterns don't lie, but people sure as hell do. Stop listening to their excuses, stop forgiving their "mistakes," and start paying attention to the bigger picture. Once you master the art of spotting recurring red flags, you'll never be blindsided by their toxic games again. Let them run their same tired patterns on someone else while you walk away, unbothered and untouchable.

2.1.2 Stay Objective: Removing Emotion From Your Observations

Two-faced people are emotional puppeteers, and guess who's holding the strings? You. That's their whole game—get you so caught up in frustration, anger, or guilt that you're too distracted to see the bigger picture. But here's the kicker: their bullshit only works if you let it. The second you take your emotions out of the equation, their power crumbles.

Let me spell it out: you're not here to play their game. You're here to observe, analyze, and dismantle. They twist the truth? Don't react. They drop some passive-aggressive bomb? Stay calm. The moment you let your emotions take the wheel, they've won. They'll flip the script, act innocent, and make *you* look like the problem. Classic move.

Example? Jake Rivers conveniently "forgets" to credit you for your work in a team meeting. Instead of blowing up, hit him with cold, hard facts: *"Actually, I sent that proposal last Thursday. Let me resend it to the team for clarity."* Boom. Game over.

Staying objective isn't about being a robot—it's about protecting your energy. Keep your reactions in check and focus on the facts. They want drama? Starve them of it. They want you rattled? Stay composed. Objectivity isn't just a tool; it's your armor. The calmer you stay, the harder it is for their manipulative crap to stick. Remember: the moment they lose control over your emotions, they lose everything.

2.1.3 Question Everything: How To Spot Inconsistencies In Their Stories

If there's one thing two-faced people suck at, it's consistency. They're so busy spinning their web of lies and playing every side that they forget one simple fact: the truth doesn't need a goddamn script. Their stories don't add up because they can't keep track of their own bullshit. Your job? Start asking questions and watch their house of cards collapse.

Don't take anything at face value. When they tell you something, ask yourself: *Does this even make sense?* Spoiler: it probably doesn't. Two-faced people thrive on vague half-truths and plausible deniability. They'll give you just enough detail to sound believable, but not enough for you to actually pin them down. That's where your questions come in.

Example? Karen says, *"Oh, I was going to include you in that email, but I wasn't sure if it was relevant to you."* Ask, *"What part of the email wasn't relevant? Can you clarify?"* Watch her stumble over her own excuse like a drunk trying to climb stairs.

The trick isn't just to ask questions—it's to ask the *right* questions. Focus on specifics. Pin them down. Two-faced people hate being boxed in because it forces them to either lie more (and get caught) or admit the truth (and look like an idiot). Either way, you win.

Here's the rule: if their story smells like bullshit, it probably is. Question everything, and don't stop until their lies fall apart. They won't see it coming, but you will.

2.1.4 Avoid Tunnel Vision: Keep An Open Mind While Staying Vigilant

Tunnel vision is a manipulator's best friend. If they can keep you hyper-focused on one part of their game, you'll miss the other ten moves they're pulling behind your back. Two-faced people are pros at distraction, misdirection, and making sure your attention is always *just* where they want it. Your job? Keep your damn eyes open and see the bigger picture.

Here's how they get you: they'll create one big, juicy drama to suck you in—something loud enough to distract you from the subtle, quieter ways they're screwing you over. Karen from accounting might be stirring up obvious gossip, but while you're busy shutting that down, she's over here positioning herself as the team MVP. Sneaky, right?

Example? Aunt Lydia makes a big deal about how *"no one appreciates family traditions anymore"* (translation: guilt trip), but meanwhile, she's sowing division between you and your siblings over who's "really" helping out the most. She's playing chess while you're stuck dealing with her little side hustle of chaos.

The fix is simple: don't get sucked into their noise. Stay vigilant without obsessing over one piece of the puzzle. Pay attention to patterns, listen carefully, and connect the dots. If you lock onto one issue, you're guaranteed to miss the full extent of their bullshit.

Here's the deal: tunnel vision makes you predictable. Keeping an open mind makes *them* vulnerable. Stay sharp, look wide, and let their next move be their downfall.

2.1.5 The Art Of Silence: Listening More To Catch Subtle Cues

Two-faced people love to talk. Why? Because the more noise they make, the harder it is for you to pick apart their bullshit. That's why your best weapon isn't some grand confrontation—it's silence. Not awkward, deer-in-the-headlights silence. *Controlled, deliberate silence.* The kind that makes them squirm while you soak up every little detail they didn't mean to let slip.

Here's the thing: people reveal themselves when you let them fill the silence. They'll over-explain, contradict themselves, or give you way more information than they intended. That's when their mask starts to crack. It's not just about what they say—it's about how they say it. Do they stumble over their words? Get defensive? Change the subject faster than Karen grabs credit for your work? All of it matters.

Example? Derek Collins insists he's "totally fine" with you hanging out with your friends, but when you don't respond, he suddenly blurts out, *"I just don't think you prioritize me enough."* Boom. Truth bomb, courtesy of your well-placed silence.

The trick is patience. Don't rush to fill the gaps or respond immediately. Let them do the heavy lifting. Stay calm, make eye contact, and give them just enough rope to hang themselves with their own inconsistencies.

Silence isn't weakness—it's power. Two-faced people hate it because they can't control it. So shut up, listen, and let their words bury them. Trust me, they will. Every single time.

Lesson 2.2: Building Boundaries

2.2.1 The Power Of "No": Saying It Without Guilt Or Explanation

Here's the thing about manipulators—they hate the word "no." It's like garlic to a vampire or truth to a politician. They thrive on your inability to set boundaries because that's how they get their hooks into you. But guess what? You don't owe them shit. Saying "no" isn't just a right—it's a goddamn power move.

The trick is to say it without guilt and, most importantly, without a damn explanation. You don't need to justify your decisions to anyone, especially not someone who's trying to use your niceness as a weapon against you. *"No, I can't help you with that project."* Done. No need to tack on, *"Because I'm really busy and feeling overwhelmed,"* because all that does is give them an opening to argue. *"Oh, but it won't take long!"* See how that works?

Example? Taylor Monroe asks you to bail her out of yet another self-inflicted disaster with some "urgent" favor. Hit her with a polite but firm, *"No, I can't."* When she presses for why, just smile and say, *"I just can't."* Watch her struggle to find a way in when you've slammed every door.

Here's the rule: "No" is a complete sentence. You don't need to soften it or sugarcoat it to spare someone's feelings, especially when they wouldn't hesitate to steamroll yours. Start saying "no" like your peace depends on it—because it does. Let them deal with their own shit for once.

2.2.2 Emotional Distance: Stop Letting Them Live Rent-Free In Your Head

If two-faced people had to pay rent for the mental space they occupy, you'd be a goddamn millionaire. They're not just manipulative—they're squatters in your brain, cluttering up your thoughts with their drama, guilt trips, and bullshit. Here's the harsh truth: the only reason they're taking up space is because you let them. Time to evict them and change the locks.

Emotional distance isn't just about ignoring them; it's about reclaiming your energy. Stop replaying their snide comments in your head. Stop dissecting every interaction for hidden meanings. Stop losing sleep over people who don't give a damn about yours. Every second you spend worrying about their next move is a second they win—and let's be clear, they don't deserve the win.

Example? Karen from accounting made yet another passive-aggressive dig in the team meeting, and now you're mentally rehearsing comebacks you should've said. Guess what? Karen's at home, blissfully unaware, while you're letting her bullshit ruin your day. Drop it. Karen isn't worth the bandwidth.

The fix is simple but not easy: whenever they creep into your head, consciously shut them out. Replace their drama with something that actually matters. Focus on your goals, your happiness, your damn lunch—anything but them. Emotional distance is your way of taking back control. They don't deserve to live in your head rent-free, and honestly, they can't afford the space. Evict their ass and move on.

2.2.3 Keep Them Guessing: Don't Reveal Your Vulnerabilities

Two-faced people are like emotional vultures—they're circling, waiting for you to expose a weakness they can pick apart. The second you let your guard down, they'll swoop in and weaponize your vulnerability faster than Karen from accounting can steal credit for your work. Your move? Keep them guessing. Don't give them a damn thing they can use against you.

Here's the deal: manipulators thrive on intel. The more they know about your struggles, fears, or insecurities, the easier it is for them to twist the knife. They'll nod sympathetically while you vent about your problems, but behind your back, they're spinning your confession into gossip or using it to undermine you. That's their game. Don't play.

Example? Taylor Monroe casually asks if you're stressed about that big project. She's not being "supportive"—she's fishing for something to use against you. Instead of unloading, hit her with a vague, *"It's a lot, but I've got it handled."* End of conversation. She can't use what she doesn't know.

Keeping them guessing doesn't mean being cold or distant—it means being smart. Share only what's necessary and nothing more. Keep your personal struggles, ambitions, and plans out of their reach. Let them think they know you while you maintain control of what they actually see.

The less ammo you give them, the harder it is for them to take a shot. Stay mysterious. Let them wonder. Their confusion is your shield, and it's one they'll never get through.

2.2.4 Boundary Maintenance: Enforce Limits With Consistency

Setting boundaries is one thing, but maintaining them? That's where the real work—and the real power—comes in. Two-faced manipulators don't respect boundaries; they see them as challenges. If you set a line in the sand, they're going to test it, push it, and see just how much they can get away with. Your job? Make damn sure they know your boundaries aren't suggestions—they're the law.

Here's the trick: consistency. You can't enforce a boundary once and then let it slide the next time they test you. That's like giving them a map to your weak spots. If you say, *"I don't discuss personal issues at work,"* then stick to it—no matter how cleverly Karen from accounting tries to bait you with her fake concern.

Example? Aunt Lydia tries her usual guilt-trip routine about you skipping a family gathering. You've already told her you're busy, but she hits you with, *"We just miss you so much; it's not the same without you."* Don't cave. Respond with, *"I understand, but I already told you I can't make it."* Repeat as necessary. She'll run out of steam before you do.

Boundaries only work when they're non-negotiable. Enforcing them consistently doesn't make you an asshole—it makes you someone who respects their own time, energy, and peace. Two-faced people hate boundaries because they can't manipulate their way past them. Good. Let them hate. It just means you're doing it right.

2.2.5 Protecting Your Time: Avoiding Energy-Drainers And Time-Wasters

Time is your most valuable resource, and two-faced people are experts at wasting it. They'll drag you into pointless arguments, guilt-trip you into doing their work, and rope you into their drama faster than a bad soap opera. Every minute you spend dealing with their bullshit is a minute you're not spending on things that actually matter. Stop giving them your time—it's not charity, and they're not worth it.

Here's the harsh truth: manipulators don't respect your time because they don't respect *you*. They'll "just need a quick favor" or "really need someone to talk to," and before you know it, you've lost hours of your day cleaning up a mess you didn't make. And the worst part? They'll act like you're the bad guy if you say no. Classic move.

Example? Jake Rivers conveniently "forgets" to finish his part of the project and asks if you can "just help out real quick" because he's "swamped." Translation: *I didn't do my job, and now I want you to do it for me.* Hard pass. Tell Jake, *"I'd love to help, but I'm slammed, too. Good luck!"* Done.

Protecting your time means saying no unapologetically, setting boundaries, and refusing to be anyone's fallback plan. Two-faced people will try to steal your time any way they can—don't let them. Guard it like it's your damn bank account, because once it's gone, you're not getting it back. Let them waste someone else's day— you've got better things to do.

Lesson 2.3: Keeping the Receipts

2.3.1 The Documentation Arsenal: What To Track And How

If you're dealing with two-faced manipulators, receipts aren't just helpful—they're your damn lifeline. These people lie like it's their full-time job, and without proof, you're stuck in a game of "he said, she said" that they'll twist to hell and back. That's why you need a documentation arsenal—because nothing shuts down bullshit faster than cold, hard evidence.

Here's what you track: **everything.** Emails, texts, meeting notes, even casual conversations if something feels off. If Karen from accounting says she'll "totally handle" that task, shoot her a quick follow-up email: *"Just confirming you're handling X by Friday, as we discussed."* Boom. You've got proof for when Karen inevitably tries to pin her laziness on you.

Example? Jake Rivers "promises" he'll handle the client follow-up but conveniently "forgets." When your boss asks why the client's pissed, you calmly forward the email where Jake said, *"I'll take care of it."* Enjoy watching him squirm.

Documentation isn't petty—it's protection. Manipulators count on you not keeping track so they can rewrite history and make you look like the idiot. Don't let them. Keep your files organized, your emails concise, and your screenshots ready.

Here's the rule: if it's not in writing, it didn't happen. Two-faced people hate receipts because they can't argue with them. So build your arsenal, and when the time comes, unleash it. Trust me, there's nothing sweeter than watching a liar choke on their own words.

2.3.2 Verbal Agreements Are Bullshit: Always Get It In Writing

Here's the first rule of dealing with two-faced manipulators: if it's not in writing, it didn't happen. Verbal agreements are their playground, a place where they can promise the world, screw you over, and later claim, *"I never said that."* Spoiler alert: they did. But without proof, it's your word against theirs, and guess who's walking away clean? Not you.

Two-faced people love verbal deals because they're slippery as hell. They'll swear they agreed to something, only to "forget" or deny it when the time comes. And if you call them out? *"Oh, there must've been a misunderstanding."* Bullshit. It wasn't a misunderstanding— it was a setup.

Example? Karen promises in a meeting that she'll take care of a key task. When she doesn't, she throws you under the bus with, *"I thought we agreed you'd handle that part."* But if you'd emailed her after the meeting—*"Just confirming you'll complete X by Friday"— *you'd have the ammo to shut her down. Now, she's left flailing.

Getting it in writing isn't just about emails. It's texts, notes, or any form of documentation that locks them into their own words. It's a paper trail they can't wiggle out of no matter how much they squirm.

Here's the rule: never trust a two-faced person to keep their word. Trust your receipts. Because when the blame game starts—and it *will* start—your proof is the only thing standing between you and their bullshit.

2.3.3 The Evidence Bank: Storing Proof For The Inevitable Showdown

When you're dealing with two-faced manipulators, consider yourself a one-person bank. But instead of cash, you're collecting evidence—and trust me, this currency is priceless. Manipulators love to twist the narrative, rewrite history, and blame you for their screw-ups. That's why your **Evidence Bank** needs to be full and ready for withdrawal when they inevitably pull their crap.

What goes in the bank? **Everything.** Emails, texts, meeting notes, screenshots—hell, even casual comments that raise an eyebrow. If Karen says in passing, *"Don't worry, I'll handle it,"* you'd better follow that up with an email: *"Just confirming you're handling X as discussed."* If it's not documented, they'll twist it faster than a pretzel at Oktoberfest.

Example? Jake Rivers claims in a team meeting that he completed a client deliverable. When it turns out he didn't, you calmly forward the email where he agreed to take care of it. Suddenly, Jake's excuse machine stalls, and you're off the hook while he scrambles to cover his tracks.

Store your receipts like they're gold. Organize them in folders, label them clearly, and make sure you can access them in seconds. When the showdown comes—and trust me, it will—you'll have the proof to expose their lies.

Here's the rule: don't wait for the chaos to start. Build your Evidence Bank now so you're always ready. Manipulators hate receipts, and nothing feels better than watching them choke on the truth they thought you wouldn't catch.

2.3.4 Digital Defense: Using Emails, Texts, And Calls To Your Advantage

If you're dealing with two-faced manipulators, digital communication is your best friend—and their worst nightmare. Emails, texts, and even call summaries are like tiny, undeniable receipts that can shut down their bullshit faster than they can spin it. Why? Because two-faced people can't argue with timestamps and written proof, no matter how good they are at twisting the narrative.

Here's the trick: make every interaction count. When they "promise" something in person or on the phone, follow up with a quick email or text: *"Just to confirm, you'll be handling X by Friday as we discussed."* They'll hate it, but too bad—it locks them into their own words and eliminates their favorite excuse: *"Oh, that's not what I meant."* Yeah, sure, Karen.

Example? Aunt Lydia calls you to complain about how no one in the family ever steps up to help. She ends with, *"You'll take care of the party decorations, right?"* You don't just agree and move on. You follow up with a text: *"Just confirming I'll handle the decorations for the party, as you requested."* Now, when she tries to act like you *offered* or didn't deliver, you've got her cornered.

Digital tools aren't just convenient—they're weapons. Use them to track conversations, clarify responsibilities, and keep a paper trail so airtight even the slipperiest two-faced manipulator can't wiggle out of it.

Here's the rule: if it's not documented digitally, it didn't happen. Let their lies meet your receipts—and watch them fold.

2.3.5 Strategic Disclosures: Knowing What To Reveal And When

When dealing with two-faced manipulators, information is power—yours *and* theirs. The more they know, the more ammo they have to twist, manipulate, and screw you over. That's why **strategic disclosure** isn't just smart; it's survival. You don't give away the whole playbook—you give them just enough to keep them guessing and nothing more.

The goal is to control the narrative without letting them control you. Share what's necessary, but hold back anything they could spin into drama. Got a big promotion coming up? Don't tell Karen until it's already signed, sealed, and announced. Working on a personal project? Don't let Jake know until it's too far along for him to sabotage. Manipulators thrive on exploiting your plans; starve them of the opportunity.

Example? Sophia Lane is fishing for details about your upcoming presentation. She says, *"I'm just curious how you're structuring it— I might be able to help."* Translation: *"I'm looking for ideas to steal."* Instead of spilling, give her something vague: *"I'm keeping it simple—nothing fancy."* Now she's got nothing to work with.

Strategic disclosure isn't about being paranoid—it's about being smart. You decide what they know, how much they know, and when they know it. Think of it like a chess game: you don't move all your pieces at once. Let them see just enough to think they've got an edge, while you quietly keep the real power in your back pocket.

Here's the rule: information is leverage. Use it wisely, and don't give manipulators an inch—they'll take a mile.

Lesson 2.4: Fortifying Your Inner Game

2.4.1 Mental Armor: Developing Emotional Resilience

If you're going to deal with two-faced manipulators, you need mental armor thicker than a bank vault. These assholes thrive on getting under your skin, poking at your insecurities, and making you second-guess every move you make. Their goal? To leave you an emotional wreck while they skate away scot-free. But here's the truth: their tactics only work if you let them.

Building emotional resilience isn't just about "staying strong" (whatever the hell that means). It's about learning how to take their bullshit, recognize it for what it is, and let it roll off you like water off a damn duck. They're trying to rattle you? Stay calm. They're pushing your buttons? Don't give them the reaction they're fishing for. The less you react, the less power they have.

Example? Karen from accounting makes yet another passive-aggressive comment during the team meeting, something like, *"Well, I guess we're just doing things differently now."* Instead of snapping back, smile and say, *"Exactly. Let's keep moving forward."* Watch her implode when her bait doesn't work.

The secret to mental armor? Realizing their attacks say more about them than they ever will about you. Their digs are about their insecurities, not your flaws. Once you understand that, you stop giving a shit. Protect your peace, shut out their noise, and let them flail while you stay unbothered. They can't win if you don't play. Let that sink in.

2.4.2 Focused Energy: Channeling Frustration Into Productivity

Dealing with two-faced people is infuriating, but here's the harsh truth: every second you spend stewing over their bullshit is a second you're handing them for free. They're living rent-free in your head while you're spinning your wheels. Time to flip the script. Take that frustration and turn it into fuel—because the best revenge is success, and nothing pisses off a manipulator more than seeing you thrive.

Focused energy means taking all that anger, annoyance, and "why the hell did they do that?" and redirecting it into something useful. Got a big project? Crush it. Feeling pissed off? Hit the gym and sweat it out. Use their nonsense as a motivator, not a roadblock.

The goal isn't just to win—it's to make their petty games look so insignificant that they're embarrassed they even tried.

Example? Jake Rivers tries to undermine you in a meeting, hinting that your project is "a little behind." Instead of spiraling into rage, use it as rocket fuel. Wrap the project up early, send a detailed progress email to the team, and cc the boss. Now Jake looks like the idiot he is, and you look like a goddamn star.

Here's the deal: your energy is yours. Don't waste it on their garbage. Channel it into something that builds you up, not something that tears you down. Let them play their little games while you turn your focus into wins. The scoreboard doesn't lie—and you'll always come out on top.

2.4.3 The Power Of Detachment: Thriving Without Their Validation

Two-faced manipulators love to keep you hooked. They dangle their approval, their attention, or some half-assed compliment like a carrot on a stick, waiting for you to jump. Here's the truth: you don't need their validation. In fact, you're better off when you stop giving a shit what they think altogether. Detachment isn't weakness—it's your secret weapon.

Detachment means cutting the emotional cord they're clinging to. They criticize you? Who cares. They try to gaslight you? Smile and let it bounce off. They're counting on you needing their approval to feel good about yourself, so the moment you stop chasing it, they lose their grip.

Example? Aunt Lydia makes her usual backhanded comment: *"I guess you're just too busy to call these days."* Old you might've scrambled to apologize. New you? Shrug and say, *"Yep, been slammed. Hope you're doing well!"* Let her stew in her passive-aggressive silence.

When you detach, you stop reacting—and nothing frustrates a manipulator more than someone who refuses to take the bait. Your happiness, success, and self-worth come from you, not from their fake praise or snide remarks. Once you realize that, they've got nothing to hold over you.

Here's the rule: don't give a damn about their opinion. Thriving without their validation isn't just liberating—it's a giant middle finger to their entire playbook. Let them choke on their need for control while you keep winning on your own terms.

2.4.4 Staying Grounded: Practices To Calm Anxiety And Build Strength

Two-faced people are chaos machines. They thrive on drama, stirring up anxiety, and making you feel like you're always on edge. The trick to beating them? Stay grounded. Because while they're busy trying to knock you off balance, you're going to stand there solid as a rock and let their bullshit bounce right off you.

Staying grounded isn't just some fluffy self-care mantra—it's a survival strategy. When you're calm, you think clearly. When you're steady, they can't manipulate you. And when you're unshakable, their little games lose all their power.

Example? Karen from accounting tries to pull you into an argument during a meeting. Instead of biting, take a deep breath, stay calm, and hit her with a neutral, *"We can revisit this later if needed."* Watch her frustration build when she realizes she can't get a rise out of you.

Here's how to stay grounded:

- **Breathe**: Literally. Deep, slow breaths keep you from reacting impulsively.
- **Stay Present**: Don't let their crap drag you into the past or make you worry about the future. Focus on *now*.

- **Move Your Body**: A workout, a walk, or even stretching can shake off the tension they're trying to dump on you.

Here's the rule: they want you frazzled, because that's when you're easy to manipulate. Stay grounded, stay calm, and don't give them an inch. Let them spin out while you stand strong. They'll hate it, and you'll love it.

2.4.5 Long-Term Strategies: Building A Life That Two-Faced People Can't Infiltrate.

Here's the ultimate power move: build a life so solid, so fortified, that two-faced manipulators can't even find a crack to slip through. These assholes only thrive where there's chaos and vulnerability. Cut off their access, and they'll flail around like fish out of water—irrelevant, powerless, and completely out of your orbit.

Step one? Tighten your circle. Surround yourself with people who are real, reliable, and drama-free. If someone shows even a hint of shady behavior, don't give them the benefit of the doubt—cut them loose. Life's too short to waste on manipulators.

Step two? Lock down your boundaries like Fort Knox. Whether it's Karen from work trying to steal your ideas or Aunt Lydia dropping guilt bombs, make sure they know your limits aren't flexible. A manipulator without access is like a thief staring at an unbreakable safe—useless.

Example? Taylor Monroe keeps prying into your personal life, fishing for dirt. You shut her down with vague responses like, *"Everything's good, thanks for asking,"* and move on. She doesn't get the satisfaction of knowing anything useful, and you keep your peace intact.

Finally, focus on what builds you up—your goals, your passions, and your well-being. The more fulfilled and self-assured you are, the less impact their games will have. Manipulators thrive on insecurity, but they've got nothing on someone who's solid, confident, and untouchable.

Here's the rule: make your life so damn good that their bullshit doesn't even register. Let them try—they won't get far.

From Defense to Destruction: Time to Drop the Hammer

You've built your armor. You've set your boundaries. You've sharpened your bullshit radar so well that manipulators don't stand a chance of sneaking past you again. But let's be real—some of these two-faced clowns won't just slink away quietly. They'll test you. They'll push. And when they realize they can't manipulate you, they'll shift gears, spinning lies and rewriting reality in real-time.

That's where the next step comes in. It's not enough to protect yourself—you have to go on the offense. When someone tries to play you, you don't just sidestep the bullshit; you flip the script and make sure they never pull that stunt again.

Chapter 3 is where we stop just blocking the punches and start landing them. You're not here to be their punching bag—you're here to call them out, expose their lies, and shut their games down for good. So buckle up. It's time to drop the hammer.

CHAPTER THREE

Exposing Lies and Bullshit

Let's be real—most two-faced manipulators rely on one thing: the fact that you won't call them out on their bullshit. They think they can play their games, twist the narrative, and walk away without consequences. Not anymore. This chapter is all about flipping the script. You're going to learn how to call them out, shut them down, and take back the power they thought they had. Armed with the right tools and a no-nonsense attitude, you'll become their worst nightmare: someone who sees through their crap and isn't afraid to say it. No more playing nice—it's time to drop the hammer.

Lesson 3.1: Mastering the Call-Out

3.1.1 Timing Is Everything: When To Strike For Maximum Impact

Calling out someone's bullshit isn't just about *what* you say—it's about *when* you say it. Strike too early, and they'll have time to wiggle out with excuses and fake apologies. Wait too long, and they'll already have spun their web of lies so tight you'll need a chainsaw to cut through it. Timing is everything, and when you hit the sweet spot, you don't just expose them—you leave them scrambling like a deer in headlights. This isn't about giving them a fair fight; it's about hitting where it hurts, when it hurts.

Why Timing Matters in a Call-Out

Manipulators are slippery little bastards. If you don't time your call-out perfectly, they'll use every trick in the book to dodge accountability. Here's why timing is the key to taking them down:

- **They're Caught Off-Guard**: The right timing doesn't give them a chance to prepare their bullshit excuses. You strike when they're least expecting it.
- **It Maximizes Their Embarrassment**: Call them out when the stakes are high—like in front of their audience of admirers—and watch their entire narrative collapse in real time.
- **It Exposes Their Game in Full**: Waiting until they've overplayed their hand gives you the receipts to rip their lies apart.

When to Strike for Maximum Damage

1. **Catch Them Mid-Bullshit**
   The best time to call someone out? When they're neck-deep in their own lies. Interrupting their performance with the truth is like pulling the curtain on a bad magician.
   - **What to Say**: "Wait, didn't you just say the exact opposite yesterday? Care to explain?"
2. **In Front of Their Audience**
   Manipulators love an audience, but the stage works both ways. Calling them out in front of their enablers exposes them to the people they're trying hardest to impress.
   - **What to Say**: "Interesting story. Mind if I share the actual version of events?"
3. **When You've Got the Receipts**
   Timing isn't just about embarrassing them—it's about having the evidence to back it up. Wait until you've got proof in hand, and then drop the hammer.
   - **What to Say**: "That's funny because this screenshot says otherwise."
4. **When They Think They've Won**
   Let them bask in the glow of their supposed victory—then rip the rug out from under them. Nothing hurts a manipulator more than thinking they've won, only to realize you've been ten steps ahead the whole time.

When NOT to Call Them Out

Timing also means knowing when to hold back. Don't waste your ammo on moments that won't hit as hard:

- **When You're Emotional**: Manipulators will use your anger or frustration to make you look like the problem. Stay calm, strike later.
- **When You're Alone**: If they can spin the story after the fact, wait until there's an audience or documentation to back you up.
- **When You're Not Ready**: A half-assed call-out won't stick. Wait until you're armed and ready to dismantle their narrative entirely.

The Bottom Line

Calling someone out isn't about playing nice or giving them a chance to explain themselves. It's about hitting at the perfect moment to expose their bullshit for what it is. Strike when the iron's hot, make it count, and leave them reeling while you walk away unbothered and victorious. Timing is your weapon—wield it wisely, and watch them crumble

3.1.2 The Calm Clapback: How To Stay Composed While Delivering The Truth

Two-faced manipulators *want* you to lose your shit. That's their entire play. They'll push, poke, and provoke until you're ready to flip the table, and the second you do? They play the victim. *"Oh my God, why are you so aggressive?!"* Don't fall for it. Instead, hit them with a calm clapback so devastating it'll leave them questioning their entire life. The key? Stay cool, stay sharp, and cut them down with precision.

The calm clapback is a weapon. You don't yell, you don't flinch, and you sure as hell don't give them the satisfaction of seeing you crack.

Instead, you keep your voice steady, your tone polite, and your words sharper than a set of Ginsu knives. *"Oh, Karen, that's interesting—I don't recall you being involved in that discussion. I must've missed your contribution. Can you remind me what it was?"* Bam. She's done.

Example? Jake Rivers pulls some crap like taking credit for your idea in a meeting. You lean back, smirk, and say, *"Glad you're aligned, Jake. Since I outlined that plan last week, it's great to see we're all on the same page."* Translation: *"Sit down, Jake, you're embarrassing yourself."*

Here's the rule: calm kills. Two-faced people expect explosions. They're not ready for icy composure paired with a brutal truth bomb. So keep your voice low, your words lethal, and watch them squirm. They started the game, but you're the one finishing it.

3.1.3 Public Vs. Private: Deciding The Best Stage For Your Confrontation

Calling out a two-faced bastard is like setting off a bomb—you've got to decide whether it's going to be a controlled demolition or a fireworks show for the whole damn crowd. The right stage depends on the stakes, and let's be clear: you don't call someone out for sport—you do it to make sure their bullshit never sees the light of day again.

Private: If it's a minor offense or you just need them to shut up and stay in their lane, pull them aside. No audience, no drama, just a surgical strike. This isn't about sparing their feelings—it's about shutting the problem down without making it a spectacle. Example? Karen screws up your project timeline but tries to blame the "miscommunication" on you. Pull her into a quiet corner and hit her with, *"Let's make sure we're clear—this was your responsibility, and it can't happen again."* Short, sharp, and impossible to ignore.

Public: When their lies are public, the takedown needs an audience. If they've been spinning a story or stealing credit, let the truth rain down like a goddamn hammer in front of everyone. Example? Jake Rivers takes credit for your pitch in a meeting. Smile and say, *"Oh, glad you liked my proposal, Jake. I sent it out last Thursday—did you want me to forward it again?"* Watch him choke on his stolen words.

Here's the rule: private for control, public for destruction. You pick the stage, and you make sure they never forget the show.

3.1.4 The Element Of Surprise: Catching Them Off Guard With Facts

Two-faced people love to play it safe in the shadows, spinning their lies and manipulation where they think no one's looking. That's why the element of surprise is your best damn weapon. They don't expect you to be watching, listening, and—most importantly—*documenting.* So when you hit them with cold, hard facts, it's like slamming a trapdoor shut under their feet.

Here's the trick: don't give them any warning. Let them think they've gotten away with their crap, and then drop the hammer when they're least prepared. Timing matters, but shock value? That's where you really hit them where it hurts.

Example? Karen "forgot" to include you in the client email chain (again) and tells the boss, *"I assumed they didn't need to be looped in."* You calmly forward the entire email thread with a note: *"Just to clarify, I requested inclusion on this last week—see below."* Watch Karen turn seven shades of red as her excuse crumbles in real time.

Surprise works because it strips manipulators of their defense mechanisms. They can't deny, deflect, or spin the narrative when the truth blindsides them like a freight train. Keep your evidence close, stay calm, and deliver the facts with the precision of a sniper.

Here's the rule: facts are your ambush, and timing is your trigger.

Let them think they've won, and then catch them off guard with the truth. They'll never see it coming—but they'll definitely feel it.

3.1.5 Knowing When To Walk Away: Picking Your Battles Wisely

Sometimes, the best way to beat a two-faced piece of shit is to not play their game at all. You've got to know when to walk away, not because you're weak, but because they're not even worth the goddamn effort. These manipulators thrive on conflict—it's their oxygen. Starve them of attention, and they'll suffocate in their own irrelevance.

Here's the thing: not every lie, every snide comment, or every sneaky move deserves your energy. You're not a referee in their pathetic game of manipulation. You're a player in your own life, and wasting time on their bullshit isn't just draining—it's a distraction from what actually matters. Walking away isn't weakness; it's knowing they're not worth your mental real estate.

Example? Aunt Lydia drops her usual passive-aggressive bomb at a family dinner: *"It must be nice to be so busy you can't even call your family anymore."* Old you might have snapped back or defended yourself. New you? Shrug and say, *"It is nice, actually. Pass the mashed potatoes."* Done. No drama. She's left flailing for attention.

Walking away doesn't mean you're ignoring the problem—it means you're choosing your battles. Save your energy for the fights that actually matter, not the petty games of insecure manipulators. The best way to win is to show them they're not even in your league. Let them stew in their own mess while you move on. Game over.

Lesson 3.2: Essential Tools of the Trade

3.2.1 The Bullshit Detector: Spotting Lies Before They Take Root

Here's the deal: two-faced people can't survive without their lies. It's their oxygen, their currency, their entire personality. Your job? Build a bullshit detector so sharp it catches their crap before it even hits the ground. They think they're slick—spoiler alert: they're not.

The first step? Stop taking anything they say at face value. Manipulators rely on vagueness, half-truths, and just enough "believability" to get you to buy in. Pay attention to the details—or lack of them. They dodge specifics because specifics can be checked, and checking is their kryptonite.

Example? Jake Rivers tells you, *"I already followed up with the client,"* but when you ask for details—like, you know, what they said—he stammers, *"Uh, they were happy, I think."* Bullshit detected. He didn't follow up, and now he's trying to cover his ass.

Next, look for patterns. Two-faced manipulators can't keep their stories straight because they're spinning different versions for everyone. The moment you catch one inconsistency, you've cracked their entire façade.

Lastly, trust your gut. If something feels off, it is. That nagging suspicion isn't paranoia—it's your brain picking up on red flags faster than you can process them. Don't ignore it.

Here's the rule: treat everything they say like it needs a fact-check. Build your detector, call out their lies early, and don't let their bullshit take root. Once you see through their game, it's over before it even starts.

3.2.2 The Fact Arsenal: Gathering Evidence To Back Your Call-Out

When it comes to dealing with two-faced manipulators, facts are your ammo, and you'd better stockpile them like you're preparing for war. These people can twist a narrative faster than a politician in a scandal, but here's the kicker: they can't argue with cold, hard proof. That's why your **Fact Arsenal** isn't optional—it's your goddamn lifeline.

Here's how you build it: document *everything*. Emails, texts, meeting notes, casual conversations—if it can be written, recorded, or timestamped, it goes in the arsenal. Manipulators thrive on ambiguity, so eliminate it entirely. Follow up verbal agreements with an email: *"Just to confirm our discussion, here's what we agreed on."* You're not being paranoid; you're being smart.

Example? Karen from accounting swears she "never got the memo" about an important deadline. You calmly forward her the email you sent last week—complete with her "Got it!" reply. Boom. The lie dies on the spot, and Karen has nowhere to run.

Your arsenal isn't just about catching them—it's about being ready for the inevitable moment when they try to pin their bullshit on you. Stay organized, keep your receipts handy, and don't hesitate to use them.

Here's the rule: facts don't lie, but manipulators do. When they come at you with their twisted version of events, hit them with the truth so hard they'll think twice before trying it again. Your facts, your power. Use them wisely.

3.2.3 The Confidence Shield: Projecting Strength Even When You're Fuming

Two-faced people love to sniff out weakness like goddamn bloodhounds. They're experts at sensing hesitation, doubt, or any sign that you're not fully in control—and the second they do, they pounce. That's why confidence isn't just important; it's your armor. You don't just need to wear it—you need to make it bulletproof.

Here's the truth: you don't have to *feel* confident to look confident. You can be fuming inside, ready to rip their bullshit apart, but if you project strength, they'll never know they've rattled you. Stand tall, make eye contact, and keep your voice steady. Fake it if you have to—because the moment they see you're unshakable, they lose their edge.

Example? Jake Rivers interrupts you in a meeting to "clarify" your point and twists it into something that benefits him. Instead of snapping, you calmly say, *"Thanks, Jake, but I think I've got it covered. Let me finish."* No panic, no anger—just a direct shutdown that leaves no room for debate. He's left looking like the overstepping idiot he is.

The Confidence Shield isn't about hiding your emotions; it's about controlling the narrative. Two-faced manipulators want you to lose your cool because it makes you easier to manipulate. Don't give them that power. Show strength, even if it's just for show, and let them flounder when their usual tactics fail.

Here's the rule: they can't mess with you if they think you're untouchable. Build that shield and make it impenetrable. Let them try—they'll regret it.

3.2.4 Strategic Phrasing: Words That Hit Hard Without Crossing The Line

Sometimes you need to tell a two-faced manipulative bastard to sit the fuck down—but you do it without *actually* saying it. That's where strategic phrasing comes in. You don't go full scorched-earth, but you sure as hell make it clear you're not buying their bullshit. The key? Precision. Every word is a loaded weapon, and you're aiming for maximum damage.

Here's the trick: don't get emotional, and don't go for the obvious insults. Instead, wrap your takedown in a layer of professional politeness so they can't even call you out for it. Example: *"Oh, I didn't realize we were redefining 'contribution.' Can you clarify what exactly you did on this project?"* Translation: *"You did jack shit, Karen, and we both know it."*

Example? Jake Rivers tries to spin a story about how he "supported" your idea. You hit him with, *"Thanks, Jake. It's great to see your enthusiasm for my work. Let me know if you'd like a* *refresher on the original plan I outlined."* Boom. He's exposed, and you didn't even raise your voice.

Strategic phrasing is about maintaining control while delivering the verbal equivalent of a gut punch. You're not playing nice; you're playing smart. Let them stew in the aftermath of your words while you sit back, cool as hell, knowing you've just burned them without breaking a sweat.

Here's the rule: keep it sharp, keep it brutal, and let your words hit harder than any screaming match ever could. Fuck subtlety—they'll know exactly what you mean.

3.2.5 The Poker Face: Keeping Your Emotions In Check While They Squirm

Two-faced manipulators live for the drama. They're like emotional vampires, feeding off your frustration, anger, or even confusion. The moment you react, they win. That's why the Poker Face is your ultimate weapon—it's like flipping them the bird without moving a muscle. You don't give them a goddamn thing. No anger, no flinching, no reaction. Let them stew in the awkward silence of their own stupidity.

Here's how it works: they poke and prod, trying to get a rise out of you. You respond with the emotional equivalent of a blank wall. No smirks, no sighs, just a calm, steady stare that says, *"I see through you, and you're pathetic."*

Example? Karen drops her latest passive-aggressive bomb in the meeting: *"Oh, I guess some people don't understand how deadlines work, but that's okay—I'll handle it."* Poker Face you leans in, locks eyes with her, and says, *"Interesting point, Karen. Would you like to clarify who you're referring to?"* The room goes silent, and Karen's left choking on her own words.

Manipulators hate the Poker Face because it takes away their power. They want you to explode so they can flip the script and act like *you're* the problem. Don't give them the satisfaction. Keep your cool, let them flail, and enjoy the satisfaction of watching them unravel.

Here's the rule: your calm is their kryptonite. Let them burn in their own awkwardness while you sit there, unbothered and untouchable.

Lesson 3.3: Tactical Approaches

3.3.1 The Subtle Exposé: Calling Them Out Without Being Obvious

Sometimes, the best way to call out a two-faced bastard is to make them expose themselves. You don't need to go full blast; you just need to plant the seeds and let their bullshit bloom in front of everyone. This is the **Subtle Exposé**—a call-out so smooth they won't even realize you're the one pulling the strings until it's too late.

Here's how it works: you don't accuse them of anything outright. Instead, you lead the conversation to a place where their lies, inconsistencies, or shady behavior come to light on their own. It's like holding up a mirror and saying, *"Take a look, asshole."* The beauty? You come off as calm, rational, and maybe even helpful, while they're left scrambling to explain themselves.

Example? Jake Rivers claims he's "taken care of everything" for the team project. Instead of calling him a liar outright (even though you *know* he hasn't), you casually ask during the meeting, *"Jake, could you walk us through exactly what you've done so far? Just so we're all aligned."* Watch him stammer and flop like a fish on dry land as the room realizes he's full of shit.

The Subtle Exposé isn't just about exposing the truth—it's about doing it in a way that leaves them no room to spin the narrative.

They fall on their own sword, and you don't even have to get your hands dirty.

Here's the rule: let their lies do the work for you. Stay calm, stay sharp, and let them dig their own grave.

3.3.2 The Direct Hit: When Blunt Honesty Is The Best Weapon

Sometimes, you don't need strategy, nuance, or subtlety—you need a damn sledgehammer. That's where the **Direct Hit** comes in. This isn't the time for polite phrasing or carefully planted seeds. This is when you grab their bullshit by the throat, drag it into the light, and set it on fire for everyone to see. It's not just a call-out—it's a goddamn demolition.

Two-faced manipulators love playing the long game, hoping you'll tiptoe around their crap forever. Guess what? You're done playing nice. The Direct Hit isn't about subtlety; it's about hitting them so hard with the truth that they don't have time to spin, deflect, or recover.

Example? Karen claims in the team meeting that she handled the client follow-up (which, spoiler alert, she didn't). You don't sit there stewing. You cut in with, *"Actually, Karen, I emailed the client myself after realizing it wasn't done. Would you like me to share the email thread so we're all on the same page?"* Boom. Public execution. Watch Karen melt into her seat.

The key to a Direct Hit is preparation. Come armed with facts, receipts, and the confidence of someone who knows they're about to wreck shop. Don't yell, don't flinch—just drop the hammer and let the fallout speak for itself.

Here's the rule: when you've got the facts, don't hold back. Hit them hard, hit them fast, and leave no room for their lies to breathe. It's not just a call-out—it's a goddamn reckoning.

3.3.3 The Diplomatic Approach: Confrontation Without Conflict

Diplomacy, huh? Sounds fancy, but let's not get it twisted—it's just a polite way of jumping into someone's shit without getting your hands dirty. You don't come at them guns blazing; you come at them with a goddamn scalpel. It's controlled, precise, and leaves them no wiggle room to deny their crap. Think of it like slapping them in the face with a velvet glove—they'll feel it, but you'll still look classy doing it.

Here's the move: you start calm, like you're just "clarifying." Ask pointed questions, drop a few well-placed facts, and let them realize you're leading them right into the grave they dug for themselves. You're not accusing—they're confessing. Genius, right?

Example? Sophia Lane "accidentally" spreads a rumor about you being difficult to work with. You corner her at a party and hit her with, *"Hey, I heard some confusion about my role on the project. Since you've been talking about it, can you clarify what exactly was said? I'd love to clear it up together."* Boom. She's choking on her own words while you stand there, smiling like a saint.

The beauty of the Diplomatic Approach is it keeps you looking cool while they're busy panicking. You're not yelling or getting emotional—you're just letting them stew in their own mess.

Here's the rule: diplomacy doesn't mean soft. It means sharp, strategic, and utterly devastating. Serve them their bullshit with a side of receipts, and watch them fold.

3.3.4 Using Humor As A Weapon: Disarming Them With Wit

Nothing pisses off a two-faced manipulator more than being taken down with a well-placed joke. They expect you to get mad, to blow up, to let them play the victim. But when you hit them with humor instead, it's like slapping them across the face with a smile. They can't deflect it, they can't twist it, and it makes them look like the jackass they are.

Here's the beauty of using humor as a weapon: it's subtle but devastating. You're not screaming or throwing accusations—you're exposing their crap in a way that makes everyone laugh *at them*. And nothing burns more than public humiliation wrapped in a joke.

Example? Karen says, *"Oh, I thought you were handling that deadline—I didn't realize I needed to step in."* You smile and reply, *"Oh, no worries, Karen. I know keeping track of deadlines is hard when you're so busy managing other people's work."* Cue the awkward silence and Karen's face turning redder than a firetruck.

Humor works because it's disarming as hell. It lets you call them out without looking angry or aggressive. Instead, you're the sharp, sarcastic genius while they're left stammering like an idiot.

Here's the rule: don't waste time yelling when you can tear them apart with a single sarcastic comment. Use your wit like a goddamn scalpel and let them bleed out while everyone else laughs. They wanted to play games? Too bad—you're better at them.

3.3.5 The Trial By Questioning: Leading Them To Expose Themselves

If two-faced manipulators had a kryptonite, it'd be their own words. They can't help but trip over their lies when you start poking holes, and that's where the **Trial by Questioning** comes in. You don't accuse them of shit—you just ask the kind of questions that make their stories collapse faster than a Jenga tower in an earthquake. They dig the hole, and you hand them the shovel.

The key? Keep it calm, keep it relentless, and let their own answers bury them. You're not the bad guy here—you're just "trying to understand." Sarcastically, of course.

Example? Jake Rivers tells the boss he handled the client presentation. You pipe up with, *"Oh, that's great! Which client was it? And when did you meet with them? Just curious so I can align my notes."* Watch him flail when he realizes his fake story doesn't have a single leg to stand on. He'll either double down on his lie (and dig deeper) or stumble into a pathetic, half-assed admission.

The beauty of the Trial by Questioning is that it doesn't make *you* look like the aggressor. You're not accusing—you're "clarifying." But in reality, you're watching them twist in the web they spun themselves.

Here's the rule: don't argue, don't accuse. Just ask, wait, and watch them implode. Their lies are their downfall, and you're just the one turning up the heat. Sit back and enjoy the show.

Lesson 3.4: Staying in Control

3.4.1 Managing The Fallout: Dealing With Their Retaliation

Calling out a two-faced manipulator is satisfying as hell, but let's be real—they're not going down without a fight. These assholes don't take being exposed lightly, and their retaliation game is strong. Lies, gossip, backpedaling—they'll throw every pathetic move they've got to try and claw back control. But guess what? You're not here to play defense—you're here to shut them the fuck down.

First, expect the tantrum. They'll cry victim, spin the narrative, and try to make you look like the bad guy. Let them. Their desperation is proof you hit the mark. Stay calm, stick to the facts, and let them drown in their own overreaction. Nothing pisses off a manipulator more than seeing you unbothered.

Example? Karen starts spreading rumors after you exposed her in a team meeting. You don't engage. Instead, you double down on professionalism and keep receipts for everything. When the boss asks what's going on, you casually forward the email thread that proves Karen's been full of shit the whole time.

Second, don't fight fire with fire. Let their retaliation burn itself out while you keep your focus sharp and your reputation clean. People will see the difference between their chaos and your calm, and trust me, it's not a good look for them.

Here's the rule: retaliation is just noise. Stay composed, stay factual, and let them implode under the weight of their own bullshit. You already won—now let them embarrass themselves trying to recover.

3.4.2 Damage Control: Repairing Relationships After The Confrontation

When you call out a two-faced manipulator, shit can get messy. They don't just come after you—they poison the well, dragging everyone around you into their little pity party. Suddenly, you're dealing with side-eye from colleagues, awkward tension at family gatherings, or friends who "just want to stay out of it." It's infuriating, but here's the deal: you can clean up their mess without stooping to their level.

Step one? Address the bullshit head-on—with the people who matter. Manipulators rely on whispers and half-truths to paint you as the villain, so counter it with the one thing they hate most: transparency. **Example?** Aunt Lydia tells the family you've "been so distant lately." You pick up the phone, call your siblings, and say, *"Hey, just wanted to clear something up—I've been busy, not distant. Lydia's spinning her usual stories again."* Now the air's cleared, and Lydia's games fall flat.

Step two? Let your actions do the talking. Be professional, be consistent, and show everyone you're not the drama queen the manipulator wants them to think you are. If Karen's gossiping at work, show up with receipts, deliver on your tasks, and let her nonsense look petty next to your results.

Here's the rule: damage control isn't about explaining yourself—it's about reclaiming the narrative. People will see the truth when you stay steady while the manipulator spirals. You can't stop their bullshit, but you can make damn sure it doesn't stick

3.4.3 Standing Your Ground: Maintaining Boundaries Post-Call-Out

Calling out a two-faced manipulator isn't a one-and-done deal. Sure, you exposed their crap, but don't think for a second they're not plotting their next move. These people don't just give up—they regroup, re-strategize, and come back swinging. That's why you can't just set boundaries; you've got to hold the damn line like your sanity depends on it—because it does.

The first step? Stop giving a shit about their fake charm or crocodile tears. Manipulators are pros at switching tactics when they're cornered. They'll go from defensive to apologetic to *"Let's just move past this"* in the blink of an eye. Don't fall for it. Standing your ground means staying firm, no matter how sweetly they smile or how convincingly they play the victim.

Example? Karen "apologizes" for her passive-aggressive bullshit but still keeps making snide comments in meetings. You shut her down immediately: *"Karen, I thought we agreed this wouldn't happen again. Let's keep things professional."* No yelling, no overexplaining—just a verbal brick wall.

Next, enforce your boundaries like a goddamn fortress. The moment you let something slide, you've opened the door for them to test you again. Be consistent, be direct, and don't waste time worrying about their feelings. You're not here to babysit their ego—you're here to protect your peace.

Here's the rule: boundaries mean nothing if you don't enforce them. Stand your ground, and let them realize they've got no way back in.

3.4.4 Learning From The Encounter: Improving Your Tactics For Next Time

Every time you go toe-to-toe with a two-faced manipulator, it's a goddamn lesson. Did they squirm? Did they retaliate? Did they find a crack in your armor you didn't even know was there? Good. That's not a failure—that's intel. The trick is using every encounter to sharpen your game so the next time they—or any other asshole—tries their shit, you're ten steps ahead.

Start by dissecting the aftermath. What worked? What didn't? Did you keep your cool, or did you let them bait you into a reaction? Did you have enough receipts to shut them down, or did they wiggle out with some half-assed excuse? Be brutally honest with yourself, because the only thing worse than dealing with a manipulator is *not learning from it.*

Example? Jake Rivers threw you under the bus in a meeting, and while you called him out, you didn't have the emails to back it up. Lesson learned: next time, you'll come armed with enough documentation to bury him before he even opens his mouth.

Every manipulative encounter is a chance to tighten your strategy. Build better boundaries. Strengthen your poker face. Perfect your clapback game. Manipulators count on people being too reactive or too passive to fight back effectively—prove them wrong.

Here's the rule: you don't just beat manipulators—you evolve. Take the lesson, refine your tactics, and make sure they—or anyone else—never get the upper hand again. Next time, you'll be unstoppable.

3.4.5 Staying Unshakeable: Building Resilience For Future Battles

Let's get one thing straight—dealing with two-faced manipulators isn't a one-time fight. These assholes are like cockroaches; for every one you squash, there's another waiting to crawl out of the woodwork. That's why you need to stay unshakeable, no matter how many of them slither into your life. You don't just win the battle—you fortify yourself for the war.

First, accept that some people are just human dumpster fires, and it's not your job to save them. Your job is to protect your peace like it's the last drink of water in the damn desert. They try to rattle you? Too bad—you're a goddamn brick wall. They spin lies? Laugh, shrug, and move on, because their bullshit says more about them than it ever will about you.

Example? Aunt Lydia takes another swipe at your character during Thanksgiving: *"Some people just don't care about family anymore."* Old you might've taken the bait. Unshakeable you? You smile and reply, *"Oh, I care, Lydia, just not enough to play your little games."* Let her stew in her own passive-aggressive nonsense.

Staying unshakeable means you don't let anyone's drama, lies, or petty bullshit crack your armor. You've been through worse, and you'll be damned if Karen from accounting or Jake the credit-stealing jackass is going to be the one to take you down.

Here's the rule: you're not just surviving manipulators—you're thriving despite them. They can throw their worst, but you're already untouchable. Let them try. You're built for this.

Flipping the Script: When Exposing Them Isn't Enough

So, you've mastered the art of the call-out, shut down their lies with cold, hard facts, and watched them squirm under the weight of their own bullshit. Feels good, doesn't it? But don't get too comfortable—because if you think manipulators just pack up and disappear once they've been exposed, you're in for a rude awakening.

See, these people don't operate on logic or accountability. They don't sit back and reflect on their failures. No, they double down.

They rewrite the story, twist the facts, and do everything in their power to make themselves the victim and you the villain. And if you're not ready for this next phase, they'll pull the rug out from under you before you even realize what's happening.

That's why Chapter 4 is all about understanding their playbook—the tricks, the mind games, the psychological warfare they use to manipulate reality itself. Because calling them out is only half the battle. The real power move? Making sure they never get to control the narrative again.

Time to flip the script. Let's go.

CHAPTER FOUR

Turning Manipulation Against Them

Two-faced manipulators love to believe they're the puppet masters of the universe, pulling strings while the rest of us dance to their bullshit tune. But here's the twist—they're not half as clever as they think they are. This chapter isn't about just surviving their games; it's about flipping the board, setting the pieces on fire, and watching them scramble when they realize you've been playing them the whole time.

You're going to dissect their playbook, expose their fragile egos, and use their own weapons against them. No more reacting, no more second-guessing—this is about seizing control and making sure they never see you as an easy target again. Welcome to the art of flipping the script.

Lesson 4.1: Understanding Their Playbook

4.1.1 The Power of the Narrative

Let's be clear—two-faced manipulators aren't just lying; they're running a goddamn propaganda machine. They don't "bend the truth"; they twist, warp, and mangle it until reality is unrecognizable, and suddenly, they're the hero of every story. They thrive on controlling the narrative, not just to convince you, but to make sure everyone around you sees the world through their bullshit-tinted glasses. The goal? Keep you confused, doubting yourself, and—most importantly—too tangled up in their nonsense to fight back.

Well, that ends now.

Why Their Narrative Holds So Much Power

Manipulators aren't necessarily *smart*, but they *are* strategic. They understand that perception is reality, and the more people they get to believe their version of events, the harder it is for you to call them out without looking "dramatic" or "unstable." They don't need the truth on their side—just enough smoke and mirrors to make everyone hesitate.

Here's why their story-twisting works so well:

- **They Play the Helpless Victim:** They could burn your house down and still convince the neighborhood that *you* gave them the match and a heartfelt speech about arson.
- **They Gaslight You Into Oblivion:** They rewrite history so often, you start wondering if *you* imagined the actual events. Spoiler alert: *you didn't*.
- **They Weaponize Public Opinion:** They tell just enough people just enough lies so that when you finally snap and expose them, they get to say, *"See? I told you they were crazy!"*
- **They Project Like a Damn IMAX Theatre:** Whatever they're guilty of, they accuse you of first. It's not *them* stirring the pot—it's you being "paranoid."

When Their Narrative Has You by the Throat

You ever feel like you're fighting an invisible enemy? Like no matter what you do, the story has already been written, and you're somehow the villain? That's by design. By the time you realize what's happening, they've already convinced half your friends, coworkers, or family that *you're* the problem. It's like showing up to a fight where they've already bribed the referee and pre-ordered your loss.

This is what their manipulation looks like in action:

- **You Call Them Out, and Suddenly *You're* the Aggressor**
  What's that? You have actual facts? Receipts? Hard evidence? Cute. The moment you bring up their bullshit, they'll gasp, clutch their pearls, and claim they "can't believe you'd attack them like this." *You're just so mean!*
- **You Try to Defend Yourself, and Now You're "Overreacting"**
  Oh, you don't like being lied about? Too bad. They'll keep their voice calm, condescending, and dripping with faux concern while you're left looking like a lunatic for—checks notes—reacting like a normal person to their gaslighting.
- **They Set You Up, and You Walk Right Into It**
  They'll "innocently" spread a rumor, conveniently in earshot of someone important, and the moment you get mad? Boom. They've got "proof" that you're the unstable one. It's a trap, and they're grinning like a smug little gremlin while you fall right into it.

When to Strike for Maximum Damage

You're not going to beat them at their own game by playing nice. If they've built their empire on a mountain of lies, your job isn't to push politely—it's to *kick the whole damn thing over*. But timing is everything. Strike too early, and they'll slither their way out with another sob story. Wait too long, and they'll have cemented their version of events so well that even *you* will start to question reality.

Here's how you take them down effectively:

- **Strike When the Lies Start Stacking**
  Let them build their fantasy world nice and high—then torch it. Expose them when they've committed *too* hard to their own bullshit, so backtracking makes them look like a damn clown.
  What to say: "Wow, so this week I'm the villain? Last week it was Derek. Who's up next?"

- **Expose Them in Front of Their Followers**
  These snakes *need* an audience. They thrive on validation. So what happens when you rip their mask off in front of their biggest fans? Humiliation. Sweet, sweet public humiliation.
  What to say: "Oh, I love this version of events—pure fiction! You should write a book. What's the title? *How to Gaslight People and Get Away With It?*"
- **When You Have the Receipts Locked and Loaded**
  There is *nothing* more satisfying than watching a manipulator's soul leave their body when you pull out undeniable proof.
  What to say: "Huh. That's weird, because this email says *exactly the opposite* of what you just claimed. Wanna explain?"
- **When They Think They've Won**
  Let them believe they got away with it. Let them bask in the glow of their bullshit. Then, when they least expect it, drop the hammer.
  What to say: "I was going to correct you earlier, but I wanted to see how deep you'd dig your own grave. You done now?"

When NOT to Engage

This is war, not a bar fight. You don't throw punches when it won't land. There are times when calling them out is a waste of energy—because *they* will never admit the truth, and *everyone else* is too far up their ass to care. Here's when you hold back:

- **When You're Too Emotional**
  They *want* you to be angry. They *need* you to lash out so they can play the victim. Keep that poker face on and make them *wait* for the fallout.
- **When They've Already Convinced the Masses**
  If they've fully poisoned the well, no amount of logic will fix it. Sometimes, you have to let them hang themselves *before* you make your move.

- **When It's Not Worth the Battle**
  Not every manipulator deserves your time. Some of these idiots are playing checkers while you're out here strategizing a damn war campaign. Let them stay in their delusions.

The Bottom Line

Two-faced manipulators don't just tell lies; they *live* them. They construct their entire reality out of smoke and bullshit, hoping you'll choke on it and stay too dazed to fight back. But now? Now you see the game. You see their strategy. And once you see it, you can *destroy* it.

So the next time one of these snakes tries to spin their tale, don't just call them out—obliterate them. Strike hard, strike smart, and make damn sure they *never* try that shit with you again.

4.1.2 Spotting Their Patterns

Manipulators don't just wake up and decide to screw with you—they **run the same tired playbook on everyone**. If you learn to **spot their patterns early**, you can shut them down before they even get started. These people aren't creative; they **rely on predictability, hesitation, and your willingness to see the best in people**. Stop giving them that advantage.

How They Condition You

It starts with **small manipulations.** A little guilt trip here, a small "misunderstanding" there. They test you, see what they can get away with, and then they **push further.** The moment you **let one slide**, they **tighten the leash.** Before you know it, you're trapped in their version of events, questioning your own damn reality. **Not anymore.**

Setting the Tone Before They Do *(Merged from Chapter 8: Establishing Boundaries)*

The first rule of dealing with manipulators? **Don't let them write the script.** If you hesitate, if you second-guess yourself, they'll **rewrite reality before you even realize what's happening.** The moment you waver, they've already decided the ending of your story, and guess what? **You're the bad guy.**

- **They thrive on hesitation**—the longer you take to call them out, the more control they take.
- **They flip the script before you react**—by the time you push back, they've already made themselves the victim.
- **They make you question yourself**—so you end up defending **your own reality** while they spin more lies.

How to Flip the Script Before They Do

- **Call them out early.** If something feels off, **say something.** Manipulators don't expect resistance—give them some.
- **Be firm and unemotional.** The second you react emotionally, **they've got you.** Keep it **cold, calm, and brutal.**
- **Reinforce the truth immediately.** If they say something twisted, **correct it fast and loudly**—don't let their version settle in.

Once you recognize **their patterns**, you strip them of their power. They rely on **people being too distracted or too forgiving to notice** their game. When you **see it, call it, and shut it down immediately**, you **break their entire strategy.** Let them find someone else to manipulate—you're **done playing their game.**

4.1.3 Exploiting Their Ego

Most manipulators are driven by an inflated sense of self-importance. Their ego is both their greatest weapon and their biggest vulnerability. They believe they're smarter, more cunning, and more deserving than everyone else, which is why they feel entitled to manipulate others. But this arrogance also blinds them to their weaknesses, making it easier for you to exploit their overconfidence.

The key to exploiting their ego is subtlety. Directly confronting them about their self-importance will only make them defensive, which isn't the goal. Instead, play into their need for validation while subtly steering the narrative in your favor. For example, if they're trying to dominate a conversation, let them feel like they've won—but only on a trivial point. Meanwhile, use their overconfidence to guide them into making mistakes. Encourage them to elaborate on their lies or inconsistencies; the more they talk, the more likely they are to slip up.

Another tactic is to use their ego against them by pretending to align with their interests. For instance, if they're trying to undermine you in a group setting, agree with them on a minor point to lower their guard. Then, introduce a counterpoint that subtly exposes their intentions. Their need to appear superior will often drive them to overreact, making their true motives more apparent to others.

4.1.4 Emotional Hooks

Manipulators know that emotions are the strings they can pull to control you. They're experts at finding your vulnerabilities and using them to their advantage. Guilt is one of their favorite tools—phrases like "I can't believe you'd do this after everything I've done for you" are designed to make you question your actions and feel obligated to comply with their demands. Fear is another common tactic, whether it's fear of losing their approval, fear of conflict, or fear of being isolated.

To break free from these emotional hooks, you need to identify and neutralize them. Start by recognizing the emotions they're trying to trigger. Are they making you feel guilty for setting boundaries? Are they instilling fear by exaggerating potential consequences? Once you've named the emotion, you can begin to detach from it. Remind yourself that their words are a reflection of their manipulation, not your reality.

One effective way to counter emotional hooks is to practice detachment. Instead of reacting emotionally, respond with calm, measured statements that acknowledge their attempt without giving it power. For instance, if they say, "You're so selfish for not helping me," you can reply, "I'm sorry you feel that way, but I've made my decision." This approach denies them the emotional reaction they're seeking, forcing them to rethink their strategy.

4.1.5 The Achilles' Heel

Every manipulator has a weak spot—a vulnerability they work hard to conceal because they know it could unravel their facade. It might be a deep-seated fear of rejection, an insecurity about their intelligence, or an obsessive need for control. Identifying this Achilles' heel is your ticket to turning the tables.

The challenge lies in finding it. Manipulators are skilled at masking their vulnerabilities, often projecting them onto others to deflect attention. Pay attention to what triggers an exaggerated reaction from them. Do they lash out when their authority is questioned? Do they become defensive when someone challenges their knowledge or expertise? These overreactions can provide valuable clues.

Once you've identified their weak spot, use it sparingly and strategically. The goal isn't to attack them outright but to subtly remind them that you're aware of their vulnerability. For example, if their Achilles' heel is their fear of being exposed, you might hint at the consequences of their actions becoming public knowledge. This approach keeps them on edge without making you the obvious aggressor.

Lesson 4.2: Shifting Power Dynamics

4.2.1 Taking Back Control

Here's the thing about manipulators: they thrive on your confusion, your second-guessing, and your willingness to let them dictate the terms. You've been playing their game long enough—it's time to flip the board and remind them who's really in charge. Taking back control doesn't require a screaming match or some dramatic confrontation. In fact, the best way to reclaim your power is to do it so subtly that they don't even realize you're pulling the rug out from under them.

Start by cutting off their oxygen supply: *your reactions.* Manipulators live for drama, so starve them of it. When they're expecting you to lash out, respond with the emotional equivalent of a shrug. "Oh, really? That's interesting," you say with a bored smile as they try to bait you into a fight. Your lack of engagement will drive them absolutely insane. Remember, the goal isn't to win their approval—it's to show them that they no longer control the narrative.

Next, set the tone. Manipulators hate it when you take the lead because it means they can't steer you into their traps. So, take the damn wheel. When they start spinning their bullshit, interrupt with, "Actually, let me stop you right there—this is what's going to happen." Your calm, authoritative tone will throw them off balance faster than a toddler on roller skates. They might try to regain control, but by staying firm and unshakable, you send a clear message: *Game over.*

4.2.2 The Art of Deflection

Manipulators are like magicians—distracting you with one hand while they screw you over with the other. The good news? You can play their game better than they can. Deflection isn't just a tactic; it's an art form. Done right, it's like watching their schemes implode in real-time.

When they come at you with their usual nonsense, don't take the bait. Instead, redirect the conversation to something they didn't see coming. Let's say they're trying to guilt-trip you for not agreeing to their latest demand. Instead of defending yourself, hit them with a casual, "Oh, speaking of plans, I was just thinking about how productive I've been lately. What have you been up to?" Watch as their face contorts in confusion, their carefully laid trap dissolving into thin air.

But deflection isn't just about steering the conversation—it's about forcing them to expose their own ridiculousness. When they make a bold claim or try to shift blame, respond with questions that turn their logic into a pretzel. "Huh, that's interesting. Can you explain how that works again? I must have missed something." The more they try to explain, the more they reveal how little sense they actually make.

The best part about deflection? It lets you maintain control without looking like the aggressor. While they're scrambling to recover, you're sitting back, sipping your metaphorical tea, and enjoying the chaos.

4.2.3 Reframing the Narrative

Manipulators rely on their ability to control the story, but here's the thing: the story is only as powerful as the audience believes it to be. If they've painted you as the villain, it's time to pick up the paintbrush and rewrite the script.

First, don't bother denying their accusations outright. They want you to waste energy defending yourself while they keep piling on the bullshit. Instead, casually dismantle their narrative by presenting a version of events that's not only more plausible but also makes them look like the manipulative clown they are. For example, if they're telling everyone you're "unreliable," don't argue. Just make a point of showing up early, being prepared, and letting your actions contradict their lies. Nothing screams "liar" louder than hard evidence to the contrary.

Next, use humor as your secret weapon. Nothing deflates a manipulator's ego faster than turning their carefully crafted drama into a joke. When they're trying to spin their story, laugh it off with, "Wow, you've got quite the imagination. Ever thought about writing fiction?" Your dismissive tone will infuriate them, especially when others start laughing along with you.

Finally, remember that manipulators can't handle transparency. When you're honest and upfront about your intentions, it throws a wrench in their plans. They thrive on ambiguity, so by being clear and direct, you strip them of the ability to twist your words. Reframing the narrative isn't just about damage control—it's about taking back the microphone and making sure everyone hears *your* version loud and clear.

4.2.4 Keeping Them Guessing

The one thing manipulators hate more than losing control is unpredictability. They want to know what you'll do next so they can stay ten steps ahead. But when you become an enigma, you're suddenly the one calling the shots.

Start by mixing up your behavior. If you're usually quick to respond to their messages, take your sweet time. If you're typically agreeable, throw in a firm "no" just for fun. The goal is to make them realize they can't predict your moves, which will leave them scrambling to adjust their strategy.

Another way to keep them guessing is to play your cards close to your chest. Manipulators love gathering information they can weaponize against you, so give them nothing to work with. When they ask probing questions, respond with vague, noncommittal answers. "What are you working on?" they might ask. "Oh, just a few things here and there," you reply with a smile. Let them stew in their own paranoia as they try to figure out what you're up to.

Finally, don't underestimate the power of silence. When manipulators try to provoke you, resist the urge to engage. A well-timed pause can be more unsettling than any comeback. Let them fill the awkward silence with their own rambling, and watch as their confidence crumbles.

4.2.5 Power Through Silence

Speaking of silence, let's talk about its real power. Manipulators rely on your words to fuel their schemes, so the less you say, the less ammunition they have. Silence is a weapon, and when wielded correctly, it can be devastating.

Think about it: what's more unnerving than someone who refuses to react? When you remain calm and quiet in the face of their provocations, you rob them of the validation they crave. Instead of getting sucked into their drama, you maintain an air of unshakable composure, which not only disarms them but also makes you look like the bigger person.

But silence isn't just about refusing to engage—it's about using pauses strategically. When they say something outrageous, don't rush to respond. Let the weight of their words hang in the air. Watch as they squirm under the pressure of their own bullshit. When you finally do speak, make every word count. A simple, "Is that so?" can carry more weight than a long-winded rebuttal.

In the end, silence isn't weakness—it's power. And when manipulators realize they can't get a rise out of you, they'll start to lose their grip on the situation. That's when you know you've won.

4.3 Rewriting the Storyline

4.3.1 Becoming the Unreliable Witness

Manipulators rely on being seen as the authority, the trustworthy voice, the poor little victim, or whatever role gets people to buy their bullshit. Your job? Undermine their credibility so thoroughly they look like they couldn't be trusted to water a plant without screwing it up.

How do you do that? Subtlety. You don't come out swinging, shouting, "They're full of crap!"—that's exactly what they want because it makes you look defensive. Instead, let them sabotage themselves. Ask seemingly innocent questions that lead them into contradictions. "Wait, didn't you say you were working late last night? Oh, you were at dinner? Wow, you must have a clone—you're everywhere!" Say it with a smirk and watch their brain short-circuit as they try to clean up the mess they just made.

Another trick: make them doubt their own story. "Really? That's not what I heard." Pause. Sip your coffee. Then change the subject. You're not even accusing them—you're just planting seeds of doubt in their audience and in their head. And the beauty? If they try to call you out, they look paranoid. Now they're the crazy one.

The key is to be calm, composed, and just shady enough that their credibility starts to crack. Once their shiny facade starts peeling, it's only a matter of time before the whole thing collapses.

4.3.2 Planting Seeds of Doubt

The manipulator's **worst nightmare** is people **questioning them.** They need their audience to believe every word **without hesitation.** So your mission? **Sprinkle a little doubt into the mix.** Think of yourself as a **gardener of chaos**, planting tiny seeds that'll grow into a **forest of skepticism.**

The Power of Subtle Doubt

The truth doesn't always need to be **loud**—sometimes, a **whisper in the right place** is enough to **undo an entire manipulation campaign.** Manipulators love to **control the story,** but they underestimate how easy it is to **plant doubt in the minds of their audience.**

Here's how you **quietly unravel their credibility without ever looking like the aggressor:**

- **Drop casual contradictions.** When they're telling their **grand narrative,** interject with a casual, *"That's interesting—I hadn't heard it that way before."* Or, *"Huh, that's not what so-and-so mentioned."* You're **not calling them a liar outright**—just **nudging** people to take a second look.
- **Use their own ego against them.** Ask them to **explain things in excruciating detail.** Manipulators thrive on **ambiguity,** so force them to **dig deep,** and their **inconsistencies will bubble to the surface.** *"Wait, if you were at that meeting, how did you also have time to call Sarah? Oh, you didn't call her? But didn't you say…?"* **Boom—implosion.**
- **Give them enough rope to hang themselves.** Instead of arguing, **let them talk.** The more they **elaborate on their bullshit,** the more tangled they get.
- **Feed selective information to others.** If someone **already doubts the manipulator,** give them **just enough** to confirm their suspicions without exposing yourself. A simple *"I don't know, something about that story doesn't add up, but maybe I'm wrong"* works wonders.

Weaponizing Fake Praise

Another **brilliant tool** in your arsenal? The **sideways compliment.** *"Wow, you always have an answer for everything! It's impressive* *how you keep track of all the details."* Let them **bask in the fake praise** while everyone else **starts wondering if their 'answers' are a little too convenient.**

4.3.3 The Strategic Leak

Sometimes, the best way to expose a manipulator is to let their actions do the talking. Enter: the strategic leak. This isn't about gossiping or stooping to their level—it's about carefully revealing just enough truth to let their lies unravel.

Step one: identify what information needs to be leaked. Is it an inconsistency in their story? A shady action they thought no one noticed? Pick something that's undeniable, something they can't weasel their way out of. Step two: choose your audience wisely. Share the tidbit with someone who has influence but isn't likely to run back to the manipulator. Think of it as planting a landmine—they won't see it coming until it's too late.

The leak doesn't have to be dramatic. In fact, the subtler, the better. "Oh, did you hear about how [manipulator] handled that situation? Kind of strange, right?" You're not making accusations; you're just starting a conversation. Once the truth starts circulating, the manipulator will be too busy putting out fires to focus on you.

And here's the kicker: manipulators are control freaks. They hate not knowing who's talking about them or what's being said. By releasing just enough information to make them paranoid, you're shifting the power dynamic. They're no longer the puppet master—you are.

4.3.4 The Counter-Narrative

Manipulators love their stories because they think they're untouchable. They craft their lies so meticulously, they believe no one would dare challenge them. Time to prove them wrong.

Creating a counter-narrative isn't about spinning your own web of lies. It's about shining a spotlight on the truth in a way that exposes their deception. First, identify the core of their story. What's the lie they're clinging to? Next, dismantle it piece by piece with facts, logic, and a touch of flair. "Oh, they said they were the ones who saved the project? Funny, because I've got the emails right here showing otherwise. Must've been a team effort."

Don't just stop at debunking their claims—take control of the story entirely. Frame yourself as the calm, rational person in contrast to their chaotic antics. Use phrases like, "I think there's been some misunderstanding," or, "I just want to clear up any confusion." These statements not only make you look like the adult in the room but also subtly imply that they've been spreading confusion (which they have).

And for the final blow? Humor. Nothing deflates a manipulator's ego like turning their grand narrative into a punchline. "Oh, I didn't realize we were rewriting history—should I grab a pen?" Delivered with a smile, this line takes the wind out of their sails and shows everyone that you're not afraid of their games.

4.3.5 The Subtle Power Play

Winning against a manipulator doesn't require a dramatic showdown. Sometimes, the most effective moves are the quiet ones—the subtle power plays that leave them scrambling while you walk away with a smirk.

One of the simplest power plays? Refuse to engage. When they try to provoke you, respond with a calm, "I see." No emotion, no argument—just a flat acknowledgment that leaves them wondering what the hell you're thinking. The less they understand your reactions, the harder it is for them to manipulate you.

Another move: control the timing. Manipulators want everything on their schedule, so take that away from them. Delay your responses, change the subject, or let their schemes stew for a while before addressing them. By refusing to play on their timeline, you're reminding them that they don't call the shots.

And let's not forget the power of confidence. Walk into the room like you own it, even if they're trying to undermine you. Speak clearly, make eye contact, and don't hesitate to throw in a sarcastic comment or two. "Oh, I didn't realize we were taking life advice from you now—what a treat." Delivered with just the right amount of bite, it shows that you're unshakable and completely unimpressed by their antics.

Subtle power plays aren't about grand gestures—they're about control. And when you master them, manipulators won't know what hit them.

4.4 Winning the Long Game

4.4.1 The Patience Strategy

When it comes to manipulators, the most dangerous weapon in your arsenal is time. They live for quick wins, snap reactions, and chaos. Why? Because rushing you into decisions keeps you off balance and them in control. Patience, on the other hand, is their worst enemy. When you slow the game down, you give yourself the power to observe, strategize, and dismantle their schemes bit by bit.

But patience isn't passive—it's strategic. Think of it as a mental chess game where you force them to make the first mistake. For example, when they start spreading rumors or trying to stir up drama, don't react right away. Let them believe they've got you cornered while you quietly gather your evidence and allies. Then, when the time is right, flip the board over and watch the pieces scatter.

Turning the Tables Twist: Manipulators thrive on emotional reactions—so give them *nothing*. When they bait you with insults, guilt trips, or false accusations, respond with cold, calculated indifference. A simple, "Interesting point," or "We'll see," is enough to keep them guessing. Let them stew in their own paranoia while you plan your next move. The less they know about what's coming, the harder it'll hit.

4.4.2 Rebuilding Your Reputation

Let's face it: manipulators love destroying reputations almost as much as they love hearing themselves talk. If they've dragged your name through the mud, it's time to remind everyone why you were never the problem in the first place.

Start by fixing the optics. Manipulators use lies to create the illusion of control, so counter them with hard, undeniable truths. Did they call you unreliable? Fine—show up early, over-deliver, and make their accusations look ridiculous. Did they paint you as the villain? Flip the narrative by being the bigger person and showing grace when it's least expected. Nothing frustrates a manipulator more than watching their smear campaign collapse under the weight of your actions.

Turning the Tables Twist: Use their attacks as fuel. If they're talking shit behind your back, make sure their audience sees you thriving. Post your successes publicly, casually mention your accomplishments, and let your victories speak for themselves. Every time they try to drag you down, you'll rise higher—and that will drive them absolutely insane.

4.4.3 The Network Effect

If manipulators are the weeds in your social garden, then your network is the fertilizer that ensures they can't take root. Build strong relationships with the people who matter most, and manipulators won't stand a chance of isolating you.

Here's how you play it: first, repair any damage they've done to your relationships. If they've driven a wedge between you and someone else, confront the issue directly. "Hey, I heard [manipulator] mentioned something about me. I just wanted to clear things up." Keep it straightforward and unflinching—no drama, no theatrics. Once people see you're willing to address issues head-on, the manipulator's credibility starts to crumble.

Turning the Tables Twist: Don't just defend your network—expand it. The more allies you have, the harder it becomes for manipulators to control the narrative. Introduce people in your circle to each other, strengthen their bonds, and create a united front. The manipulator will soon realize they're not just up against you—they're up against an entire ecosystem of support.

4.4.4 Lessons from the Battle

Surviving a manipulator's games is like surviving a car crash: painful, disorienting, but ultimately, a learning experience. And if you don't learn from it, you're just setting yourself up to get hit again. So let's take stock of the wreckage and make sure you're stronger the next time some two-faced idiot comes along.

First, identify what worked. Did you shut them down with humor? Outlast them with patience? Rally your allies to expose their lies? Whatever it was, add it to your toolbox. Next, figure out what didn't work. Maybe you got sucked into their drama too quickly, or maybe you underestimated how far they'd go to win. That's fine—own it, learn from it, and move on.

Turning the Tables Twist: Keep a "manipulator playbook." Every time you deal with one of these clowns, jot down their tactics, your responses, and the outcome. Over time, you'll have a personalized guide to spotting and neutralizing manipulators before they even get started. Think of it as your secret weapon for staying ten steps ahead.

4.4.5 Making Yourself Untouchable

Here's the final, most satisfying step in the long game: becoming completely, gloriously untouchable. When you reach this level, manipulators won't just lose—they won't even bother trying to mess with you in the first place.

Start with unshakable boundaries. Manipulators test limits, so make sure yours are bulletproof. The moment they try to cross a line, shut it down with zero hesitation. "That's not up for discussion," is all you need to say. Don't justify, don't explain, don't give them an inch to work with.

Next, cultivate independence. Manipulators rely on your need for validation, approval, or support. Take those needs away, and they have no leverage. Build a life that's so fulfilling, so full of confidence and self-assurance, that their petty games can't even dent your armor.

Turning the Tables Twist: Use your unshakable confidence to intimidate them. Walk into every room like you own it, speak with authority, and don't hesitate to call out bullshit when you see it. "Oh, is that the story we're going with? Fascinating." Delivered with a smirk, it lets them know you're onto their games—and that they're completely outmatched.

Checkmate: Beating Manipulators Before They Make Their Move

You've flipped the script. You've turned their own tactics against them, ripped their bullshit narratives apart, and left them scrambling to regain control. But let's be real— manipulators don't go down easy. They regroup, re-strategize, and come back with even slicker tricks, hoping you'll let your guard down just long enough for them to sink their claws back in.

That's why stopping them isn't enough—you have to *outsmart* them.

Chapter 5 isn't about defense anymore. It's about staying ten steps ahead, seeing through their games before they even start, and making sure they *choke* on their own manipulation. You're not just shutting them down—you're making sure they never even get the chance to try again.

Welcome to the next level: Outsmarting the Manipulators.

CHAPTER FIVE

Outsmarting the Manipulators

Manipulators think they're the smartest people in the room, but here's the reality—they're predictable as hell. Their tactics aren't genius; they're just polished bullshit they've used on enough people to make it look convincing. Outsmarting them isn't about stooping to their level—it's about being ten steps ahead and making them choke on their own games. This chapter is your playbook for dismantling their tricks, exposing their lies, and walking away victorious every damn time. They want a mental chess match? Good. You're about to checkmate their manipulative asses.

Lesson 5.1: Cracking The Manipulators Code

5.1.1 Recognizing Common Manipulation Tactics: How They Fuck With Your Head

Manipulators don't reinvent the wheel—they just keep rolling out the same tired, toxic tricks and hope you're too distracted, polite, or trusting to notice. The thing is, once you learn to spot their go-to tactics, they stop being sneaky masterminds and start looking like what they really are: pathetic, predictable amateurs who peaked in high school. Recognizing manipulation isn't rocket science—it's pattern recognition for bullshit. And by the time you finish this snippet, you'll be able to see their tricks coming from a mile away.

Their Greatest Hits: The Manipulator's Playbook

1. **The Guilt Trip Symphony**
   These assholes are virtuosos of guilt. They'll twist the situation so hard, you'll end up apologizing for *their* fuck-ups.

- ○ **Example**: "I can't believe you'd do this to me after everything I've done for you!" Oh, shut up. You didn't do jack shit except create problems.

2. **The Sob Story™**
Suddenly, they've got the saddest life ever, and somehow, you're the only person who can save them.
- ○ **Example**: "No one else understands me like you do." Newsflash: no one else *wants* to deal with your crap, and neither do I.

3. **Gaslighting 101**
The classic "You're imagining things" move. They'll deny, deflect, and rewrite history until you're questioning your own sanity.
- ○ **Them**: "I never said that."
- ○ **You**: "Funny, because I have the receipts right here."

4. **The Fake Ally Act**
They pretend to have your back, but behind the scenes, they're stirring the pot and making sure you're the one who looks bad.
- ○ **Example**: "I only told them because I thought it would help you!" Sure, Jan.

5. **The Silent Treatment Power Play**
They'll go radio silent, making you think you've done something wrong, all while they sit back and enjoy watching you squirm.
- ○ **What to Do**: Let them stew in their silence. You've got better things to do.

Why These Tactics Work (Until You Wise Up)

Manipulation works because it targets your emotions. They'll twist your empathy, kindness, and guilt into weapons they can use against you. But once you spot the patterns, their tactics lose their power. Here's why they're effective—until they're not:

- **They Exploit Your Need to Please**: Manipulators bank on the fact that you don't want to rock the boat.
- **They Weaponize Your Emotions**: Whether it's guilt, pity, or anger, they know how to push your buttons.
- **They Count on Confusion**: If they can keep you second-guessing yourself, they can keep controlling the situation.

How to Shut Down Their Tactics Like a Pro

1. **Call Out Their Bullshit**
   The second you spot a manipulative move, name it for what it is. Manipulators hate being exposed.
   - **What to Say**: "You're trying to guilt-trip me, and it's not going to work."
2. **Stick to the Facts**
   Don't let them drag you into an emotional spiral. Keep the conversation grounded in reality.
   - **Example**: "I'm not discussing how you feel about this—I'm sticking to what actually happened."
3. **Refuse to Engage**
   Some tactics, like the silent treatment, only work if you react. Don't give them the satisfaction.
   - **What to Do**: Walk away and let them play their little games alone.
4. **Hold Your Boundaries**
   Manipulators hate boundaries because they're used to getting their way. Stand firm, and don't apologize for protecting your peace.
   - **What to Say**: "I'm not comfortable with this, and I'm not going to change my mind."

The Bottom Line

Manipulators think their tactics are clever, but once you see the playbook, their whole act falls apart. Recognizing their tricks is your first step to outsmarting them and taking back control. Let them run their tired games on someone else while you stand tall, unbothered, and completely immune to their bullshit. You're smarter than their manipulative crap, and now they know it.

5.1.2 The Language Of Deception: Spotting Lies In How They Talk

Manipulators don't just lie—they turn it into a goddamn art form. They're not bold enough to give you outright bullshit (at least not all the time); instead, they use vague language, half-truths, and carefully chosen words to spin their web. But here's the thing about lies: no matter how pretty they dress them up, the cracks are always there if you're paying attention.

One of their favorite tools? **Vagueness.** They'll dodge specifics like a politician at a press conference. *"I think we agreed on that last week,"* or *"I was under the impression you were handling it."* Translation: *"I didn't do shit, and I'm trying to cover my ass."*

Then there's **overexplaining.** When someone's telling the truth, they get to the point. But a liar? They'll give you a goddamn novel of excuses, all in an effort to make their story sound "convincing." The irony? The more they explain, the faker it sounds.

Example? Jake Rivers claims he "forgot" to loop you in on a critical email chain. When pressed, he starts rambling about how *"It must've been when I was swamped with other tasks, and, you know, things just got so hectic."* Yeah, Jake. Sure.

Finally, manipulators love **redefining words.** They'll twist the meaning of something you said to fit their agenda. *"Well, when you said you'd help, I assumed you meant you'd handle everything."* Nice try.

Here's the rule: listen closely. Their words are their weapon, but they're also their weakness. Spot the cracks, and their whole narrative crumbles.

5.1.3 The Emotional Bait: How They Use Your Feelings Against You

Two-faced manipulators aren't just liars—they're emotional con artists. They don't need to outsmart you because they're too busy outplaying your feelings. They dangle emotional bait like guilt, fear, or even fake flattery, and the second you bite, they've got you hooked. The worst part? They make you feel like you walked right into the trap. Spoiler alert: you didn't—it's their entire strategy.

Here's the move: they use guilt to make you think you owe them something. *"I just thought you'd care enough to help,"* they'll sigh, with their best "poor me" face. Translation? *"Let me manipulate you into doing my dirty work because I'm too lazy to do it myself."*

Fear is another favorite. They'll threaten consequences, real or implied, to keep you under their thumb. *"If you don't step up, this whole thing might fall apart,"* they'll say, knowing damn well the problem is *them,* not you.

And let's not forget the classic: fake flattery. *"You're the only one who can handle this,"* they gush. What they really mean is, *"I'm about to dump a mess on you because you're competent, and I'm a manipulative slacker."*

Example? Taylor Monroe lays it on thick: *"I couldn't have done this without you—you're amazing!"* Next thing you know, you're carrying her workload while she takes credit.

Here's the rule: emotional bait only works if you bite. Recognize the trap, call it out, and let them deal with their own damn problems. You've got better things to do than play their emotional puppet.

5.1.4 The Illusion Of Innocence: Why They Always Play The Victim

Manipulators have a signature move, and it's as predictable as it is infuriating: they play the fucking victim. No matter how much chaos they cause, no matter how many lies they spin, they somehow twist the narrative to make themselves look like the poor, misunderstood saint in a world full of assholes. Spoiler alert: they're the asshole.

Here's their playbook: they screw up, stir the pot, and when they get called out? Boom—they flip the script. *"I didn't mean it like that,"* or *"I was just trying to help, but no one ever appreciates me."* Yeah, sure, Karen, you're practically a goddamn martyr.

The illusion of innocence is their shield, their escape hatch, and their golden ticket out of accountability. They rely on the fact that most people hate conflict and will back off if someone starts crying crocodile tears or looking hurt. Don't fall for it.

Example? Aunt Lydia guilt-trips you for not attending her last-minute dinner. When you explain that you had plans, she hits you with, *"I just thought family was more important."* Translation? *"I'm going to make you feel like shit because I didn't get my way."* Fuck that.

Here's the rule: just because they play the victim doesn't mean they're innocent. Call out the game for what it is. Let them whine, let them pout, and let them wallow in their fake-ass sorrow. You're not here to babysit their fragile ego. Their innocence? It's a goddamn illusion, and you're about to shatter it.

5.1.5 *The Web Of Control: Understanding The Layers Of Their Manipulation*

Two-faced manipulators don't just play one game—they're running a whole fucking operation. Think of their bullshit as a web: every lie, every guilt trip, every passive-aggressive comment is a thread designed to pull you in and keep you stuck. The longer you stay in their web, the harder it is to see the strings they're pulling—and that's exactly what they're counting on.

The web of control works in layers. First, they isolate you. They'll whisper behind your back, plant seeds of doubt, and make you feel like no one else has your back. Then comes the guilt and fear—classic emotional blackmail. *"You don't want to disappoint me, do you?"* or *"If you don't step up, this whole thing could fall apart."* Translation: *"Do what I want or I'll make your life hell."*

Finally, they throw in a little love-bombing to keep you hooked. One second they're making you feel like shit, and the next they're telling you how much they "appreciate" you. It's manipulation on steroids, and it's designed to make you question your every move.

Example? Jake Rivers blames you for missing a deadline but follows it up with, *"I know you're doing your best—I just want to make sure we're all on track."* Fuck off, Jake. We both know you're just covering your ass.

Here's the rule: see the web for what it is—a trap. Once you recognize the layers of their manipulation, you can tear it down thread by thread and leave them stuck in the mess they created.

Lesson 5.2: Countering Their Moves

5.2.1 The Reverse Play: Using Their Tactics Against Them

Manipulators think they've got the monopoly on mind games, but here's the truth: their playbook isn't that complicated. The Reverse Play isn't just about defense—it's about turning their own weapons against them and leaving them gasping for air.

Take their favorite move: interrupting. They love to bulldoze conversations to stay in control. Flip it on them. Cut them off mid-sentence with something like, "Oh, sorry, I thought we were done with your bullshit." Watch their smug composure crack. They're not used to being outmaneuvered in their own game.

And let's talk about guilt trips. These assholes are experts at playing the victim, making you feel like the bad guy for setting boundaries. Here's how you break them: agree, but make it sting. When they whine, "You've changed," hit back with, "You're damn right I have. Got tired of your crap." They won't know whether to cry or applaud.

Then there's silence—your secret weapon. Manipulators thrive on reaction. Starve them of it. When they're spinning their tale of woe, sit there like a stone-cold judge. No nodding, no interruptions, just a blank stare that screams, *You're boring me to death.* They'll unravel faster than a cheap sweater.

The best part? You don't have to outsmart them—you just have to show them they're not as clever as they think. Play their game better, and you'll leave them with nothing but their own pathetic reflection.

5.2.2 The Power Of Questions: Undermining Them With Strategic Inquiry

Manipulators hate questions, especially the kind that make them squirm. Their whole strategy relies on throwing you off balance, so flipping the script with sharp, strategic inquiries is like shining a spotlight on their bullshit. They won't know whether to answer or run for cover.

The trick? Keep your tone calm, like you're genuinely curious. "Wait, can you explain that again?" is your new best friend. Make them repeat their lies. Every time they do, they'll trip over a detail or contradict themselves. You're not just poking holes—you're tearing the whole damn thing apart.

Then there's the killer move: ask *why*. Manipulators hate "why" questions because it forces them to justify themselves. "Why did you do that?" or "Why didn't you mention this before?" puts them on the defensive, and guess what? They're not nearly as good at improvising as they think they are. They'll flounder, stall, or worse—double down on their nonsense, which only makes them look guiltier.

And let's not forget the nuclear option: the rapid-fire interrogation. Hit them with a barrage of specific questions—when, where, who, how. It's like pulling threads on a cheap suit. Pretty soon, the whole thing unravels, and they're left standing there in their metaphorical underwear.

Questions aren't just a tool—they're a weapon. Use them wisely, and you'll leave manipulators exposed, humiliated, and scrambling to find an exit.

5.2.3 Disarming With Logic: Exposing Flaws In Their Arguments

Manipulators hate logic. It's their kryptonite. They thrive on chaos, emotions, and confusion—because facts? Facts expose them for the conniving frauds they are. So, here's the play: stay calm, stay sharp, and weaponize logic like a damn sniper.

First, strip their argument down to the bare bones. They'll say something vague like, "You always make me feel this way." Always? Really? Hit them back with, "Define 'always.' Are we talking 24/7, or just when you don't get your way?" Watch them stutter and squirm as their bullshit crumbles under its own weight.

Next, pin them down with specifics. Manipulators thrive on grey areas, but when you ask for dates, times, or examples, their whole narrative falls apart. "When exactly did that happen? Because I seem to remember it going a little differently." They'll panic, backpedal, or try to change the subject. Don't let them. Keep the pressure on.

And when they try to shift blame or guilt-trip you? Double down on the logic. "So, let me get this straight—you're mad because I didn't let you walk all over me? Yeah, that makes total sense." Spoiler: it doesn't, and they damn well know it.

Logic isn't sexy, but it's devastatingly effective. While they're scrambling to spin their next lie, you'll be calmly dismantling their whole argument brick by pathetic brick. Nothing says "game over" like cold, hard facts.

5.2.4 Staying Unemotional: How To Keep Your Cool While They Lose Theirs

Manipulators feed off your emotions like goddamn vampires. They thrive on chaos, tears, and that moment when you lose your shit. But here's the kicker: if you keep your cool, they've got nothing. Nada. Their power dissolves faster than a cheap aspirin in water.

Staying unemotional doesn't mean you're indifferent—it means you're playing the long game. When they're baiting you with their petty bullshit, don't bite. They want you to scream, cry, or flip a table. Instead, hit them with a deadpan, "That's cute. Are you done?" Watch their face as their attempt to rile you up crashes and burns.

Here's the magic of staying calm: it makes *them* look unhinged. The louder and more frantic they get, the more you look like the rational adult in the room. It's a power move, plain and simple. Let them dig their own grave while you stand there with a metaphorical shovel, ready to bury their nonsense.

And when they really push your buttons—because let's face it, they'll try—take a beat. Breathe. Remind yourself that their bullshit isn't worth your energy. You're not here to match their drama; you're here to outclass it.

Keeping your cool isn't just a strategy; it's a goddamn flex. Because while they're busy throwing their tantrum, you're already ten steps ahead, cool as ice and ready to take them down.

5.2.5 The Element Of Confusion: Throwing Them Off Their Game

Manipulators think they're the smartest fuckers in the room. They've got their scripts, their rehearsed lines, and their little bag of tricks. So what do you do? Burn their damn playbook. Hit them with the one thing they can't handle: pure, unfiltered confusion.

First rule: answer their questions with questions. When they say, "Why are you acting like this?" fire back with, "Why do you care?" or, "What exactly do you mean by 'this'?" Watch their gears grind to a halt. They'll either have to explain their bullshit (which they can't) or shut the hell up. Either way, you win.

Next, throw in a curveball they don't see coming. Change the subject completely. They're mid-rant about something you "did wrong," and you hit them with, "Hey, did you hear about the weather tomorrow?" It's so random it'll short-circuit their brain. Manipulators need control, and this move yanks it right out of their sweaty little hands.

And don't underestimate the power of contradiction. Agree with them in a way that's so absurd it makes their own argument look ridiculous. "You're right—I probably do plot against you in my free time. It's all I live for." Say it with a straight face, and they'll be left wondering if you're crazy or if they just walked into their own trap.

Confusion isn't just a tactic—it's a goddamn art form. Leave them dazed, disoriented, and second-guessing every move they make. Welcome to the mental Thunderdome, where you always come out on top.

Lesson 5.3: Building an Ironclad Defense

5.3.1 The Importance Of Boundaries: Ensuring They Can't Cross The Line

Let's get one thing straight: boundaries aren't optional—they're mandatory. They're the goddamn electric fence that keeps manipulative assholes out of your mental backyard. Without them, you're basically inviting these parasites to waltz in, set up camp, and wreck your shit. No thanks.

Setting boundaries isn't about being nice—it's about survival. And yeah, it's going to piss people off. Good. If someone gets offended because you won't let them walk all over you, that's a *them* problem. You're not responsible for their fragile ego or their inability to take "no" for an answer. You're responsible for keeping your sanity intact.

Here's the deal: you can't just talk about boundaries—you have to enforce them. Say it loud, say it clear, and don't flinch. "I'm not available for this conversation right now." Boom. Done. And when they try to guilt-trip you or push back? Double down. "Did I stutter? I said no." If that feels harsh, good. They need to hear it.

The reality is, manipulators test your boundaries like toddlers testing bedtime rules. The moment you let one slide, they're taking an inch, a mile, and then your goddamn soul. So don't budge. Hold the line like your peace of mind depends on it—because it does.

Boundaries aren't just a defense; they're a statement: *I'm in charge here, not you.* And if someone doesn't like it, they can fuck all the way off.

5.3.2 Spotting The Setup: Recognizing Traps Before You Fall For Them

Manipulators don't just wait for opportunities—they build their own traps. These sneaky bastards are like spiders, weaving intricate webs of bullshit designed to catch you slipping. But here's the secret: if you know what to look for, you can spot their setups from a mile away and walk right the fuck around them.

The first red flag? Anything that feels *too good to be true.* Compliments out of nowhere, sudden generosity, or over-the-top enthusiasm? Yeah, that's not kindness—it's bait. They're buttering you up so when the trap springs, you're too blindsided to fight back. Don't fall for it. Smile, nod, and keep your guard up.

Next, watch for leading questions. "Don't you think it's weird how *so-and-so* treated me?" Translation: they're fishing for ammo to twist your words into a weapon. Respond with something noncommittal, like, "I hadn't noticed," and let their little fishing expedition sink.

And let's not forget the classic guilt setup. They'll say something like, "I just feel like you don't care anymore," to see if you'll trip over yourself to prove them wrong. Don't take the bait. Let them stew in their self-pity while you calmly sip your metaphorical tea.

The truth is, manipulators are predictable as hell once you start paying attention. They rely on patterns, and when you break those patterns—by refusing to engage—you leave them with nothing but an empty trap and a bruised ego.

5.3.3 Strategic Retreats: Knowing When To Step Back To Stay Ahead

Sometimes, the smartest move in the game is to walk the hell away. Not because you're weak, but because manipulators aren't worth the effort it takes to keep swatting their bullshit out of the air. A strategic retreat isn't surrender—it's a power move that says, "I've got bigger fish to fry than your sorry ass."

The first rule of retreat: don't announce it. Manipulators love a scene, so don't give them the satisfaction of some dramatic exit. Just stop engaging. No explanations, no justifications, no long-winded speeches. Silence is your mic drop, and trust me, it'll drive them insane.

When you step back, manipulators lose their favorite toy: *you*. They can't play their games without an audience, and nothing pisses them off more than realizing you've taken yourself out of the equation. Let them spiral. Their tantrums are proof that your retreat hit exactly where it hurts.

And don't think of a retreat as a loss—it's a regroup. While they're flailing around trying to regain control, you're using that time to recalibrate, reassess, and plan your next move. It's not running; it's playing the long game.

Remember, not every battle is worth fighting, and not every manipulative asshole deserves your energy. Sometimes, the best way to win is to leave them standing in their own pile of bullshit while you walk away, head held high, completely unbothered.

5.3.4 The Network Shield: Using Allies To Counter Their Influence

Manipulators think they're lone geniuses, pulling the strings while the rest of us dance like clueless marionettes. But here's the reality check they don't see coming: you've got a network, and when you use it right, their little solo act doesn't stand a chance.

First off, stop trying to handle everything solo. That's exactly what these sneaky assholes want—they thrive on isolating you so they can work their manipulative magic. Instead, loop in the right people. Build your network of trusted allies who can see through the bullshit just as clearly as you can.

The trick? Don't just go running to your friends with, "Look what this jerk did." Manipulators expect that. Instead, subtly plant seeds. "Have you noticed how *so-and-so* always seems to stir things up?" Let your allies start connecting the dots on their own. Once they see the pattern, it's game over for the manipulator.

And don't underestimate the power of a united front. Manipulators rely on dividing and conquering—if you and your network stay consistent, their influence shrinks faster than their credibility. Call out inconsistencies as a group, shut down gossip, and make it crystal clear that their games won't work here.

The beauty of the network shield? It's not just about protection—it's about making the manipulator realize they're outnumbered and outclassed. They'll either retreat or self-destruct, and you get to watch it all unfold without breaking a sweat.

5.3.5 Controlling The Narrative: Keeping Their Version Of Events In Check

Manipulators love to twist the narrative to fit their bullshit story. They'll take a conversation, sprinkle in some lies, and leave you looking like the villain. Well, guess what? It's time to show them who's really in charge of the story. Spoiler alert: It's not them.

The first rule of narrative control is simple: don't let them define the terms. If they try to frame you as the bad guy, stop them dead in their tracks. "Actually, that's not what happened, and I'm not going to let you rewrite history." Say it with confidence. They'll try to push back, but your calm, firm stance will make them second-guess their little script.

Now, when they start spinning their yarn of lies, don't react— *counter*. Throw the truth in their face like a brick. "So, you're saying I did *that*? Funny, because I remember it a little differently. Let me refresh your memory." Don't let them control the narrative from the sidelines. Take it back, piece by piece.

If they try to manipulate others into believing their version of events, stop them in their tracks. "I'm not sure where you're getting your information from, but that's not the full story. Let me explain what really went down." Nothing makes a manipulator more uncomfortable than when their bullshit starts unraveling in front of an audience.

In the end, controlling the narrative isn't about being louder or more aggressive. It's about being unapologetically clear. If you can stand firm in your truth while they squirm in their lies, you've already won.

Lesson 5.4: Winning the Mental Game

5.4.1 Developing Emotional Intelligence: Outmaneuvering Them With Self-Awareness

Emotional intelligence? Yeah, it's not some buzzword—it's your goddamn secret weapon. Manipulators bank on your emotions, using them as leverage to twist your reality and pull the strings. But here's the thing: when you've got emotional intelligence on lock, they can't get inside your head. Not even close.

First off, emotional intelligence isn't about being a robot. It's about being hyper-aware of how you're feeling *and* knowing how to use that to your advantage. Manipulators want you to lose your cool, snap, and give them the satisfaction of seeing you fall apart. You know what? Screw that. Stay cool, stay collected, and make them wonder if they're dealing with a human—or a goddamn Zen master.

You need to know when you're being manipulated—and not just react out of anger or frustration. That's what they're hoping for. They'll throw some emotional grenade your way, baiting you to feel guilty, defensive, or even enraged. But when you recognize what's happening, you can take a step back and say, "Nice try, but I'm not biting." Watch them squirm as they realize their emotional play didn't land.

And here's the best part—emotional intelligence lets you stay in control of the narrative. When you react from a place of self-awareness, you not only avoid their traps, you outsmart them. They think they're pushing your buttons, but in reality, you're the one pushing theirs—by keeping your shit together while they implode.

Manipulators are good at reading emotions, but guess what? You're better. You've got this emotional chess game figured out while they're still stuck on checkers.

5.4.2 The Power Of Patience: Waiting For The Perfect Moment To Strike

Patience isn't just a virtue—it's a goddamn power move. Manipulators think they control the clock, but guess what? You're not in a rush. You're the one biding your time, watching, waiting, knowing that when the right moment comes, you'll strike with the precision of a goddamn sniper.

Here's the thing: manipulators love to operate fast, pushing people into decisions or emotional reactions before they've had time to think. They don't realize you're sitting there, cool as a cucumber, with your plan brewing under the surface. You don't need to jump in every time they throw a tantrum. No, you just wait for them to dig themselves a hole, and then you toss the shovel in their lap.

Patience means you're never out of control. You don't let your emotions or their chaos rush you into a reaction. Manipulators want you frantic, knee-deep in their mess, but you're too smart for that. You're just watching them flail and stumble, while you're silently preparing to deliver the knockout punch. That's the beauty of patience—it lets you stay above the fray, watching the storm from your quiet perch, waiting for the perfect strike.

And when that moment finally comes? You'll be ready, and they'll be blindsided. They won't even know what hit them. You've played the long game, and now it's checkmate. Manipulators don't know how to deal with someone who isn't panicking, who's waiting for their opening—and that's why you always win.

5.4.3 Maintaining Confidence: Staying Strong Even Under Their Pressure

Manipulators can't stand it when you're unshakable. They need you rattled, doubting yourself, and second-guessing every damn move you make. And guess what? They're never going to get that from you. The moment you let them see a crack in your armor, they pounce. So here's the secret: stay *fucking* confident.

It doesn't matter what they throw at you—gaslighting, guilt trips, or emotional manipulation—they want you to feel small. But here's the deal: confidence isn't about being perfect. It's about not giving a single shit about what they think. Stand tall, speak clearly, and don't let their petty attempts to undermine you even get under your skin. It's not arrogance; it's survival.

When they try to push you off balance, stay centered. Hold your ground, no matter how much they try to rattle your cage. A manipulator feeds off your discomfort. So when they see you unphased, they'll start to realize they've got nothing. You're not here to play their games. You're here to remind them who's in charge.

And here's the kicker—real confidence doesn't need to scream. It doesn't need to be loud or flashy. It's the calm assurance that says, "I know who I am, and you can go fuck yourself if you think I'm going to doubt that." That's the kind of energy manipulators can't touch. So when the pressure comes, you just stand there like a goddamn rock while they flail around like the emotional toddlers they are.

5.4.4 Turning The Tables: Shifting From Defense To Offense

You want to know the best way to handle a manipulator? Stop playing defense. Stop waiting for their next move and put them on the goddamn back foot. Turn the tables and hit them with a reality check they never saw coming.

When they start pulling their usual crap—twisting your words, guilt-tripping you, or trying to control the situation—*don't play their game.* Hit them with questions that make them uncomfortable, like, "So, what exactly is it you want from me?" or "Why are you trying to make me feel responsible for your issues?" You're not here to clean up their mess; you're here to make them realize they've been bullshitting you the whole time.

Now, it's time to play offense. Manipulators thrive on the illusion that they're in control. When you call them out and force them to explain their bullshit, they're thrown off their game. You've just shifted the narrative. You've put the pressure on them instead of you, and now they're scrambling.

And here's where the magic happens: the more they scramble, the more desperate they get. The moment they're on the defense, they lose. Because manipulators aren't good at taking heat. They're not built for being questioned, held accountable, or exposed for the assholes they are. The second you stop defending yourself and start putting their dirty laundry in the spotlight, they start to look like the fools they are.

So, stop playing nice. Stop reacting. Start making them react. They're not prepared for that. And when you're the one calling the shots, they'll have no choice but to back off, or worse—fall apart completely.

5.4.5 The Final Checkmate: Leaving Them With No Moves Left To Play

Here's the thing about manipulators: they think they can outsmart you, control you, fuck with your head until you're too dizzy to fight back. But the final checkmate? That's when you leave them standing there with absolutely no moves left to play. They're done. Over. Game's fucking up. And it's your move.

The trick is simple: don't just win the battle—*end the war*. You've got them right where you want them, and now it's time to put them in a position where they can't escape your grip. When they try to pull one last "innocent" little move—maybe a sob story or some fake-ass apology—shut it down before it even starts. "Nice try, but I'm done with your shit." No hesitation. No second-guessing. You've already seen through their game, and they're not getting another chance.

At this point, they'll try to gaslight you. They'll try to twist the story again and pull you back into their toxic bullshit. But you've got your boundaries set and your mind made up. You walk away. Don't look back. Don't give them a chance to worm their way back in. They've had their shot. They've lost.

And when they try to rebuild their bullshit, they'll realize something: there's no more room for them in your life. Their manipulative tactics don't work anymore because you've taken control. They're no longer the ones pulling the strings—they're just pathetic little puppets flailing around.

That's the real victory: when they've got nothing left, no narrative, no lies, no ways to manipulate you. And you? You're free. Completely unbothered. While they're left standing in their own steaming pile of bullshit.

Burning Down the Fallout

You've outplayed the manipulators, outmaneuvered their tricks, and left them choking on their own bullshit. Feels good, doesn't it? But before you pop the champagne, there's one last mess to deal with— the aftermath. Because let's be real, these two-faced clowns don't just disappear without leaving a trail of chaos behind them. They smear your reputation, wreck relationships, and create a storm of drama that lingers long after they're gone. And guess who's left standing in the wreckage? You.

Chapter 6 isn't about justice—it's about cleanup. This is where you assess the damage, set the record straight, and make damn sure they don't leave lasting scars on your life. It's about reclaiming control, shutting down their lingering influence, and making sure their toxic bullshit is wiped out for good. Because you're not just surviving this—you're making sure they *never* get the chance to pull this shit again.

Time to clean up the **shitstorm.**

CHAPTER SIX

Cleaning up the Shit Storm

Let's face it: manipulators don't just stir up trouble—they leave behind a goddamn wreckage of lies, chaos, and shattered trust in their wake. And guess who's left holding the mop? You. Cleaning up their mess isn't just frustrating—it's infuriating, especially when you realize they probably walked away without a scratch while you're stuck picking up the pieces. But here's the deal: this chapter isn't about playing nice or fixing their problems for them. It's about taking control, minimizing the damage, and making damn sure they never pull this shit again. You're not their janitor—you're their worst fucking nightmare.

Lesson 6.1: Assessing the Damage

6.1.1 Assessing the Damage: Knowing What You're Dealing With

Before you can clean up the mess left by some two-faced, drama-addicted asshole, you need to figure out just how bad it really is. Are we talking a small spill or a full-blown toxic waste disaster? Because manipulators don't just create problems—they create chaos. They're like emotional arsonists, setting fires everywhere and then blaming you for the smoke. Step one in damage control is taking a hard look at the mess they've made, without sugarcoating or denial, so you can figure out your next move.

Why Assessing the Damage Matters

You can't fix what you don't fully understand. Ignoring the problem or downplaying it only gives them more room to cause even more havoc. Here's why you need to assess the mess head-on:

- **It Exposes Their Lies**: Once you start digging, you'll see the full scope of their manipulative bullshit—and trust me, it's bigger than you think.
- **It Puts You Back in Control**: Knowing exactly what you're dealing with takes the power out of their hands and puts it back in yours.
- **It Helps You Plan Your Comeback**: Whether you're cleaning up your reputation, fixing relationships, or salvaging your sanity, a clear picture of the damage gives you the blueprint to rebuild.

How to Assess the Damage Like a Pro

1. **Follow the Trail of Chaos**
   Start at the source of the drama and work your way out. Who's been affected? What lies have they spread? How far has the ripple effect gone?
   - **What to Ask**: "Who's been pulled into their bullshit, and how do I set the record straight?"
2. **Separate Fact from Fiction**
   Manipulators thrive on blurring the lines between truth and lies. Your job is to untangle the web and figure out what's real.
   - **What to Do**: Check the facts, gather receipts, and don't take anyone's word for it—especially theirs.
3. **Identify the Collateral Damage**
   Their chaos doesn't just hit you—it hits everyone around you. Figure out who else has been caught in the crossfire so you can address it.
   - **What to Ask**: "Who's been dragged into this mess, and how do I make it right?"
4. **Check Your Own Feelings**
   Manipulative assholes don't just leave external damage—they fuck with your head, too. Take stock of your own emotional state so you can start rebuilding.
   - **What to Ask Yourself**: "How has this affected me, and what do I need to heal?"

What NOT to Do When Assessing the Damage

- **Don't Minimize It**: "Oh, it's not that bad." Yes, it is. Don't downplay the chaos—they're counting on you too.
- **Don't Rush to Fix Everything**: You're not a superhero, and you're definitely not their janitor. Take your time to assess before you act.
- **Don't Blame Yourself**: Their mess is their fault, no matter how much they try to pin it on you.

Assessing the damage is about facing the chaos head-on and taking stock of exactly what you're dealing with. It's not fun, it's not fair, and it sure as hell isn't your fault, but it's the first step toward taking back control. Once you know the full scope of their mess, you can start cleaning it up—on your terms, not theirs. Let them stew in their own bullshit while you rebuild stronger than ever.

6.1.2 Separating Facts From Fiction: Distinguishing Truth From Their Fabricated Lies

Let's get this straight: two-faced assholes love to twist the truth into a nice little pile of steaming lies. And guess who gets to clean up their mess? Yep, you. So, before you get all tangled up in their web of bullshit, you need to separate the facts from the fiction. It's not a guessing game—it's about cutting through their lies with the precision of a goddamn surgeon.

Start by looking at what they've said and asking yourself: *Is this even remotely true?* Spoiler alert: it probably isn't. They'll craft stories that paint them as the victim and you as the villain. Sounds familiar, right? You've been framed in their narrative while they've been off playing the innocent martyr. But here's the catch—manipulators suck at keeping their story straight. One minute, it's one thing. The next, it's a completely different set of lies. They can't keep their story together long enough to even convince themselves.

Now, start picking apart their fabricated tales. Look for inconsistencies. If they said one thing to you and a completely different thing to someone else, it's game over. And when you catch them in the act? Don't let them worm their way out of it. Call their bullshit for what it is. Counter their lies with cold, hard facts. The truth has a way of shutting down manipulative games—fast.

Don't fall for their crap. You've got a front-row seat to their show, and it's about time you exposed it for the circus it is.

6.1.3 Who's Affected: Understanding How Their Mess Has Spread

So, who's caught in the crossfire of this goddamn shitshow? The manipulators have pulled their usual stunt, and now it's time to figure out exactly who's been dragged into their mess. Spoiler alert: it's not just you. They don't blow up your life without leaving a trail of destruction behind. And guess what? You're not the only casualty here.

Start by looking around—who's been sucked into this clusterfuck? Is it your friends? Your family? Hell, even your coworkers? You need to figure out who's been on the receiving end of their lies and manipulation. The more people they rope into their nonsense, the more complicated this mess gets. You can't just focus on your own damage; you have to map out who else is tangled in their web. These assholes don't just affect you—they make sure everyone around you feels the burn too.

You need to take stock of every person they've manipulated or lied to. Is there someone who's now pissed at you because they've swallowed the manipulator's version of events? Did they turn people against you with their sweet, venomous lies? Welcome to the fallout, where everyone's been touched by their toxic bullshit.

It's not just about figuring out who's been hurt—it's about understanding *how deep* the damage goes. When you start seeing the full scope of their destruction, you can begin the cleanup. But first, you've got to assess the wreckage and understand just how far their chaos has reached. It's bigger than you think.

6.1.4 The Fallout Map: Charting The Immediate And Long-Term Consequences

Alright, now that you've got a good look at the damage, it's time to draw the fucking map. You're no longer just reacting to their bullshit—you're laying out the entire land of destruction they've caused. Immediate consequences? That's the obvious mess. But the long-term fallout? That's where the real fun begins, because this shit doesn't just disappear overnight.

First, let's start with the now. Who's pissed off right this second? Who's throwing you dirty looks? Who's calling you out for shit that isn't even your fault? These are the people you need to fix, and fast. Their anger is like a ticking time bomb, and you can't afford to let that shit fester. Clean that mess up before it gets worse. But here's the truth: It's not going to be easy. Some people you might be able to smooth over with the truth, but others? They're too far gone in the manipulator's twisted version of events. Deal with it. Move on.

Now, the long-term consequences? That's where it gets sticky. Who's going to remember this shit months or even years from now? Who's going to have a scar from this that never quite heals? Think about the damage to your reputation, the relationships that might never be the same, the trust that's been broken and can't be rebuilt overnight. The manipulator might have moved on to their next target, but you're left dealing with the fallout for as long as it takes for people to forget or forgive. Spoiler alert: that could take a while.

You need to map this out. You need to know exactly who's affected, what it's going to cost you, and how long you're going to be cleaning up their goddamn mess. Because the sooner you face the full consequences, the sooner you can start fucking fixing it.

6.1.5 The Emotional Toll: Recognizing How Their Actions Have Impacted You

Let's cut the crap for a second—this whole damn situation isn't just about the mess they've made in your life; it's about the emotional wreckage they've left behind. Manipulators have this beautiful way of ripping up your mental and emotional state like they're tossing out trash. And guess what? It's *fucking* exhausting.

You've been through the wringer, no doubt. Maybe you're pissed off, maybe you're drained, or maybe you're just flat-out fucking numb. Whatever it is, it's real. These assholes didn't just damage your relationships or reputation—they've got their claws deep into your emotional well-being. You feel it in the way your head spins when you think about it, the stress eating at your gut, the frustration building up like a pressure cooker.

But here's the thing: you can't ignore it. You need to recognize the toll this shit has taken on you, because if you don't, you're just setting yourself up for the next round of manipulation. It's easy to get caught up in cleaning up everyone else's mess, but if you don't take a second to check in with your own mental health, you're just kicking the can down the road for future you to deal with.

This isn't some "get over it" kind of situation. The emotional toll is *real* and it's fucking heavy. The sooner you own up to how much damage this has done to you emotionally, the sooner you can start fixing it. But first, acknowledge the wound. It's there. You're hurt, and it's okay to admit it. The real damage doesn't just show up on your calendar—it's inside your head, your heart, and your soul.

Lesson 6.2: Containing the Chaos

6.2.1 Damage Mitigation: Stopping The Problem Before It Gets Worse

Listen up, because this is where the rubber meets the road: You can't just sit around whining about the chaos. If you want to fix this shitshow, you've got to *stop the bleeding* before it gets worse. Every second you waste letting this nonsense fester is a second the manipulator's mess is spreading like cancer.

Damage mitigation isn't a waiting game. It's not about hoping things will magically fix themselves. You've got to take immediate action, or you're fucked. So what do you do? First, put out the fire wherever it's burning the hottest. Are relationships crumbling? Step in, shut down the lies, and get the truth out there before their twisted version of events spreads further than it already has. The longer you wait, the harder it gets to put the pieces back together.

Next, get your reputation under control. You're not going to charm people into forgetting the lies; you've got to *own your side of the story* and force them to hear it. You're not some passive victim in this—if you're not vocal about the damage and clearing the air, no one's going to believe you. Manipulators love a silent target. They thrive on people who sit back and let their narrative run wild.

The key here is action, not reaction. You've got to move fast and clean up the mess while it's still manageable. Let this thing get out of hand, and you're looking at long-term fallout that you can't even begin to fix. Step in now, and take control. Before it *really* gets ugly.

6.2.2 Repairing Relationships: Mending Fences With Those Affected By Their Games

Alright, time to face the music. If you want to fix this fucking disaster, it's not just about cleaning up the mess—it's about mending the relationships that got torched by this two-faced asshole. And guess what? This isn't going to be a walk in the park. People have been lied to, manipulated, and thrown under the bus, so don't expect them to roll over and forget about the damage.

The first step? You've got to own the truth. No half-assed apologies, no sugarcoating, just straight-up honesty. "Yeah, I got caught in their bullshit. I was fucked over, and I'm not gonna let that shit happen again." You need to call the manipulator out, but *don't use them as an excuse.* No one wants to hear you whine about how you were the victim of someone else's game—own your part, and let them know how you're fixing it.

Next, make sure you're not just talking the talk. You need to show people that you're not the same person who got wrapped up in this mess. Don't just say you're sorry—prove it with your actions. If they see you squirming or playing victim, they'll write you off. You've got to show them that you've learned from this and that you've got your shit together.

People don't forget, and trust? That's a whole other mountain to climb. But if you put in the effort, show up, and own your mistakes without making excuses, there's a shot at repairing what was broken. But don't think it'll be easy—it'll take time, patience, and a hell of a lot of consistency. You've got to prove to them that you're not another weak link in their manipulative chain.

6.2.3 Cleaning Up The Lies: Countering Their Misinformation With The Truth

Here's the thing: manipulators are nothing without their lies, and the longer you let their bullshit hang around unchallenged, the worse it gets. Their little fabrications are like wildfire—they spread, they grow, and they burn everything in their path. If you want to stop the damage, it's time to douse the flames with some cold, hard truth. But here's the kicker: don't expect it to be pretty.

You need to hit the ground running and correct the record wherever their lies have taken root. People might have already bought into their crap, and that's your battle now. You can't be passive about this—you've got to actively inject truth into the situation, no matter how uncomfortable it is. Don't wait for them to "admit" they're lying—*call them out*. If someone's spreading their version of events, cut in with your own. "That's not how it went down. Let me tell you what actually happened." Say it loud, say it proud. Let them squirm.

And don't get cute with it. This isn't the time for subtlety. You need to bulldoze their lies with clarity, logic, and, above all, confidence. If you start getting defensive or wishy-washy, you're giving them an opening to spin their next web of deceit. You need to be firm and unrelenting—don't let them weasel their way out. Countering their lies isn't a fucking debate, it's a declaration.

Sure, some people will still believe their nonsense, and that's fine. But your job is to get the truth out there and make sure their lies don't go unchallenged. You'll sleep better knowing you fought the good fight, even if some assholes are too stubborn to listen.

6.2.4 Rebuilding Trust: Regaining Confidence From Those Who Doubted You

So, you've cleaned up the mess, put out the fire, and you think you're done? Guess again. The real battle now is rebuilding the trust that the manipulator's lies and your own stupidity (yes, I said it) have destroyed. It's going to be a grind, so if you're looking for a quick fix, go ahead and grab a fucking magic wand because it ain't happening. Trust isn't something you can just "earn back" with a few nice words. It takes consistency, humility, and—let's be real here—time.

First off, stop playing the victim. Yeah, you've been wronged, but no one cares about your sob story. They care about what you're doing *now* to prove you're not the same person who got caught up in all that drama. The quicker you accept that, the faster you'll start rebuilding your reputation. Walk the walk, don't just talk the talk. You want people to trust you again? *Show* them you've changed by being reliable, honest, and above all, *consistent*. Actions speak louder than any apology or excuse you can throw at them.

And listen, not everyone's going to forgive you. Some people will look at you like you're a fucking joke, and that's fine. Let them. You don't need to win everyone back. But for the ones that matter—the ones you really care about? You need to prove that you've learned from the mess. You've gotta show them that you're better than the manipulator's bullshit and you're not going to repeat the same mistakes. Trust takes a long time to build and about five minutes to ruin, so buckle up. This is going to be a slow climb.

6.2.5 The Power Of Transparency: Using Honesty To Reclaim Your Credibility

Here's the deal: when shit hits the fan, the last thing you want to do is start spinning more lies to cover up the mess. That's the exact bullshit that got you into this situation in the first place. If you want to reclaim your credibility and show the world you've got your shit together, you need to embrace the most terrifying weapon you've got—*honesty*.

Now, I know you're probably thinking, "But I've been honest all along, right?" Wrong. If you haven't laid everything out there, exposed the full scope of the damage, and shown the world that you're not hiding behind half-truths, then you're still playing the manipulator's game. Transparency is the only way to truly stop the bleeding. When people see you owning the full scope of the chaos, it'll hit them differently. They won't be able to twist your story, because you've already fucking told it—every messy detail, every bad decision, and every moment you fucked up.

But here's the catch: *don't over-explain*. Manipulators are masters at talking in circles to cover their asses. You're not doing that. You're not trying to justify yourself, you're just laying the truth out there, cold and raw. You'll feel exposed, sure—but that's how you rebuild the trust that's been lost. You stop pretending to be perfect and show people that you're human. You'll find that transparency is a far more powerful tool than hiding behind more lies. It's time to stop being afraid of the truth and use it to get your damn life back on track.

Lesson 6.3: Guarding Against Future Attacks

6.3.1 Strengthening Boundaries: Ensuring They Can't Cause More Harm

Alright, here's the hard truth: if you don't build up your fucking walls now, you're going to get run over again by the same manipulative assholes. You've cleaned up the mess, but that doesn't mean they won't try to waltz back into your life with their bullshit once things settle down. It's your job to make sure that doesn't happen. So, what's step one? *Fortify those boundaries like your life depends on it—because it does.*

These two-faced bastards thrive on chaos, and they're experts at slipping through the cracks if you're not vigilant. If you're still giving them even an inch of access, you're basically inviting them to come back in and make a new mess. Your boundaries need to be fucking impenetrable, and that means setting clear limits and sticking to them, no matter how much they try to push you.

Start with the basics. Who can you trust to stay in your circle? Who's shown their true colors, and who's earned a second chance? Cut the dead weight. You don't need people in your life who can't respect your boundaries. That means no more excuses for toxic people, no more "Well, maybe they didn't mean it" bullshit. Anyone who tries to invade your personal space, your time, or your mental peace needs to be shut down. Block them, mute them, whatever it takes. If they can't get the message, you'll have to make it loud and clear. No more games.

Building boundaries is uncomfortable. You'll have to be firm, maybe even a little harsh. But that's the cost of not letting these fuckers walk all over you. If you want peace, you've got to make sure they can't break in again.

6.3.2 Documenting Everything: Creating A Paper Trail To Defend Yourself

Let's get one thing straight: manipulators are fucking skilled at twisting the truth and covering their tracks. They can spin a story and make you look like the crazy one in five seconds flat. And guess what? If you don't have proof of what really went down, you're screwed. That's where documentation comes in. You're not just going to sit there and let them rewrite history; you're going to create a paper trail so solid that even their best lies can't stand up to it.

Every conversation, every email, every text, every fucking interaction? You need to document it all. Get it in writing. Keep records. I don't care if it's a casual chat or some back-and-forth on social media—if it's important, *take notes*. If they said something shady, screenshot it. If they tried to manipulate you into doing something, write down the details. This isn't about playing nice or being a tattletale; this is about protecting yourself from the bullshit storm they're going to unleash when things go south.

And here's the kicker—don't just keep it all in one place. Store it in multiple spots: cloud, physical records, whatever works. You need to make sure that if they try to pull some sneaky stunt later, you've got the receipts to shut them down. Trust me, you don't want to be in a situation where you're the one looking like a liar because you didn't cover your ass.

This is war, and documentation is your armor. Don't go into battle without it.

6.3.3 Identifying Weak Points: Closing The Gaps They Exploited

So, the manipulator's out there somewhere, licking their wounds, waiting for the next opportunity to fuck with you. Here's the thing: if you don't figure out where they slipped past your defenses, you're setting yourself up to get taken for a ride again. You need to find the weak points in your life and plug the goddamn holes before they come back and exploit them.

Think about it. Where did they get in? Was it because you were too nice? Too trusting? Maybe you let your guard down in certain areas—family, work, friendships—and that's where they weaseled their way in. If you don't find those gaps, if you don't recognize where you dropped the ball, it's only a matter of time before they come knocking.

Look for patterns. When did you give them an inch? When did you let them bend your rules? Maybe it was a lack of clear boundaries or a moment of weakness when you needed something from them. Whatever it was, figure it the fuck out. Identifying those weak points is the first step in making sure this doesn't happen again.

Once you've found them, *fix them*. Harden your boundaries. Make sure you're not repeating the same mistakes. If your trust has been abused in certain areas, stop giving it away so easily. The manipulator may not be a mastermind, but they sure as hell know how to exploit your blind spots. So, plug those gaps, double down on your boundaries, and stop leaving yourself exposed. If you don't do this now, you'll just be an easy target again.

6.3.4 The Exit Strategy: Knowing When And How To Cut Them Off

Here's the harsh truth: not everyone is worth saving, and not every relationship is worth fixing. There comes a point when you need to accept that some people are just too toxic to have in your life. The manipulator? Yeah, they're one of those people. It's time to cut them off, and I don't mean "cut them off for now" or "just distance yourself a little." No, I mean *rip that shit out of your life like a bad tooth that's about to infect the rest of you.*

Knowing when to cut them off is crucial. It's not a decision you make out of anger; it's a decision you make out of self-preservation. If they've shown you, time and time again, that they can't be trusted or that they're actively fucking with your peace, then you don't owe them any more of your time, energy, or attention. The longer you keep them around, the longer you let them drag you back into their manipulation. So, do yourself a favor: cut the cord and don't look back.

Now, the *how* of cutting them off? It's simple. Don't make it a dramatic spectacle. Don't get caught up in a long, drawn-out confrontation where they can twist things in their favor. Just quietly block them, mute them, or shut them down. Don't explain. Don't apologize. Just make it clear: *You're done.* If they try to manipulate you into a conversation, ignore it. They don't deserve any more of your mental space.

The exit strategy isn't a "maybe" thing—it's a *necessary* thing. And if you've learned anything from this mess, it's that you need to start cutting the toxic shit out of your life, or you'll end up repeating the same goddamn cycle.

6.3.5 Learning From The Experience: Turning Their Mess Into A Valuable Lesson

So, you've survived the goddamn circus of manipulation, lies, and chaos. Now what? Do you just move on like it was no big deal? Absolutely fucking not. You've been through the ringer, and it's time to squeeze every bit of wisdom out of this shitshow before you walk away. If you don't learn from this experience, then you've wasted your time—and you'll just end up falling into the same mess again.

Start by asking yourself the hard questions: *How did I get here? What signs did I ignore?* Maybe you were too trusting, too forgiving, or just too fucking naïve. It's okay—own it. Recognizing where you fucked up isn't about beating yourself up, it's about making sure you never repeat the same mistakes. These assholes didn't get the better of you because you're weak; they got you because you missed the red flags. Don't let that slide.

Now, take those lessons and use them to build a better version of yourself. Strengthen your boundaries. Trust fewer people, but trust them more deeply. Be more discerning. The shit you've been through will make you a hell of a lot tougher if you let it. But if you just let the pain be a wasted experience, you'll end up right back in the same position—getting taken for a ride by the next manipulative asshole who comes along.

In the end, this whole mess wasn't just some random act of chaos. It was a lesson in survival, and you've got to make sure you take the knowledge with you. That's the only way you'll ever come out on top.

Lesson 6.4: Reclaiming Control

6.4.1 Restoring Your Peace: Finding Emotional Balance After The Storm

You've been through hell. Your life's been turned upside down by a manipulator, and now, you're supposed to just "move on" and find peace? It's not going to happen overnight, and it sure as hell won't happen by pretending everything's fine. You've gotta fight for your peace, and it starts with getting your emotions back in check.

The first step is simple, but it's also the hardest: *stop giving a shit about their bullshit.* Let it go. It's easy to stay pissed off, to stay wound up in the chaos they left behind. But guess what? The more you stay angry, the more you let them win. You're holding onto their mess like it's your personal trophy. No more. This is your life now, and it's time to reclaim it. *Let go of the emotional baggage—it* doesn't serve you. It's not helping you heal, it's just keeping you tied to them.

Now, finding emotional balance? That's a process. You've got to rebuild from the inside out. Take time for yourself, do the things that calm your mind and center your soul. For some, it's getting lost in a hobby, for others, it's just taking quiet walks or diving into a good book. Whatever it takes to cut out the noise and find a little slice of peace again, do it. No more overthinking, no more rehashing the past. You need to be present, not living in their drama.

It's your life, not theirs. Don't let them keep fucking with your peace just because they're too immature to let go of their manipulative games. You've survived, now it's time to thrive again.

6.4.2 Reinforcing Your Reputation: Showing Others You're Unshaken

Listen, when someone comes into your life, screws it up, and leaves, the last thing you need to do is let them take your reputation with them. The manipulator might have tried to slander you, twist your story, and drag your name through the mud—but you're not just going to sit back and let that shit stick. It's time to reinforce your reputation, and guess what? That starts with showing the world you're *unfuckingshaken*.

Don't let their lies define you. You've been through the chaos, you've been painted as the bad guy, and now it's time to flip the script. People know who you are—*show them*. Don't waste time defending yourself. Instead, focus on doing the things that speak louder than any lie they've told. Work hard. Be consistent. Show up and do what you do best. Your actions will speak so fucking loudly that no one will give a damn about the manipulator's toxic narrative anymore.

But here's the thing: this isn't about proving something to the manipulator. It's about proving it to yourself. You've got to believe, deep down, that their mess doesn't affect you, that their lies don't touch your core. The more you stand firm in your own integrity, the less room there is for anyone to question your character.

If they try to come back and stir the pot, don't even waste a breath. Just keep doing your thing. Watch their little manipulative games crumble in the face of your unshakable reputation. You're not just surviving anymore—you're thriving, and they can't touch that.

6.4.3 Using The Mess To Your Advantage: Spinning Their Chaos Into Opportunity

You've survived the goddamn disaster, and now you're sitting on top of the wreckage. So, what do you do now? Let the manipulator win and sit in the ashes? Hell no. It's time to take all the chaos they've thrown at you and flip it on its fucking head. This is your chance to spin their mess into an opportunity that benefits you. You've been handed a pile of shit—now turn it into gold.

First, let's talk about perspective. Sure, this whole thing was a shitshow, but it's also given you a front-row seat to see exactly what kind of people are out there—and what kind of bullshit you're capable of surviving. You're stronger now. You know exactly what red flags to look for, what to avoid, and how to spot a manipulator from a mile away. That's not just surviving—it's *learning* and adapting. The kind of growth that only comes from being tested by fire.

But it's not just about personal growth. Use this situation to prove to others that you're more than capable of handling the shit life throws at you. Show people that even when things fall apart, you can pick up the pieces, get the job done, and move forward. You think your manipulator is the only one who can make moves? Think again. Take that energy, that knowledge, and turn it into something that positions you ahead of the game.

Their chaos was a disaster—but it's your fucking opportunity now. Don't waste it.

6.4.4 Long-Term Strategies: Building Resilience For The Next Challenge

Let's not kid ourselves—life's not going to stop throwing curveballs. That manipulator may have fucked up your world, but guess what? Someone else will come along eventually, trying to fuck with your peace again. The key to all of this isn't just surviving the storm; it's learning to weather the next one without losing your shit. So, how do you do that? You build resilience. You become the kind of person who doesn't just bounce back from bullshit—you *bounce forward*.

First, start with a rock-solid mindset. Stop expecting things to always go your way. Life is unpredictable, and if you think it's all going to be smooth sailing, you're setting yourself up for disappointment. Instead, train your brain to *adapt* to whatever comes at you. The more you get used to rolling with the punches, the less power people have over you. Build your emotional muscle like you're hitting the gym for a mental workout. Learn how to stay calm when the world is burning around you, because that's what separates the survivors from the losers.

Next, keep expanding your toolkit. Learn from every challenge. That manipulator didn't win because they're smarter; they won because they caught you off guard. The next time someone tries their bullshit, you'll be ready with a full arsenal of strategies to shut them down before they even get the chance to start. Build boundaries. Keep your circle tight. Learn how to spot the red flags, and don't waste time on people who don't deserve it.

Resilience is about being un-fucking-breakable. Life's going to throw more bullshit your way, but when you've got your mental game locked in, nothing can touch you. So next time? You won't just survive—it'll feel like nothing even fazed you.

6.4.5 The Final Clean Sweep: Making Sure Their Mess Doesn't Linger

Alright, this is it—the last step. The final goddamn clean sweep. You've fought through the chaos, you've rebuilt, and now it's time to make sure that manipulator's mess doesn't hang around like a bad smell. You can't just half-ass this part and hope everything "works itself out." No, you need to make sure their bullshit is *gone* for good. No lingering bad vibes, no open wounds left for them to crawl back into. This is how you close the chapter once and for all.

Start by cleaning up the last of the emotional debris. Sure, you might've moved on in a lot of ways, but if you're still holding onto grudges, guilt, or resentment, you're letting their mess live on inside your head. Do yourself a favor—*let it go*. Let go of the anger, the frustration, and the feeling of being wronged. They don't get to control that anymore. It's yours, so take it back. Burn it down mentally, emotionally, and move the fuck on. No more wasted energy on someone who doesn't deserve it.

Next, eliminate any remaining access they have to your life. That means cutting ties—blocking them, muting them, *erasing them*. If they left any lingering emotional or social connections, shut that shit down. They don't deserve to have any foot in the door. And while you're at it, make sure to clean up the mess they left in your relationships, too. If anyone still believes their narrative, fix it. Set the record straight with people who matter, but don't waste time on those who can't see through the bullshit.

The final sweep isn't just about closing doors; it's about making sure no traces of them—no emotional residue, no lingering doubts—are left behind. When you're done, you'll know. And when you're standing in that space, free of their toxic mess, you'll realize: You're fucking unstoppable.

Ripping the Masks Off the Frauds

You've cleaned up the wreckage, shut down the chaos, and put every manipulator in your path exactly where they belong—out of your damn way. But let's be real, the game doesn't stop here. There's always another type of two-faced fraud lurking, waiting to pull their own brand of bullshit. And these ones? They're the worst kind of parasites.

Just because you've handled the immediate fallout doesn't mean the battle is over. Some people don't just manipulate situations—they manipulate perception itself. They steal credit, twist stories, and thrive on smoke and mirrors, using deception as their ticket to influence. You've dealt with the wreckage they leave behind, but now it's time to stop them before they even get started.

Chapter 7 isn't about fixing the damage—it's about exposing the fakers before they have a chance to rewrite your reality. The frauds, the clout chasers, the empty shells who talk big but have nothing to back it up. It's time to drag them into the light and rip the masks off for good.

CHAPTER SEVEN

Living Two-Faced Free

*Let's get one thing straight—freedom from manipulative, two-faced bullshit isn't just some feel-good dream. It's a **fucking requirement** if you want to live a life that isn't one endless cycle of dealing with liars, users, and energy-sucking parasites. This chapter isn't about playing nice. It's about **burning the goddamn bridge, pissing on the ashes, and walking away without a second thought.***

*You've wasted enough time getting tangled in their lies, cleaning up their messes, and questioning your own sanity while they sat back and laughed. Enough. This is where you cut the cord, slam the door, and make damn sure they **never** find a way back in. No more fixing. No more forgiving. No more getting dragged into their toxic circus. This is where you **win.***

Lesson 7.1: Breaking Free from the Cycle

7.1.1 Recognizing The Chains: Understanding How They've Kept You Stuck

Let's not sugarcoat this: you've been played. You've been running their errands, cleaning up their messes, and handing over your mental peace like it's some kind of fucking charity. And why? Because they wrapped you in chains so subtle you didn't even realize you were shackled. These manipulative assholes have been living rent-free in your head, spinning their drama, guilt-tripping you into submission, and watching you dance to their tune like you're their goddamn puppet. Every time you bent over backward to fix their problems or keep the peace, they tightened those chains a little more. And let's be honest, you let them.

But here's the thing: it wasn't your fault. They're experts at this shit. They know exactly how to push your buttons, how to make you feel guilty for even thinking about yourself, and how to manipulate you into believing their chaos is your responsibility. Spoiler alert—it's not. They've been stringing you along, feeding on your loyalty and kindness while keeping you trapped in a cycle of emotional servitude. The worst part? They've convinced you that stepping away makes you the bad guy. Newsflash: the only thing you're guilty of is giving a fuck about the wrong person.

Why Recognizing the Chains Matters

- **They've Conditioned You**: They've trained you to jump at their every whim while making you think it was your choice.
- **It's a Power Game**: Their goal was never connection—it was control.
- **You're Not the Problem**: Their manipulative tactics are about their own insecurities, not your worth.

How to Break Free

1. **Spot the Manipulation**
   - Look at the patterns: guilt trips, playing the victim, twisting your words to suit their narrative. Recognizing their tactics is the first step to shutting them down.
   - *What to say to yourself*: "Their games are not my problem."
2. **Call Out the Lies**
   - Stop believing the stories they fed you. Their "loyalty," "love," or "friendship" wasn't real—it was a leash.
   - *What to do*: Write out the ways they've manipulated you. It's time to get brutally honest with yourself.
3. **Own Your Role, Then Let It Go**
   - You stayed because you cared. That's not weakness; it's humanity. But now? You're done playing the fool.

    ○   *What to say*: "I cared for the wrong person. Now I care about me."

What Not to Do

- **Don't Make Excuses for Them**: "Oh, they're just damaged" doesn't cut it. They knew what they were doing.
- **Don't Cling to the Chains**: Nostalgia is a liar. If it was toxic, it wasn't worth it.

The Bottom Line

Here's the raw truth: they used you. They latched onto your kindness, your loyalty, and your desire to help because it made their life easier. They weren't a friend, a partner, or anything worth keeping around—they were a parasite, feeding on your emotional energy while giving you nothing but stress in return. Recognizing the chains isn't about beating yourself up; it's about waking the fuck up.

And now? You're done being their personal fixer, their emotional punching bag, or their go-to problem solver. The second you see the chains for what they are—manipulation and control disguised as connection—they lose their grip. You're not their pawn anymore. You're breaking every single fucking link, one by one, until the only thing left is your freedom. And when they try to guilt you into putting the chains back on? Laugh in their face and keep walking. You're free now. Act like it.

7.1.2 The Clean Break: Severing Ties Without Looking Back

You know what? *Fuck them.* You've been stuck in their drama for far too long, letting them crawl into your life like an emotional parasite, sucking the life out of you. And now? It's time for the *clean break*. No more explanations, no more second chances, and absolutely no more playing the victim for their manipulation. This isn't some casual "I'll take a break from them" shit. This is *severing ties* like you're cutting dead weight off your back. Clean. Final. Over.

They'll try to guilt-trip you, make you feel bad for "leaving them in a hard time" or tell you "they'll change" if you just give them one more shot. Fuck. That. Noise. You've been down this road a million times, and every time they've pulled you back into their toxic bullshit, like you're some kind of emotional yo-yo. Not anymore. When you make the break, you make it permanent. You're done.

And guess what? The second you stop entertaining their lies, their drama, their games, they'll throw a tantrum. They'll try to pull out all the stops—more guilt, more "but we're family/friends," more "I don't know what I'll do without you" crap. *Let them.* That's their last pathetic attempt to reel you back in. Stick to your guns and cut the emotional leash for good.

The best part? Once you make that clean break, you don't even look back. The moment you start questioning whether you've done the right thing, remind yourself: you're *free.*

7.1.3 Emotional Unhooking: Letting Go Of Guilt, Anger, And Resentment

Here's the truth: manipulators don't just steal your time, they steal your fucking peace. They drag you through a toxic mess of guilt, anger, and resentment until you're so twisted up inside, you can't remember what it feels like to be calm. They want you stuck in that emotional quicksand because as long as you're drowning in negativity, they get to walk away unscathed. But here's the kicker: it's time to *unhook* yourself from all that bullshit.

You've been carrying this weight for far too long, letting them twist your feelings, making you feel guilty for things you never did, angry over shit that wasn't your fault, and resentful because *they* fucked you over. Stop. Right. Now. The first step is realizing this—their shit isn't your shit. Their manipulation, their games, their lies—they don't get to control your emotional state anymore. That guilt you've been holding onto? Let it go. It's theirs, not yours. The anger you're holding? That's *your* fuel, not a shackling chain. The resentment?

Fuck that. It's a wasted emotion and one that keeps you chained to them.

Start by cutting the emotional cord. You don't need to forgive them, you don't need closure, you just need to free yourself from the mess they left behind. It's time to take your peace back. You've been playing their game long enough, and guess what? You can step off the battlefield and walk away with your head high. Because when you finally let go of their emotional baggage, you'll realize that the only person who's been hurting you... *was you*.

7.1.4 Cutting Their Influence: Eliminating Their Access To Your Life

Let's be blunt: manipulators don't deserve any access to your life. They've taken enough—your time, your energy, your emotions— and it's time to *cut them off* completely. You don't need to be polite. You don't need to "explain" your decision. You don't owe them a single thing. Their influence in your life has been nothing but a toxic drain, and it's time to pull the fucking plug.

These assholes are like weeds in your garden—if you don't rip them out by the roots, they'll keep coming back. And trust me, they will. They'll find ways to sneak back in, manipulate the situation, and make you feel like you *should* let them back in. "I'm sorry," they'll say. "I've changed," they'll promise. Don't buy that shit. It's the same old game, and you're smarter than that now.

The key here is *total removal*. Social media? Block them. Phone number? Delete it. Any possible way they can creep back into your life—whether through a friend, a family member, or some random bullshit excuse—they need to be cut off. Period. You need to be so damn firm that there's no question in their mind: *you are out of my life, for good*.

They'll try to manipulate, guilt-trip, and convince others that you're the problem. Let them. Their inability to respect your boundaries is their fucking issue, not yours. Keep your distance, protect your peace, and remember—eliminating their influence is the only way to take your life back.

7.1.5 Sticking To Your Decision: Staying Firm Despite Attempts To Pull You Back

Oh, they're gonna try it. The manipulative assholes are gonna circle back with all their tricks, their guilt trips, and their half-assed apologies, trying to wiggle their way back into your life. They'll promise "things will be different this time" and play the "I've changed" card like it's a fucking free pass. But here's the truth— *don't buy their bullshit*. You've already made the decision to cut them out, and it's time to *stick to it*. No exceptions.

They're desperate now. They'll try to manipulate your emotions, make you feel guilty for walking away, or pull some sob story about how lost they are without you. *Don't fall for it*. Stick to your decision like it's your lifeline because guess what? It *is*. Every time you entertain their manipulative antics, you give them the chance to worm their way back in, and the cycle starts all over again. The only thing they respect is consistency—and you can't afford to let them think they've got another shot.

If they try to guilt-trip you, remind yourself why you left in the first place. Think about the stress, the drama, the lies. All of that is *their shit*, not yours. When you stand firm, you're not just protecting yourself from them—you're proving to yourself that you're *better* than that bullshit. You're stronger, smarter, and way above their games.

So, when they come knocking, don't even hesitate. Close the door in their face, block them from your life, and keep moving forward with the peace you've worked so hard to rebuild. You don't owe them a damn thing.

Lesson 7.2: Building a Healthier Circle

7.2.1 Quality Over Quantity: Choosing Relationships That Add Value To Your Life

Let's get one thing straight: not everyone deserves a seat at your table. You've spent enough time letting people into your life who just take, take, take and offer jack shit in return. The manipulators, the emotional vampires, the leeches—they've drained you dry. But here's the reality check: *you don't need a crowd.* You need the *right* people. Quality over quantity, every damn time.

Stop trying to fill your life with a bunch of superficial bullshit. "Oh, but they're my friend," you'll say. "We've known each other forever." Well, guess what? If they're not contributing anything real to your life—if they're just taking up space and filling your head with drama—*cut them the hell out.* You don't need fake friendships to make you feel validated. The only thing they're doing is keeping you tied to their toxic mess.

Start building relationships that actually *add value* to your life. Real friends—real supporters—are the ones who uplift you, challenge you, and *get* you. They don't make you feel like shit or use you for their own gain. These are the people who show up, who respect your boundaries, and who genuinely care about your well-being. And guess what? You don't need a hundred of them. A few solid, real relationships will get you further than a thousand fake ones ever will.

So stop wasting time on people who bring nothing to the table but drama and manipulation. Build a circle of people who help you grow, who make you better, and who *respect* the person you are. That's how you create a life worth living.

7.2.2 Recognizing True Supporters: Spotting Those Who Genuinely Have Your Back

Ah, true supporters. You know the ones—the real friends who don't try to manipulate, who aren't there just when it's convenient, and who actually give a shit about your well-being. The fakers? They're easy to spot—they love the attention, love using you as a pawn in their little games, and, when things get tough, they're nowhere to be found. But the true supporters? They don't just show up when you're winning. They show up when everything's falling apart. And those are the people who matter.

Here's the thing—true supporters don't need to be constantly validated. They don't need to make sure you know how great they are by one-upping your struggles with their own stories of "hardship." They listen. They don't try to fix you or tell you what you *should* do—they just *support* you. They don't bring the drama or try to inject themselves into every situation. They stay the hell out of your way when you need space, and they offer help when you need it without expecting anything in return.

True supporters are the ones who make *your* life easier, not harder. They respect your boundaries, celebrate your wins without jealousy, and are there to help you up when you fall—without making you feel like you owe them for it. So, how do you spot them? Simple: they're the ones who stick around even when they're not benefiting from it. If they're just riding your coattails or showing up when it's easy, they're not real supporters. They're just leeches.

So, clear out the fake ones and keep the ones who prove, time and time again, that they've got your back—not because they have to, but because they *want to*.

7.2.3 Creating Mutual Trust: Building Connections Rooted In Honesty

If you've been living in a world of manipulation and half-truths, it's time to flip the damn script. *Mutual trust* isn't something that comes with playing games or keeping secrets. It's not about who can outsmart who or who can keep the upper hand. Real, solid trust is built on one thing and one thing only—honesty. And if you've been running around in circles with people who don't give a shit about being real with you, it's time to cut that dead weight.

Here's the reality: trust isn't earned by saying the right things—it's earned by doing the right things. It's about showing up when you say you will, being upfront when things go wrong, and owning your mistakes instead of throwing everyone else under the bus. You don't get to keep someone's trust if you're constantly lying or hiding shit. That's manipulation, not *trust*. So, if you want people to trust you, start by being *fucking honest*. Be raw. Be real. Don't dance around the truth just to make someone feel comfortable. If they can't handle the truth, then they're not worth your time.

Mutual trust is a two-way street, and it starts with you. Stop entertaining relationships that are built on secrets, passive-aggressive nonsense, or fake facades. Build something real. Create connections where both sides know they can be themselves, completely unfiltered, without fear of judgment or betrayal. When you both give each other the space to be completely honest, that's when trust forms.

The fakers? They'll never get this. They're too busy trying to play the game. But you? You've already moved on to something better. Something real.

7.2.4 *Identifying Early Red Flags: Avoiding New Toxic Relationships*

You've been burned enough times by manipulators, liars, and emotional leeches, right? So why the hell would you let another one sneak into your life? Here's the deal: you need to start seeing the red flags *before* they become a goddamn forest fire. The minute someone shows up in your life and starts giving you bad vibes, *trust that gut instinct*. It's not paranoia—it's survival.

These fakes don't always come with neon signs. No, they're sneaky. They'll charm their way into your life, act like they've got it all together, and make you feel like they're a blessing. But guess what? *That's exactly what they want you to think.* They're sizing you up, figuring out how to manipulate you into thinking they're your best friend, while they're secretly playing a game behind your back.

So, what do you look for? First off, *patterns.* Does this person constantly make everything about them? Are they always playing the victim card, even when the shit they've caused is their own damn fault? Do they love dropping passive-aggressive comments and then act like it's "no big deal"? If they're doing any of this, the red flag should be flashing in your face. You don't need to go diving into their backstory or trying to psychoanalyze them—you just need to trust the fact that if they're manipulating now, they'll be doing it again.

Don't make the mistake of thinking you can fix them, or that they'll change. They won't. They're only gonna bring drama and chaos, and you've had enough of that shit. Cut them off early, trust your instincts, and save yourself the headache. You're not a charity for manipulators.

7.2.5 Celebrating Healthy Boundaries: Why Real Friends Respect Your Limits

You want to know why fake-ass relationships fail? Because they don't respect boundaries. Manipulators? They test, stretch, and break every damn limit you set, just to see how far they can push you before you break. But here's the truth: real friends *get it.* Real connections are built on mutual respect, and when you set a boundary, they don't question it—they *respect it.*

If you're constantly in relationships where you're bending over backwards for people who don't give a shit about your needs, it's time to wake up. Stop playing the martyr, and stop feeling guilty for wanting your peace. Real friends understand that boundaries aren't walls meant to keep people out—they're fucking guidelines that say, "This is who I am. If you can't respect that, then get the hell out."

Healthy boundaries don't just protect you—they also protect the relationship. If someone's constantly pushing, disrespecting your limits, or trying to make you feel bad for wanting space, that's not friendship—that's manipulation. And guess what? You don't need that toxic shit. Real friends know that if you say no, it's not personal. It's just you taking care of your mental health, your peace, and your fucking sanity.

So, celebrate your boundaries. Don't apologize for them. Don't backpedal when someone tries to guilt you into doing shit you don't want to do. The people who respect your limits are the ones who really deserve to be in your life. The rest? Fuck 'em.

Lesson 7.3: Resilience for the Future

7.3.1 The Power Of Self-Reflection: Learning From Past Encounters

Let's get real—if you don't learn from the past, you're just destined to repeat your mistakes, and who the fuck wants that? Sure, manipulators have done their best to mess with your head, but here's the deal: *they only win if you don't learn.* Self-reflection is your most powerful tool in making sure you never get caught in the same toxic web again. You've survived their bullshit once, but that doesn't mean you should let them do it again.

The first step? Take a goddamn step back and look at what just happened. How did you let them manipulate you in the first place? What signs did you ignore? Maybe you were too trusting. Maybe you thought you could "fix" them. Maybe you overlooked red flags because you were desperate for connection. Whatever it is, face it. Don't make excuses. *Own your role in the mess.* You're not here to blame yourself, but you are here to learn from it.

And here's the kicker—you've got to be honest with yourself. It's easy to fall into the trap of saying, "Oh, they were so convincing, I didn't know better." Fuck that. You *knew* something wasn't right. You just didn't trust your gut. Next time, *you will*. The trick is learning to spot the signs early—before they get their claws in too deep.

Self-reflection isn't about beating yourself up. It's about *arming yourself* for the next time a manipulative asshole tries to mess with you. And when you've learned the lesson, you're already ahead of the game. No one's playing you. Not anymore.

7.3.2 Developing Emotional Armor: Staying Strong Without Becoming Hardened

Alright, time for a reality check. You've been burned by manipulative assholes who've played with your emotions, twisted your words, and left you questioning your own sanity. It's fucked up, but here's the truth: you can't let it turn you into some cold, emotionless shell. You need emotional armor—not to shut people out, but to *protect* yourself without turning into a bitter, jaded wreck who pushes everyone away.

The key here is building emotional strength without becoming *hardened*. Sure, you need to stop letting people walk all over you. You need to stop letting fakers pull you into their drama and use your vulnerabilities against you. But that doesn't mean you stop feeling. The goal is to stay *grounded*—to know what you're worth, to know where your boundaries are, and to never let anyone, manipulator or not, cross them without consequences.

Start by identifying what really triggers you. What makes you vulnerable to their bullshit? Do you second-guess yourself too much? Do you care too much about what others think? Do you bend too easily when someone manipulates your empathy? Whatever it is, you need to face it head-on and fortify that weakness. Build yourself up with solid, unwavering confidence in your decisions, your worth, and your ability to deal with assholes without losing your cool.

But don't lose your humanity in the process. You can be strong and still compassionate. You can protect your emotions without becoming a cold-hearted cynic. *That* is emotional armor—the ability to stand firm while still being human enough to feel, to connect, and to choose who deserves a place in your life.

7.3.3 The Confidence Shield: Believing In Your Ability To Handle Anything

Let's get one thing straight: confidence is your fucking armor. You can't walk around waiting for life to hand you some easy, bullshit path of least resistance. Life's a battleground, and the only way to win is to believe *you can handle anything* that comes your way. These manipulators want you to doubt yourself, to second-guess your decisions, to let their games shake you to your core. But guess what? They can't touch you if you're walking around with a shield made of pure, unapologetic confidence.

Here's the trick: it's not about being cocky. It's about being rock solid in who you are and what you're capable of. You've been through the fire, dealt with their games, and guess what? You're still standing. *That's your proof.* You've faced their manipulations, their lies, their attempts to make you question yourself—and you didn't crumble. You're stronger than they ever thought you could be, and that's exactly what pisses them off.

So, how do you build this confidence shield? You remind yourself, every damn day, that you *know* your worth. You're not perfect, you don't need to be. But you know you can handle anything they throw at you. You trust your decisions, your gut, your ability to bounce back from anything they try to do to you. You don't wait for external validation or approval. You give it to yourself. Because when you believe in your ability to handle anything, *nothing* they do can ever touch you.

Walk into every room with that confidence—like you've already won. And watch how quickly the manipulators start to shrink in your presence.

7.3.4 Cultivating Inner Peace: Practices To Stay Grounded In Chaotic Times

Look, life's a fucking storm, and these manipulative assholes are just the wind, trying to blow you off course and knock you over. But here's the thing—you don't need to get swept up in their chaos. Cultivating inner peace isn't some zen, meditation bullshit that works for five minutes before everything falls apart. No. This is about building a core that's solid as steel, no matter how much the world tries to shake you. When you've got peace inside, nothing external can fuck with you.

So, how do you stay grounded when the manipulator's out here stirring the pot? First off, *stop letting their bullshit get under your skin*. Don't engage in every petty drama they try to drag you into. Their chaos? That's their problem. *Your peace? That's sacred.* Protect it. You've got to learn how to walk away when they try to pull you into their emotional shitshow. Take a breather, walk away, and remember, *none of this is your fight.*

Next, find what centers you. It's not about some Instagram-worthy self-care routine (though that helps). Find your real, tangible peace—whether that's working out, writing, journaling, or just *shutting the fuck up and being by yourself for a minute*. Whatever keeps you in control and reminds you that your life isn't about reacting to their manipulations.

You don't need to rise to every occasion they throw your way. Stay focused on your own goals, your own path, and don't let them be the storm that knocks you off course. When you learn how to stay grounded in your own peace, *they'll never be able to rattle you again.*

7.3.5 Becoming Unshakeable: Thriving Even When Manipulators Cross Your Path

Let's get something straight—manipulators are not going anywhere. They're like cockroaches, always finding a way to sneak back into your life and try to mess with your vibe. But here's the key to winning: *you become unshakeable*. You stop letting these assholes have any power over you. Their games, their lies, their manipulations? *Irrelevant*. You are so fucking solid, so grounded in who you are, that no matter what they throw at you, it doesn't even make a dent.

You've been tested, and now you've got the armor. They'll try to rattle you—gaslight you, guilt-trip you, pull every shitty trick in the book to get you off track. But here's the thing: when you're unshakeable, they don't stand a chance. You don't need to argue with them. You don't need to explain yourself. You don't need to scream and shout to get your point across. You just *keep going*, steady as hell, doing your thing. And every time they try to drag you into their drama, you walk away, unbothered.

The real magic here? You're not just surviving their bullshit—you're thriving despite it. You've learned the power of detachment, the art of emotional resilience, and the strength of saying, "Fuck you, I'm not playing your game." When you let go of their control, when you stop giving them a say in your life, you realize something—*you're the one in charge*.

They can cross your path, but they'll never knock you off course. You're not just getting by—you're *thriving*, and they're stuck trying to catch up.

Lesson 7.4: Designing a Two-Faced-Free Life

7.4.1 Creating Peaceful Spaces: Building An Environment That Supports Your Growth

Let's be real for a second—if you're still allowing toxic, manipulative people into your space, you're making life harder than it needs to be.

You want peace? You've got to *create* it. This isn't about hoping things will magically calm down or waiting for someone else to do the work for you. It's about *taking control* and building an environment that nurtures your growth, your peace, and your goddamn sanity.

The first step? *Eliminate the chaos.* If there are people in your life who suck the energy out of you, who drain your mental health with their constant drama and manipulation, cut them the fuck off. Block them, mute them, delete them—whatever it takes. You don't need them lurking around like emotional leeches, sucking up every ounce of peace you have left. Surround yourself with people who respect you, who uplift you, and who don't need to play mind games to feel important.

Next, focus on creating a space—both physical and mental—that helps you thrive. This means getting rid of distractions, clutter, and negativity. You want your environment to *support* your growth, not hold you back. Keep things that inspire you, that remind you of your worth and your goals. Create a space where you can think clearly, make decisions, and move forward without being held down by past bullshit.

You can't change the world, but you can control your space. Make sure it's one that supports *you*—because if you don't make peace a priority, nobody else will.

7.4.2 Living With Intent: Prioritizing What Truly Matters

You know what the problem is with most people? They're too busy chasing bullshit—shiny distractions, other people's opinions, things that don't fucking matter. They're living like it's some kind of goddamn race to get somewhere, anywhere, just as long as they're not facing the truth. But here's the truth: *life is about living with intent.* You don't just float through this world hoping things magically work out. You decide what you want, you make a plan, and then you fucking go for it.

You have to get clear about what really matters to you. Is it the opinions of people who can't even see your worth? Is it the drama that other people want to pull you into, trying to get you to fight for scraps of their validation? Hell no. It's about your peace. It's about your goals. It's about the relationships that actually build you up, not tear you down.

Living with intent means waking up every day knowing exactly what you're going to do and why. You don't waste time on shit that's not serving you. If someone's wasting your energy with their fake bullshit, you cut them out. If something's not aligned with your values, you let it go. If you're not working toward your goals, you figure out why and fix it.

So, stop fucking around. Stop letting the world dictate your pace and start living with purpose. You're not here to keep up with anyone else's expectations. You're here to create a life that *you* want, and that means putting your time and energy where it truly matters.

7.4.3 Protecting Your Energy: Avoiding Drama And Toxic Influences

Let's be clear—your energy is *everything*. You only have so much of it to give, and these manipulative assholes? They want to drain it. They thrive on chaos, drama, and feeding off of your emotional bandwidth, like emotional vampires. They want to pull you into their mess, make you carry their burdens, and leave you with nothing but exhaustion. But here's the deal: *you don't have to play that game*. Protect your energy like it's the only fucking currency that matters.

Stop letting people who bring nothing but negativity into your life have a seat at your table. You don't owe anyone your time, your mental space, or your fucking peace just because they're *family* or *friends* or *whatever title they've earned in your life*. If they bring drama, guilt, or manipulation into the mix, *cut them out*. You don't need that in your life.

It's not just about avoiding toxic people—it's about actively *protecting* your energy. You don't let anyone disrupt your peace for the sake of their nonsense. You don't entertain drama. You don't engage with people who are trying to suck you into their emotional turmoil. They can keep their shit to themselves.

Guard your peace fiercely. Set boundaries that protect your energy and don't let anyone cross them. Don't let them drag you into their toxic world, because once you let them, it's like a black hole sucking the life out of you. You're too valuable to waste your energy on people who don't deserve it.

7.4.4 Embracing Positivity: Surrounding Yourself With Uplifting People

If you're still hanging out with toxic assholes, playing the "fixer" or "savior" role, *cut that shit out.* You're not here to carry the weight of people who can't even carry their own baggage. It's time to embrace the positivity that's been waiting for you, and to do that, you've got to *surround yourself* with people who lift you the fuck up—not drag you down with their drama, insecurities, and manipulative bullshit.

You're not a therapist, you're not a fixer, and you sure as hell aren't a goddamn emotional punching bag. So why waste another second on people who can't appreciate you or respect your boundaries? Surround yourself with people who inspire you, who challenge you to grow, and who genuinely want the best for you—not just when it's convenient for them. Real friends, real supporters—they'll be there when shit hits the fan, but they won't be throwing more chaos on top of your already messy life.

And it's not just about people. *Your environment matters.* If you're living in a toxic, cluttered, and draining space—change it. Get rid of the crap that doesn't serve you. Fill your world with things that make you feel good, whether it's your home, your work, or your hobbies. Positive energy isn't just a feel-good phrase; it's the foundation of building a life that doesn't make you want to scream every time you open your eyes in the morning.

You're here for a fucking reason—to thrive, to grow, and to live a life that's not bogged down by toxic influences. So, get rid of the negativity, and embrace the positivity that *actually* adds value to your life. You deserve it.

7.4.5 Thriving Without The Drama: Living Your Best Life Without Looking Back

Let's be honest here—life is too short to waste on drama, manipulation, and toxic bullshit. So why the hell are you still letting it control your existence? You've already done the hard part—*you've broken free* from the mind games, the emotional rollercoasters, and the fakes who tried to bring you down. Now, it's time to live your best fucking life, and the best part? You don't have to look back.

Thriving without the drama isn't some pipe dream—it's a conscious decision you make every goddamn day. You don't get sucked into the messes people try to drag you into. You don't waste your energy on people who can't respect your boundaries. You don't let anyone fuck with your peace. Instead, you focus on what truly matters: your goals, your happiness, and your growth. If someone doesn't align with that, *kick them to the curb*—no guilt, no hesitation.

Living your best life is about choosing to be around people who bring you up, not drag you down. It's about prioritizing your mental health and self-care, not making sure everyone else is okay while you fall apart. You've got one shot at this life—so stop wasting it on people who think it's okay to play with your emotions. Cut the drama out, and put yourself first.

The truth? Once you stop letting people manipulate, guilt-trip, or drain you, *you'll be unstoppable*. And guess what? The drama? It's not even part of your story anymore.

When Family and Friends Are the Real Two-Faced Threat

You've cut out the manipulators, walked away from the two-faced bullshit, and finally built a life where you're not constantly looking over your shoulder. But here's the catch—some of the worst offenders aren't just out in the world. They're in your circle. Sometimes, they're sitting across from you at family dinner or blowing up your phone with "concern" that's really just another attempt at control.

Because let's be real: **toxic friends and family** are a special breed of nightmare. These aren't just some random assholes you can block and forget. These are people who **think** they have a permanent VIP pass into your life just because they share a last name with you or once held your hair back at a party. They weaponize history, guilt, and loyalty to keep you on their leash— because if you're not bending over backward to meet their demands, you're the bad guy.

But not anymore.

You've dealt with the frauds—the backstabbing friends, the fake supporters, the jealous nobodies who couldn't handle your success. You've exposed their games, burned the bridges that needed burning, and cleared the dead weight from your life. But what happens when the two-faced manipulators **aren't just "friends" or acquaintances**—when they share your blood, sit at your dinner table, or pretend to have your back simply because of a family title?

Two Faced Friends and Family

Two-faced friends are bad enough, but when the betrayal comes from inside the house? That's a whole different level of mindfuckery. Family and close friends **know your weak spots, your history, and exactly how to twist the knife while making it look like a hug.** These are the ones who guilt-trip, gaslight, and manipulate

148

under the excuse of "love"—as if being related gives them a free pass to treat you like crap.

Chapter 8 rips the mask off these **toxic relatives and fake-ass "lifelong" friends.** You'll learn how to spot their bullshit, shut down their guilt trips, and decide whether to call them out, cut them loose, or keep them at arm's length. Because blood might be thicker than water, but it sure as hell isn't thicker than self-respect.

CHAPTER EIGHT

Toxic Two-Faced Friends & Family

Let's call it what it is: dealing with two-faced family members and friends is a special kind of hell. These manipulative assholes hide behind fake smiles, shitty excuses, and phrases like "we're family" or "you know I'm always here for you," while they sharpen their knives for your back. They've perfected the art of emotional manipulation, guilt-tripping, and passive-aggressive nonsense, all while pretending to be on your side.

Spoiler alert: they're not. *This chapter rips the mask off their bullshit, teaches you how to set boundaries that even these toxic parasites can't cross, and helps you decide whether to confront, forgive, or cut them loose for good. Get ready to shut their shit down and remind them that being family or a "friend" isn't a license to treat you like crap.*

Lesson 8.1: Navigating Family Dynamics

8.1.1 The Family Facade: Why Two-Faced Behavior Thrives In Families

Let's not sugarcoat it—family is often where the worst of human behavior is born, raised, and perfected. Two-faced relatives thrive in this cesspool because they've had years to learn every little weakness, every soft spot, and every emotional trigger you have. They weaponize their so-called "love" like a damn scalpel, slicing you open while smiling sweetly and reminding you how much "family means everything." Newsflash: family doesn't mean shit when it's used as an excuse to manipulate, control, and emotionally drain you.

Here's the dirty truth: the family dynamic is a breeding ground for this crap. It's built on unspoken rules, outdated expectations, and a whole lot of "don't rock the boat" nonsense. Toxic family members know exactly how to exploit that. They'll act supportive and loving in public, playing the role of the perfect sibling, parent, or cousin. But behind closed doors? They're planting seeds of guilt, stirring up drama, and pulling the strings like the little puppet masters they are. And the worst part? They get away with it because *you let them*.

How They Get Away With It

Two-faced family members don't just survive—they thrive—because they've mastered the long game. They'll do just enough nice things to keep you questioning yourself. "But they helped me when I was in a tough spot!" Yeah, because they wanted to hold it over your head for the rest of eternity. Their favorite weapon? The "blood bond." You'll hear it on repeat: "But we're family!" Like that's some magical get-out-of-jail-free card for treating you like garbage. Spoiler alert: it's not.

And let's not forget how they spin the narrative. You set a boundary? Suddenly, you're the villain. You say no? Now you're selfish. They'll cry to anyone who will listen, painting themselves as the poor, misunderstood victim while you're the heartless monster who dares to prioritize your sanity. It's a masterclass in manipulation.

Here's the deal: family isn't a free pass to act like an asshole. If someone is treating you like crap, "family" doesn't mean you have to take it. Recognize the facade for what it is—a mask for their two-faced nonsense—and stop playing along. You don't owe anyone blind loyalty, no matter how much they guilt you into thinking otherwise.

8.1.2 Recognizing Toxic Patterns: Spotting Manipulative Relatives

If you've ever walked away from a family gathering wondering how the hell you ended up feeling like the bad guy, congratulations—you've just been played by a two-faced family manipulator. These toxic assholes don't just know how to push your buttons; they installed half of them. Their manipulation isn't random—it's a goddamn blueprint, and they run the same playbook every time. Recognizing their patterns is your first step toward flipping the script.

1. The Puppet Master

This one operates behind the scenes, pulling strings while pretending to "help" you. They don't tell you what to do directly—that'd be too obvious. Instead, they nudge, suggest, and "advise," making sure every decision you make benefits *them*.

Signs you're dealing with a Puppet Master:

- They offer unsolicited "advice" about your life choices, but it always aligns with their interests.
- When things go wrong, they blame *you* for not listening to them.
- If you resist, they play the victim: "I was just trying to help!"

How to shut them down: Stop explaining yourself. Say no without a goddamn essay. "Thanks, but I've got it handled." Repeat as needed.

2. The Martyr

Ah, the family guilt machine. The Martyr has sacrificed *so much* for you, or at least that's the story they keep telling. Their favorite tool? Guilt-tripping you into doing what they want by making you feel like a selfish prick.

Signs you're dealing with a Martyr:

- "After everything I've done for this family, and this is how you repay me?"
- Constant reminders of their "sacrifices," no matter how irrelevant or fabricated.
- They love making you feel like you owe them something— forever.

How to shut them down: Stop buying their sob story. You didn't ask for their sacrifices, and you don't owe them shit. When they start whining, hit them with: "I appreciate what you've done, but my decisions are my own."

3. The Shit-Stirrer

This chaos-loving jackass thrives on drama. They don't just drop bombs into conversations; they light the fuse and walk away, watching the fallout like it's their favorite soap opera.

Signs you're dealing with a Shit-Stirrer:

- "I don't want to cause trouble, but did you hear what [insert relative's name] said about you?"
- They never confront anyone directly—just spread rumors and let the drama unfold.
- Somehow, they're always in the middle of every family fight, but they never take responsibility.

How to shut them down: Call out their bullshit. "Why are you telling me this? What are you trying to accomplish?" Watch them squirm as their little game unravels.

4. The Fake Ally

This one pretends to have your back but turns on you the second it benefits them. They're all smiles to your face and full of criticism behind your back.

Signs you're dealing with a Fake Ally:

- Over-the-top compliments in public, but constant undermining in private.
- They "accidentally" let private details about your life slip to others.
- They align with whoever's in power at the moment—it's always about their gain.

How to shut them down: Keep them at arm's length. Don't give them ammo. Share as little as possible and make your boundaries crystal clear.

5. The Perpetual Victim

This person is never responsible for anything. Every problem in their life is someone else's fault, usually yours. They twist every situation to make themselves look like the wounded party.

Signs you're dealing with a Perpetual Victim:

- "I can't believe you'd do this to me. Don't you care about how this affects me?"
- They turn every conversation into a pity party for themselves.
- They're quick to accuse you of being "mean" or "uncaring" when you set boundaries.

How to shut them down: Refuse to engage. When they pull the victim card, stick to the facts and don't apologize for things you didn't do.

How to Take Your Power Back

Recognizing these toxic patterns isn't just about calling out their bullshit—it's about protecting your peace and taking control of your life. Here's how you do it:

- **Stay Emotionally Detached**: Two-faced manipulators feed off your reactions. Don't give them the satisfaction.
- **Set Firm Boundaries**: Make it clear what behavior you won't tolerate. Enforce those boundaries like your mental health depends on it—because it does.
- **Stop Explaining Yourself**: You don't owe anyone a justification for living your life. No is a complete sentence.
- **Document Everything**: For the real pros at manipulation, keep receipts. If they twist your words, you'll have proof.

Family might be forever, but their access to your peace of mind sure as hell isn't. Recognize the games, refuse to play, and let these toxic assholes stew in their own drama while you live your life on your terms.

8.1.3 The Guilt Factor: How They Use "Family" To Excuse Bad Behavior

Guilt. It's the two-faced family manipulator's bread and butter. They wield it like a damn chainsaw, cutting down your confidence, boundaries, and sanity in one fell swoop. And the worst part? You probably don't even realize it's happening until you're neck-deep in their emotional quicksand, apologizing for things you didn't even do. If you want to stop drowning, you've got to recognize how they use guilt to control you—and call them out on their bullshit.

1. The Emotional Blackmailer

This one doesn't just make you feel guilty; they *weaponize* your emotions against you. They'll remind you of everything they've ever done for you—every favor, every time they showed up, every crumb of support they gave—just to make you feel like you owe them the world.

Signs you're dealing with an Emotional Blackmailer:

- "After all I've done for you, this is how you treat me?"
- They conveniently forget that their "sacrifices" were things they chose to do.

- Every interaction leaves you feeling indebted, even if they've done nothing extraordinary.

How to fight back: Acknowledge their manipulation for what it is: emotional extortion. The next time they start their guilt monologue, shut it down. "I appreciate what you've done, but my decisions are mine to make." No apologies, no explanations. Let them stew.

2. The Martyr Extraordinaire

The Martyr doesn't just guilt-trip you—they make a goddamn spectacle of it. They've "given up so much" for the family, and they'll tell anyone who will listen. Their sob stories are as endless as they are exhausting, and the endgame is always the same: to make you feel like a selfish monster for daring to prioritize yourself.

Signs you're dealing with a Martyr:

- "I sacrificed so much for this family, and you can't even [insert minor request here]."
- They drop their sacrifices into conversations like landmines.
- Their tone? Equal parts martyrdom and smug superiority.

How to fight back: Don't take the bait. "I didn't ask for that, and I don't owe you anything for it." Sure, they'll pout, but their tantrum is not your problem.

3. The Nostalgia Manipulator

Ah, the sentimental assassin. They'll drag out every cherished memory from your childhood, twist it into a guilt weapon, and beat you over the head with it. "Remember when we used to be so close? What happened to us?" They know exactly what strings to pull to make you feel like you're the one who let the family down.

Signs you're dealing with a Nostalgia Manipulator:

- Constant reminders of "how things used to be."
- Accusations that you've changed (because God forbid you set boundaries).
- Subtle digs about how you're not "who you used to be."

How to fight back: Don't let their weaponized nostalgia get to you. People change, and that's okay. "Things are different now, and that's not a bad thing." They can take their walk down memory lane without dragging you along for the ride.

4. The Guilt Grenadier

This one doesn't hold back. They go straight for the emotional jugular, dropping bombs like, "If you cared about this family, you'd do [insert ridiculous demand here]." They don't even try to disguise it—they just want to overwhelm you with guilt until you cave.

Signs you're dealing with a Guilt Grenadier:

- They use phrases like "If you loved me, you would…"
- They escalate quickly, from subtle guilt to full-on emotional terrorism.
- You constantly feel like you're being manipulated into doing things you don't want to do.

How to fight back: Call out the manipulation directly. "Guilt isn't going to work on me. Let's talk when you're ready to be respectful." End the conversation. Walk away if you have to.

How to Stop Guilt Dead in Its Tracks

Here's the thing about guilt: it only works if you let it. These two-faced manipulators rely on your need for approval, your loyalty, and your fear of being the "bad guy." But guess what? You're not the bad guy for protecting your peace.

- **Recognize the Patterns:** Pay attention to how they twist your emotions. Once you see it, you can stop falling for it.
- **Own Your Boundaries:** Don't let their guilt trip derail your decisions. No is a complete sentence.
- **Refuse to Engage:** When they start pouring on the guilt, shut it down immediately. You don't owe them an explanation.
- **Put Yourself First:** Your peace of mind is more important than their manipulative tantrums. End of story.

Guilt is a cheap trick, and once you stop letting it work, their power over you crumbles. Let them stew in their self-made pity party—you've got better things to do than play their emotional games.

8.1.4 Handling Family Gatherings: The Dysfunctional Shitshow Survival Guide

Ah, family gatherings—where everyone pretends to love each other while sharpening their metaphorical knives behind their backs. These events are a two-faced person's paradise, and if you're not careful, you'll end up as their entertainment for the night. Let's be real: family get-togethers aren't about bonding; they're about dodging the emotional landmines these toxic jackasses scatter everywhere. Here's how to survive without losing your sanity—or flipping the table (unless you really want to).

Step 1: Know the Players in This Circus

Every family has their roster of toxic performers, and these clowns come to every gathering armed and ready. You've got Aunt Karen, the Queen of Passive Aggression, who asks shit like, "Are you still working *that* job?" with a fake-ass smile plastered on her face. Then there's Cousin Debbie, the Drama Dealer, who "accidentally" spills your secrets while pretending to care. And let's not forget Uncle Bob, the loudmouth know-it-all who thinks his unsolicited opinions are a gift to humanity.

Pro tip? Expect their nonsense and beat them at their own game. Karen drops a backhanded compliment? "Thanks, Karen! Always love your support." Debbie starts spilling tea? "Wow, Debbie, that's almost accurate. I should've known you'd get it half right." Uncle Bob opens his mouth? Ignore him entirely—your silence will piss him off more than any argument ever could.

Step 2: Boundaries Are Your Best Weapon

If you don't walk into that gathering with steel-reinforced boundaries, you're screwed. These people will bulldoze right over you, then blame *you* for the damage. Decide what's off-limits—your personal life, your career, your relationship status—and stick to it like your mental health depends on it. Because it does.

When someone tries to pry, shut them the fuck down. "Oh, I'm not talking about that today. How's your divorce going?" Flip the script and watch them scramble. Toxic relatives hate it when you don't play along, and the look on their faces is worth every second of awkward silence. If they push harder, double down. "I said I'm not talking about it. Don't make me repeat myself."

Step 3: Get the Hell Out When You Need To

You are not a hostage at this shitshow. Repeat that to yourself. If things start spiraling into a full-blown circus of passive-aggressive digs and drunken rants, *leave*. Seriously, fake a phone call, claim a migraine, or just stand up and say, "Well, this has been fun, but I'm out." Let them stew in their dysfunction while you go home and binge something on Netflix in peace. You owe them nothing—not your time, not your energy, and definitely not your patience.

Family gatherings aren't about connection—they're about survival. Know the players, stay two steps ahead, and don't let these two-faced manipulators drag you into their toxic vortex. Set boundaries like your life depends on it, clap back when necessary, and never hesitate to get the hell out. At the end of the day, their drama is *their problem.* If they want to gossip about you after you leave, let them— it just proves you're living rent-free in their heads. And isn't that the sweetest revenge of all?

8.1.5 Setting Firm Family Boundaries: Your No-Bullshit Survival Shield

Let's be brutally honest: toxic family members hate boundaries. Why? Because boundaries ruin their fun. They can't manipulate you, guilt-trip you, or steamroll you if you've got a wall of "fuck no" standing between you and their nonsense. But here's the kicker— they're not going to respect your boundaries unless you *make* them. So buckle up, because it's time to lay down the law.

Step 1: Stop Explaining Yourself

The first rule of boundaries? No goddamn explanations. Toxic relatives love loopholes, and every time you justify your decisions, you're handing them a crowbar to pry those boundaries wide open. "I can't make it to the party" doesn't need a follow-up like, "because I'm busy, and I have plans, and blah blah blah." Nope. Just say, "I won't be there." Period. If they push, hit them with, "I've already made my decision." It's not a debate— it's a declaration.

Step 2: Enforce Like a Dictator

Setting a boundary is the easy part. The hard part? Enforcing it. Toxic family members will test your limits like toddlers in a candy store. If you don't enforce your rules, they'll bulldoze right over you. Say no to lending them money? They'll "forget" and ask again next week. Shut that shit down. "I've already said no, and that's not going to change." Repeat as needed, louder if necessary. Boundaries aren't suggestions—they're goddamn laws. Act like it.

Step 3: Anticipate the Guilt Bombs

You're not going to set boundaries without backlash. Get ready for the tears, the gaslighting, and the dramatic declarations of betrayal. "I can't believe you're doing this to *family*! What happened to loyalty?" Spoiler alert: loyalty doesn't mean letting someone treat you like garbage. Their guilt trips are nothing more than emotional manipulation dressed up as concern. Don't fall for it. Your peace of mind is not up for negotiation.

Step 4: Limit Access to Your Life

Here's a revolutionary idea: you don't have to give toxic family members full access to your life. Keep them on an information diet. The less they know, the less they can use against you. Don't share your plans, your struggles, or your successes—they'll just twist them into ammunition. Keep conversations light and surface-level, like discussing the weather or how Aunt Linda's casserole still sucks.

The Bottom Line

Boundaries aren't about keeping people out; they're about keeping your sanity in. Toxic relatives will push, test, and guilt you, but you're not here to play their game. Set your rules, enforce them without apology, and stop giving a damn about their tantrums. They can cry, complain, or call you selfish all they want—it doesn't change the fact that your mental health is more important than their manipulative bullshit. If they can't handle it? Too bad. That's their problem, not yours.

Lesson 8.2: Friendships Gone Two-Faced

8.2.1 The Shift In Loyalty: Recognizing When A Friend Turns Against You

Loyalty isn't just a buzzword—it's the backbone of any relationship. So when a friend decides to shift their loyalty and flip on you like a cheap mattress, it feels like a gut punch. One minute they're laughing with you over drinks, and the next, they're whispering your secrets to anyone who'll listen. It's a betrayal wrapped in bullshit, served with a side of smugness. If you've ever felt blindsided by a backstabbing "friend," welcome to the club—it sucks, but it's not your fault.

Spotting the Shift

Here's the thing about disloyal friends: they don't announce their betrayal with a neon sign. No, they're sneakier than that. They'll start small, testing the waters before they dive into full-blown betrayal. Pay attention to these red flags:

- **Sudden Distance**: They stop texting, stop calling, and when you reach out, they give you half-assed excuses. "Oh, I've been *so busy* lately!" Translation: I've already decided you're not worth my time.
- **Weird Vibes**: Conversations feel off. They're less engaged, overly neutral, or suspiciously defensive when you bring up anything personal. That's not them being tired—that's them mentally checking out of the friendship.
- **Friendly Fire**: You hear through the grapevine that they've been talking shit about you. They'll deny it, of course. "I didn't mean it like that!" Sure, Jan. You don't "accidentally" run your mouth about someone you supposedly care about.
- **Switching Teams**: They start cozying up to people they know you don't like or who don't like you. It's not just a coincidence—it's a goddamn power move.

Why They Turn

Disloyalty usually boils down to one thing: insecurity. Maybe they're jealous of your success, bitter about something you said, or just tired of pretending to be a decent person. Whatever the reason, it's not about you—it's about their inability to handle their own shit. Instead of being upfront, they take the coward's route, slowly phasing you out or stabbing you in the back when they think you're not looking.

What to Do

When you notice the shift, don't ignore it. Pretending it's not happening will only give them more time to screw you over. Here's how to handle it like a boss:

1. **Confront Them**: Call out the behavior directly. "I've noticed you've been distant and heard some things. Is there something going on?" They'll probably deny everything, but at least you're putting them on notice.
2. **Protect Yourself**: Stop sharing personal details with them. If they're already disloyal, the last thing you want to do is give them more ammo.
3. **Decide if They're Worth It**: Not all friendships are built to last, and some people are better off left behind. If their betrayal is a one-time thing and they're genuinely sorry, maybe you can work through it. But if it's a pattern? Drop them like a bad habit.

The Bottom Line

Disloyalty isn't an accident—it's a choice. And when someone makes that choice, they're showing you exactly who they are. Believe them. You don't need people in your life who treat loyalty like a suggestion. Spot the shift, confront the bullshit, and if necessary, show them the door. You deserve better, and if they can't deliver, they can fuck right off.

8.2.2 Spotting Hidden Jealousy: Why Some Friends Secretly Resent Your Success

Jealousy: the silent killer of friendships. It's the venom that turns someone you trust into a two-faced snake, smiling sweetly to your face while secretly praying you crash and burn. And the worst part?

They don't even have the guts to admit it. No, they'll wrap their jealousy in fake compliments, subtle digs, and passive-aggressive bullshit until you're left wondering why every conversation feels like walking through a minefield. Spoiler alert: it's because they can't handle your success.

The Signs of Jealousy They Think They're Hiding

Two-faced people suck at subtlety. They think they're masters of disguise, but their jealousy is about as obvious as a neon sign screaming, "I CAN'T HANDLE YOUR HAPPINESS." Here's how to spot it:

- **Backhanded Compliments**: "Wow, that's great you got the promotion! I mean, it's not like it's *that* hard in your field, right?" Oh, thanks for the shade, Cheryl. Your jealousy's showing.
- **Weirdly Competitive**: You share good news, and instead of being happy for you, they turn it into a dick-measuring contest. "Oh, you ran a 5K? That's cute—I just signed up for a marathon." Calm down, Karen. It's not a competition.
- **Downplaying Your Achievements**: You're excited about a big win, and they hit you with, "That's cool, I guess." Excuse me? *Guess?* Sit down, Cheryl. Your bitterness is hanging out.
- **Talking Shit Behind Your Back**: Jealousy makes them sloppy. If people start telling you they've been bad-mouthing you, believe it. They're too spineless to say it to your face, so they're spreading their insecurities like wildfire.

Why They're Jealous

Jealousy isn't about you—it's about them. Your success is a mirror that reflects everything they *haven't* done. They hate that you're thriving because it reminds them of their own mediocrity. Maybe they're stuck in a job they hate, or their relationship's falling apart, or they're just bitter that life didn't hand them a golden ticket. Instead of fixing their own shit, they'd rather tear you down to their level.

How to Deal with Their Jealous Bullshit

- **Call It Out**: If their jealousy is spilling into your conversations, don't let it slide. Hit them with a, "You seem a little off about my success—what's going on?" Watch them stammer as they try to backpedal.
- **Stop Oversharing**: Don't give them ammo. If they can't handle your wins, stop sharing them. Keep the conversation surface-level and let them wallow in their own bitterness.
- **Protect Your Energy**: Jealousy is toxic as hell, and if they can't work through it, it's time to create some distance. You don't need their negativity polluting your life.

The Bottom Line

Jealousy turns friends into frenemies faster than you can say, "Congrats." If someone in your circle is throwing shade at your success, they're not rooting for you—they're rooting for your failure. And here's the truth: you don't owe them shit. You worked for what you've got, and if they can't clap for you, they can fuck right off. Let them stew in their own insecurities while you keep winning.

8.2.3 The Gossip Betrayal: Dealing With Friends Who Spill Your Secrets

There's nothing worse than finding out that the friend you trusted with your deepest secrets has turned into a human megaphone, blasting your private shit to anyone with ears. These two-faced gossips are the lowest of the low, weaponizing your vulnerability to boost their social currency. You didn't just confide in them—you handed them ammunition, and they didn't hesitate to pull the trigger. And the cherry on top? They'll act like it's no big deal. "Oh, I didn't think it was *that* private!" Screw that. It was private because you fucking told them it was.

How Gossip Betrayal Happens

Gossips don't just slip up—they make calculated choices. The second you tell them something sensitive, they're already weighing how much social clout they can squeeze out of spilling it. "This is just between us" translates in their tiny, toxic minds to, "I can't wait to tell someone else." They don't care about your trust—they care about how they can use your secrets to climb some imaginary ladder of relevance.

It starts small. Maybe they "accidentally" share something trivial, just to test the waters. Then, when they see there are no consequences, they move on to the big stuff: your fears, your failures, your mistakes. They spread it like wildfire, all while pretending to be your biggest supporter.

Red Flags You're Dealing with a Gossip Snake

- **They Know Everyone's Business**: If they're constantly spilling tea about other people, don't think for a second that you're exempt. You're just next in line.
- **Your Business is Suddenly Public**: You tell them something in confidence, and two days later, you're getting side-eyes from strangers who shouldn't know a damn thing about it.
- **They Downplay the Damage**: "Oh, I didn't think it was a big deal!" Bitch, it's a big deal if I told you not to tell anyone.

Why They Do It

It's simple: they crave attention. Gossip is their currency, and your secrets are their jackpot. They don't care if spilling your shit damages your reputation, your relationships, or your trust—they're too busy enjoying the momentary rush of being "in the know." It's pathetic, but it's who they are.

How to Deal with the Betrayal

1. **Confront Them**: Don't let it slide. Sit them down and say, "Why the hell are you telling people my business?" Watch them squirm as they try to justify their crap.

2. **Cut the Supply**: Stop telling them anything. If they don't have access to your secrets, they've got nothing to spread. Keep conversations surface-level and boring as hell.

3. **Decide Their Fate**: Some friendships can survive a betrayal like this—*if* they own up to it and change. But let's be honest, most gossips don't. If they've betrayed you once, chances are they'll do it again. Know when to walk away.

The Bottom Line

A gossiping friend isn't just careless—they're dangerous. They've shown you exactly where their loyalty lies, and it's not with you. You deserve friends who protect your secrets, not ones who pimp them out for attention. Confront them, cut them off if you need to, and move the hell on. Let them choke on their own irrelevance while you surround yourself with people who actually respect you.

8.2.4 Confronting the Faker: Tearing the Mask Off the Two-Faced Fraud

There's nothing more infuriating than realizing someone you called a friend is nothing more than a sneaky, two-faced piece of shit. They smile in your face, play the loyal companion, and then turn around and trash you behind your back. These fakers thrive on deception, but the moment you confront them? Their carefully crafted mask shatters faster than their dignity. It's time to stop tiptoeing around their crap and call them out for the frauds they are.

Step 1: Spot the Bullshit

Before you go to war, make sure you've got your intel. Fakers are slippery as hell, and they'll deny everything the second you confront them. Look for these classic faker moves:

- **They're Two Different People**: Sweet and supportive in private, cold and distant in public—or worse, bad-mouthing you behind your back.
- **They Talk in Circles**: Ever notice how their stories don't add up? It's because they're busy spinning their web of lies.
- **Your Gut Says They're Full of It**: Listen to your instincts. If something feels off, it probably is.

Step 2: Call Them Out

When you're ready to confront the faker, don't hold back. Start with something direct: "I know what you've been saying/doing behind my back, and I'm not putting up with it anymore." No fluff, no sugarcoating—just straight to the point.

They'll deny it. They'll deflect. Hell, they might even try to gaslight you: "I have no idea what you're talking about!" Don't let them squirm out of it. Hit them with the receipts. "Oh, really? Then why did [insert mutual friend] tell me you said [insert their bullshit]?" Watch their face as the color drains—*chef's kiss*.

Step 3: Make Them Choose

Once you've exposed their two-faced antics, it's decision time. Lay down the law: "If you want to stay in my life, this behavior stops now. Period." Give them a chance to own up, but don't hold your breath. Most fakers are too deep in their own lies to change. If they try to weasel their way out with excuses or fake apologies, you've got your answer: they're not worth it.

Step 4: Burn the Bridge If Necessary

Here's the harsh truth: some people are irredeemable. If their betrayal runs deep or they refuse to take responsibility, it's time to cut your losses. You don't owe a two-faced faker a second chance to screw you over. End it with no room for debate. "This friendship isn't working for me anymore. Good luck, but I'm done." Then walk away and don't look back.

Step 5: Protect Yourself Going Forward

Once the faker is out of your life, tighten your circle. Share your trust sparingly and keep an eye out for similar patterns in others. Fakers are everywhere, but now you know the signs—and how to handle them.

The Bottom Line

Confronting a faker isn't just about calling them out—it's about reclaiming your time, energy, and trust. You deserve real friends who've got your back, not phonies who stab you in it. Tear the mask off, expose their crap, and let them deal with the fallout. You've got better things to do than babysit someone else's insecurities. Let them go rot in their own mess while you move on with your life.

8.2.5 Deciding to Stay or Go: Cutting Loose or Clinging to Dead Weight

So, you've unmasked the faker, spotted the jealousy, and called out the bullshit. Now it's time to ask yourself the ultimate question: Is this relationship even worth saving? Let's be brutally honest—just because someone's been in your life for years doesn't mean they deserve to stay. Loyalty is a two-way street, and if you're the only one driving, it's time to get out of the car and let them walk their ass home.

Step 1: Weigh the Damage

Start with the facts. How bad did they screw you over? Was it a minor slip-up that can be fixed, or are they a repeat offender who couldn't spell "loyalty" if you spotted them all the vowels? Look at the patterns. Are they always stirring shit, playing both sides, or subtly tearing you down? If this is just who they are, no amount of second chances is going to turn them into a decent human being.

Ask yourself: Do you feel better or worse after spending time with them? If it's worse, that's your gut screaming, *Drop this asshole already.*

Step 2: Test Their Response

If you've confronted them and they owned up to their behavior, great—maybe there's hope. But let's not kid ourselves. Most two-faced people are so full of excuses and deflection they should be writing political speeches. Watch their actions, not their words. Are they actually trying to change, or is it just more empty promises and crocodile tears? If they're not putting in real effort, it's because they don't care enough to fix things.

Step 3: Ask Yourself What They Bring to the Table

Friendships are supposed to add value to your life, not suck the soul out of it. What's this person contributing? Are they supportive, uplifting, and trustworthy? Or are they just another source of drama and stress? Nostalgia isn't a good enough reason to keep someone around. If all they bring is chaos and fake smiles, it's time to let them go.

Step 4: Make the Call

Once you've assessed the situation, make a decision and stick to it. If they've shown they're willing to change and you believe the friendship is worth salvaging, set some boundaries and move forward cautiously. But if they've proven time and time again that they can't be trusted, do yourself a favor and cut them loose. Don't waste your energy trying to fix what's already broken beyond repair.

Step 5: Burn the Bridge (If Needed)

Sometimes the best way to deal with a two-faced friend is to light that bridge up like it's the Fourth of July. No drawn-out explanations, no guilt-ridden goodbyes. Just a clean break. "This friendship isn't working for me anymore. Take care." Done. Let them stew in their own toxicity while you move on to bigger and better things.

The Bottom Line

Deciding to stay or go isn't easy, but it's necessary. If the relationship brings more pain than joy, what the hell are you hanging onto? Loyalty doesn't mean tolerating toxic behavior, and forgiveness doesn't mean giving someone free rein to screw you over again. Choose yourself, cut the dead weight, and let the two-faced assholes deal with the fallout. You're better off without them.

Lesson 8.3: Balancing Forgiveness and Self-Respect

8.3.1 The Art Of Forgiveness: When To Let Go And When To Hold The Line

Let's get one thing straight right out of the gate: forgiveness isn't about them—it's about you. When someone screws you over, especially a two-faced family member or so-called friend, holding onto that rage feels good at first. But eventually, it eats at you like acid. Forgiveness, however, doesn't mean handing them a goddamn free pass. It means saying, "You no longer have control over my peace." It's about letting go of the grudge without letting them off the hook.

What Forgiveness *Isn't*

Before we dive into the art of forgiveness, let's debunk the fairy tale nonsense. Forgiveness doesn't mean you're besties again. It doesn't mean you forget what they did, and it sure as hell doesn't mean you invite them back into your life for a second chance at screwing you over.

- **It's Not a Reset Button**: They don't get a clean slate just because you decide to forgive. Their betrayal happened, and you're not obligated to pretend otherwise.
- **It's Not About Closure**: Let's face it: most two-faced assholes aren't going to give you the heartfelt apology you deserve. Forgive them anyway—*for yourself*, not for their benefit.
- **It's Not Tolerance**: Forgiveness doesn't mean you keep putting up with their toxic crap. Boundaries still exist, and you enforce them like your sanity depends on it.

Why Forgiveness Matters

Hanging onto anger feels righteous—until it doesn't. You're replaying the betrayal in your head on a loop while they've probably moved on to their next victim. That grudge isn't hurting them; it's poisoning you. Forgiveness is about reclaiming your energy. It's about saying, "You're not worth this mental real estate."

How to Forgive Without Losing Your Edge

1. **Acknowledge the Hurt**: Don't sugarcoat what they did. Name it, feel it, and process it. Forgiveness isn't about denial—it's about facing the pain head-on so it doesn't control you.
2. **Take Your Time**: Forgiveness isn't a goddamn race. Maybe you'll get there in a week, or maybe it'll take years. There's no deadline, and anyone who pressures you to "move on" can shove it.
3. **Don't Forget the Lesson**: Forgiving someone doesn't mean trusting them again. Keep the lesson but ditch the emotional baggage. Fool me once, shame on you. Fool me twice? Not a fucking chance.
4. **Make It About You**: Forgiveness isn't about letting them off the hook. It's about unhooking yourself from the bullshit they dragged you into.

The Bottom Line

Forgiveness is an act of power, not weakness. It doesn't mean forgetting, tolerating, or excusing what they did. It means cutting the cord, reclaiming your peace, and refusing to let their betrayal dictate your future. So, forgive—not for them, but for you—and keep it moving. And if they mistake your forgiveness for a green light to screw you over again, well, they're in for one hell of a wake-up call.

8.3.2 The Danger of Reconciliation: Don't Get Played Twice

Let's talk about reconciliation—the shiny, feel-good concept that makes therapists and rom-com writers drool. On paper, it sounds great: you patch things up, hold hands, and skip off into the sunset. But in real life? Reconciliation with a two-faced asshole is like giving a snake a second chance to bite you. Sure, they might say all the right things, but don't kid yourself—leopards don't change their spots, and manipulators don't suddenly find Jesus because you forgave them.

Why Reconciliation is a Trap

Two-faced people love the idea of reconciliation because it gives them access to you again. They get to weasel their way back into your life, pretending to have learned their lesson while plotting their next betrayal. It's not about fixing the relationship—it's about resetting the stage for another round of their toxic bullshit.

Here's how they play the game:

- **The Sob Story**: "I've been doing a lot of thinking, and I realize I made mistakes." Oh, really? And I'm supposed to believe you've changed in the three weeks since you stabbed me in the back? Sure, Jan.
- **The Faux Accountability**: They'll admit just enough to make it seem like they're owning up to their behavior, but they'll conveniently leave out the worst parts. "I know I hurt

you, but I was going through a tough time." Translation: *I don't actually take responsibility, but I hope you're too stupid to notice.*

- **The Empty Promises**: "I'll never do it again." Wanna bet? Because history says otherwise.

When Reconciliation Works (Rarely)

Let's be fair—some people do change. But those people don't just apologize; they back it up with consistent, genuine actions over time. If they're showing:

- Real accountability (not just lip service),
- Tangible effort to rebuild trust, and
- A clear understanding of what they did wrong (without excuses or justifications), then maybe—*maybe*—they're worth a second chance. But let's be honest: those people are unicorns in the world of two-faced manipulators.

How to Protect Yourself

If you're even *considering* reconciliation, you better armor the fuck up. Set boundaries like your life depends on it and enforce them with military precision.

- **Test Their Behavior**: Are they actually following through on their promises, or are they slipping back into old habits?
- **Keep Your Distance**: Reconciliation doesn't mean rolling out the red carpet. Let them prove themselves before you fully let them back in.
- **Trust Your Gut**: If something feels off, it probably is. Don't let nostalgia or guilt cloud your judgment.

The Bottom Line

Reconciliation is a gamble, and the stakes are your sanity. If you're dealing with someone who's genuinely changed, fine, give it a shot—*cautiously*. But if their apology feels hollow, their actions don't match their words, or they're just repeating the same toxic patterns? Cut your losses and walk away. You've got better things to do than babysit someone else's redemption arc. Let them "grow" on their own time while you thrive without their bullshit weighing you down

8.3.3 Protecting Your Heart: Forgive, But Don't Be Stupid

Here's the deal: forgiveness is for you, but protection is for your future. Just because you've decided to let go of the grudge doesn't mean you're opening the gates for someone to waltz back in and wreck your life all over again. Protecting your heart is about drawing the line—firmly, loudly, and unapologetically. If they don't like it? Too bad. That's their problem, not yours.

Why Forgiving Without Forgetting Matters

The phrase "forgive and forget" is the biggest load of crap ever peddled. Forgetting isn't just unrealistic—it's dangerous. Forgetting what someone did gives them the perfect setup to screw you over again. You didn't endure their betrayal just to give them a free pass to hit repeat. Forgiveness is about letting go of the anger, not wiping the slate clean for round two.

- **They've Shown Their True Colors**: Betrayal isn't an accident; it's a choice. If they've chosen to hurt you once, it's on you to make sure they don't get another chance.
- **Boundaries Are Your Best Friend**: Protecting your heart means enforcing limits so ironclad even a bulldozer couldn't break through.
- **It's About Power, Not Revenge**: Forgiving someone doesn't mean you're weak—it means you're strong enough to take back control. Forgetting, on the other hand? That's just handing them the keys to screw you over again.

How to Guard Your Peace

1. **Keep the Lessons, Ditch the Pain**: Their betrayal taught you something valuable—what to watch for, who to trust, and where to draw the line. Keep those lessons close, and let the rest of the bullshit go.
2. **Create a Firewall**: No more blind trust. Keep things on a need-to-know basis. They don't need full access to your life just because you forgave them.
3. **Pay Attention to Patterns**: People who've betrayed you once often have a habit of doing it again. If they start slipping into old behaviors, call it out immediately or cut them loose.
4. **Don't Feel Guilty About Boundaries**: Protecting your heart isn't selfish—it's survival. If someone whines that you're being "cold" or "distant," that's just their manipulative ass trying to guilt you. Stick to your guns.

What Protecting Your Heart Doesn't Mean

- **It Doesn't Mean Being Bitter**: Protecting yourself doesn't mean shutting everyone out or becoming a fortress of doom. It's about being smarter, not angrier.
- **It Doesn't Mean Letting Them Off the Hook**: Just because you're not dwelling on what they did doesn't mean they get a free pass. They're still responsible for their actions.

The Bottom Line

Protecting your heart is about building a fortress, not a prison. Forgive them if you need to, but don't forget the lesson. Don't hand them the blueprint to hurt you again. Keep your peace, enforce your boundaries, and let them deal with the fact that they'll never have full access to you again. If they don't like it, tough shit. Your heart isn't their playground—it's your fortress, and you hold the key.

8.3.4 Respecting Yourself First: Stop Being Everyone's Doormat

Respecting yourself isn't just a warm, fuzzy concept—it's the backbone of dealing with two-faced manipulators and toxic assholes. If you don't respect yourself, guess what? Nobody else will, especially the people who thrive on walking all over you. Forgiveness and boundaries don't mean shit if you're not putting yourself first. It's time to stop bending over backward for people who wouldn't even lean sideways for you.

The Golden Rule of Self-Respect

Here's the harsh truth: people treat you the way you allow them to. Every time you let someone's bullshit slide, you're handing them permission to keep pulling the same crap. Respecting yourself starts with realizing that you are not a doormat, a punching bag, or a guilt sponge for someone else's insecurities.

- **Stop Explaining Yourself**: "No" is a complete sentence. You don't owe anyone a PowerPoint presentation on why you're setting boundaries or cutting them off.
- **Put Your Needs First**: If someone calls you selfish for taking care of yourself, that's just their manipulative way of saying they can't use you anymore. Let them whine.
- **Cut the Toxic Out**: Respecting yourself means recognizing when someone is adding zero value to your life and letting them go. No regrets, no apologies.

Why Self-Respect Pisses Off Toxic People

Two-faced manipulators thrive on your self-doubt. They count on you second-guessing yourself, apologizing for things you didn't do, and bending over backward to keep the peace. But the second you start respecting yourself? Oh, they hate that. They'll call you cold, distant, or even a "bitch." Good. That just means you're doing it right.

- **They Can't Control You Anymore**: Toxic people lose their grip the moment you put yourself first.
- **They'll Try to Guilt-Trip You**: "I don't even recognize you anymore!" No shit, Karen. That's because I'm not putting up with your crap anymore.
- **They'll Spread Drama**: When they realize they can't manipulate you, they'll badmouth you to anyone who'll listen. Let them. Your self-respect isn't up for debate.

How to Prioritize Yourself

1. **Set and Enforce Boundaries**: Decide what behavior you will and won't tolerate, and stick to it. If they push, shove back harder.
2. **Stop People-Pleasing**: You don't need to make everyone happy. Focus on your own happiness—anyone who doesn't like it can fuck right off.
3. **Celebrate Yourself**: Stop waiting for others to validate you. Respecting yourself means recognizing your own worth, no cheerleaders required.
4. **Cut the Parasites**: If someone's only in your life to drain your energy, it's time to say goodbye. Respect yourself enough to walk away.

Self-respect isn't optional—it's non-negotiable. It's about putting your peace, your priorities, and your sanity above someone else's manipulative agenda. If they can't handle the new, boundary-setting, self-respecting version of you? That's their problem, not yours. Respect yourself first, last, and always. Let them choke on their drama while you thrive.

8.3.5 Moving Forward with Clarity: Leaving the Bullshit Behind

Moving forward after dealing with two-faced people isn't just about cutting them out of your life—it's about making sure their toxic bullshit doesn't linger in your mind, your decisions, or your relationships. Clarity isn't about "forgive and forget"—it's about seeing things for what they really are, learning the lesson, and walking away with your head held high while they drown in the mess they made.

Step 1: Ditch the Emotional Baggage

First things first—stop carrying the weight of what they did to you. Yes, they were manipulative, two-faced, and probably made you feel like crap. But dragging that anger and hurt around only gives them power they don't deserve. Dump that baggage at the curb like yesterday's trash and drive the hell away.

- **Acknowledge the Hurt**: Be honest about how their actions affected you. Name it, process it, and let it go.
- **Don't Seek Closure from Them**: Most two-faced assholes aren't going to give you the apology you deserve. Closure doesn't come from them—it comes from you deciding to move the fuck on.

Step 2: Learn the Lesson

Every betrayal has a lesson. Maybe it's about recognizing red flags earlier, setting stronger boundaries, or trusting your instincts when something feels off. The lesson isn't to stop trusting everyone—it's to stop ignoring your gut when someone's behavior doesn't match their words.

- **Spot the Patterns**: What did this situation teach you about the kind of people you let into your life?
- **Upgrade Your Filters**: Moving forward with clarity means being more selective about who gets access to your time, energy, and trust.

Step 3: Rebuild Your Confidence

Betrayal can shake your sense of self, but let's be real—it says more about them than it does about you. You're not the problem; they are.

Moving forward means rebuilding your confidence and reminding yourself that their bullshit doesn't define you.

- **Celebrate Your Wins**: Focus on what you've achieved despite their crap. You're stronger than their manipulation, and that's worth celebrating.
- **Surround Yourself with Real Ones**: The best way to heal is to invest in relationships with people who actually have your back.

Step 4: Make Peace with the Past

Making peace doesn't mean pretending it didn't happen—it means accepting it for what it was and refusing to let it control your future. The past is done; the only thing left to decide is how you're going to use it to grow.

The Bottom Line

Moving forward with clarity isn't about pretending the betrayal didn't happen—it's about refusing to let it hold you back. Leave the two-faced manipulators in the rearview mirror, take the lessons with you, and rebuild a life free from their toxic influence. You've got better things to do than dwell on their bullshit. Let them stay stuck while you move on, stronger, smarter, and completely unbothered.

Lesson 8.4: Creating Healthy Relationship Dynamics

8.4.1 Communicating Effectively: Setting Expectations With Family And Friends

Let's be honest: communicating with toxic, two-faced people—or anyone with a flair for manipulation—feels like playing chess with a pigeon. No matter how strategic you are, they'll knock over all the pieces, shit on the board, and act like they won. That's why effective communication isn't about pleasing them—it's about making yourself crystal clear, so there's no room for their bullshit to take root.

Step 1: Say What You Mean (and Mean What You Say)

Two-faced manipulators thrive on ambiguity. If you leave room for interpretation, they'll twist your words faster than a pretzel at a carnival. "I'm not sure" becomes "Yes," and "Maybe later" becomes "You owe me forever." Stop dancing around the point and get straight to it.

- **Example 1**: Instead of saying, "I don't know if I can help," say, "No, I'm not available." Done. No wiggle room, no debate.
- **Example 2**: Replace "I'd prefer if you didn't do that" with "Stop doing that. Now." Tone matters—leave no doubt.

Step 2: Keep It Short and Brutal

Let's be real: these people aren't looking for clarity; they're looking for leverage. The more you ramble, the more ammunition you're handing them. Keep your communication direct, to the point, and as emotionless as a robot with a vendetta.

- **Don't Apologize for Being Clear**: Saying no doesn't require an apology or a soliloquy. "No, that doesn't work for me" is more than enough.
- **Avoid Emotional Overloads**: These manipulators *love* when you lose your cool— it gives them something to weaponize. Stay calm, stay sharp, and watch them squirm.

Step 3: Set Expectations Like a Goddamn Boss

If you don't lay out clear expectations, you're practically inviting chaos into your life. Set boundaries in a way that leaves zero room for negotiation, and repeat them like a mantra if they keep testing you.

- **What to Say**: "If you keep bringing this up, I'm ending the conversation." And then *do it*. Empty threats are just invitations for them to keep pushing.
- **Enforce Consequences**: When they cross a line—and they will—follow through. If you said you'd cut them off after one more slip-up, don't stick around for a second one.

Step 4: Call Out Their Bullshit

Effective communication doesn't mean letting things slide to "keep the peace." When someone tries to twist your words, gaslight you, or outright lie, shut that shit down on the spot.

- **Example**: "That's not what I said, and you know it. Don't put words in my mouth." Watch as their face freezes because they weren't expecting you to call them out.

Step 5: Protect Your Peace

Not every conversation deserves your time, and not every person deserves a response. Sometimes the most effective communication is silence. Refusing to engage sends a louder message than words ever could.

The Bottom Line

Communicating effectively with toxic people isn't about "understanding each other"—it's about shutting down their manipulative games before they even start. Be clear, be direct, and don't give a single inch. You're not responsible for how they feel about your boundaries or your words. If they can't handle it? That's their problem, not yours. Speak your mind, stand your ground, and let them deal with the fallout.

8.4.2 Building Mutual Respect: A Two-Way Street, Not a Dead-End

Mutual respect isn't just a nice idea—it's the bare minimum for any relationship worth keeping. And let's get one thing straight: if respect isn't a two-way street, it's a dead-end, and you're the one stuck paying the emotional toll. Two-faced people don't give a damn about respect—they only care about control. So, if you're going to deal with these assholes, you've got to demand respect like your peace of mind depends on it—because it does.

Step 1: Stop Handing Out Free Passes

Respect is earned, not given out like Halloween candy. If someone isn't respecting your time, boundaries, or energy, stop making excuses for them. "That's just how they are" is the kind of bullshit that keeps you stuck in toxic relationships. If they can't act like a decent human being, they don't deserve a spot in your life.

- **What to Do**: Call out disrespect the second it happens. "I don't appreciate that," or "You're crossing a line." Short, sharp, and leaves no room for debate.
- **Why It Works**: Two-faced people count on your silence. The moment you speak up, you're taking away their power.

Step 2: Enforce Reciprocity Like a Boss

Respect is a two-way exchange, not a charity. If you're giving respect and getting nothing but drama in return, you're in a one-sided relationship, and it's time to balance the scales.

- **Set the Standard**: "I'm willing to respect you, but I expect the same in return." If they can't meet that bar, let them take their bullshit somewhere else.
- **Stop Overgiving**: You're not a vending machine of kindness. If they're not reciprocating, stop wasting your time.

Step 3: Define What Respect Looks Like

Let's be real: some people don't know what respect is because no one's ever required it from them. That doesn't mean you have to teach them, but it does mean you need to set clear expectations.

- **Respect Your Time**: "Don't show up late and expect me to wait."
- **Respect Your Space**: "Don't invade my boundaries and then act surprised when I shut you down."
- **Respect Your Effort**: "If I'm putting in the work, I expect you to meet me halfway."

Step 4: Walk Away When It's Not Mutual

Here's the hard truth: you can't force someone to respect you. If they're not willing to meet you halfway, stop trying to drag them across the finish line. Respect yourself enough to walk away from relationships that don't serve you. Yes, it's uncomfortable. Yes, it might feel like you're burning a bridge. But if that bridge leads to nowhere, why the hell are you trying to keep it intact?

The Bottom Line

Building mutual respect isn't about begging someone to treat you well—it's about demanding it and cutting ties when they can't deliver. Two-faced manipulators thrive in relationships where respect is one-sided, but the moment you enforce boundaries and reciprocity, their games fall apart. Don't waste your energy on people who don't respect you. Raise your standards, demand better, and let the disrespectful assholes choke on their own irrelevance.

8.4.3 Recognizing Genuine Support: Identifying People Who Truly Have Your Back

In a world full of two-faced manipulators and backstabbing bastards, figuring out who's genuinely got your back can feel like trying to find a needle in a haystack—except the haystack is on fire, and someone keeps throwing more hay on top. But here's the deal: genuine support isn't hard to recognize when you know what to look for. The problem? You've been too busy giving people the benefit of the doubt to see the red flags waving in your face.

What Genuine Support Actually Looks Like

Let's cut the crap. Real support isn't just someone liking your social media posts or saying, "I'm here for you," with no follow-through. It's about actions, not empty words. Here's what real support looks like:

- **They Show Up**: Genuine people don't just talk about being there for you—they actually show the fuck up. Whether it's a late-night phone call, celebrating your wins, or backing you up when someone's talking shit, they prove they're in your corner.
- **They Don't Make It About Themselves**: They listen without flipping the script to their own problems. When you're venting, they're not waiting for their turn to speak— they're actually paying attention.
- **They're Honest Without Being Assholes**: They'll call you out when you need it but do it with respect. Real friends tell you the truth, not to tear you down but to help you level up.
- **They Don't Disappear When Things Get Messy**: Fake supporters scatter the second you're not "fun" or "convenient" anymore. Real ones stick around, even when the going gets tough.

Signs You're Dealing with Fake Support

Of course, not everyone clapping for you wants you to win. Some people are just sticking around to see how they can benefit or waiting for you to fail so they can say, "I told you so." Watch out for these red flags:

- **Inconsistent Behavior**: One day, they're hyping you up; the next, they're nowhere to be found. Genuine support doesn't come and go with their mood swings.
- **Backhanded Compliments**: "Wow, I didn't think you'd pull that off!" Translation: They didn't believe in you but are pretending to now.
- **They're Only Around for the Good Times**: If they're all-in during your wins but MIA when shit hits the fan, they're not supportive—they're opportunistic.

How to Keep the Real Ones Close

Once you've weeded out the fakes, it's time to hold onto the people who actually give a damn about you. Here's how:

1. **Show Appreciation**: Don't take genuine support for granted. Thank them, acknowledge their efforts, and let them know they matter.
2. **Reciprocate**: Support isn't a one-way street. Be the kind of person you'd want in your corner.
3. **Prioritize Quality Over Quantity**: You don't need an army of supporters. A few solid people are worth more than a crowd of fake cheerleaders.

The Bottom Line

Recognizing genuine support is about paying attention to actions, not words. Real supporters don't just talk—they show up, they stick around, and they cheer you on without expecting anything in return. Cut the fakes, keep the real ones, and stop wasting your energy on people who wouldn't lift a finger for you. Life's too short for half-assed friendships and two-faced "allies." Find your crew and stick with them. The rest? Let them choke on their own mediocrity.

8.4.4 Maintaining Healthy Distance: Keep the Assholes at Arm's Length

Let's face it—sometimes, cutting people off completely isn't an option. Maybe it's a family member you can't fully escape, or a coworker you're stuck with until one of you finally quits. Whatever the case, you don't have to let them waltz into your life and plant their toxic flag. The solution? Keep those assholes at arm's length while protecting your sanity like your life depends on it—because it does.

Step 1: Master the Art of Detachment

Detachment is your best friend when dealing with toxic or two-faced people you can't fully kick to the curb. It's not about being cold-hearted—it's about self-preservation. You're not their emotional dumpster, and you're not obligated to engage with their drama.

- **Stay Surface-Level**: Keep conversations basic. "How's the weather?" or "How about those Dodgers?" is just fine. Anything deeper is just giving them ammunition.
- **Don't Take the Bait**: When they inevitably try to provoke you, let their bullshit roll off your back. "That's interesting" is a great catch-all response for their nonsense.

Step 2: Control the Access

The key to maintaining healthy distance is controlling how much of you they get—and it shouldn't be much. They don't need to know your plans, your struggles, or your wins. Keep it vague, keep it minimal, and keep your private life private.

- **Don't Overshare**: They'll twist your words into a weapon the first chance they get. The less they know, the less damage they can do.
- **Set Time Limits**: If you have to interact, keep it brief. You're not obligated to spend hours listening to their bullshit.

Step 3: Enforce Boundaries Like a Bouncer

Boundaries are the line in the sand that separates your peace from their chaos. The trick is not just setting them but *enforcing* them like your sanity depends on it. Because, newsflash: it does.

- **Example Boundary**: "I'm not discussing [insert topic] with you." If they bring it up, end the conversation immediately.
- **Follow Through**: If they cross the line, don't let it slide. Shut it down. "We've already talked about this. I'm done."

Step 4: Use Them Strategically (If You Must)

Sometimes, maintaining distance means playing the game smarter than they do. If they're unavoidable, figure out how to keep the interaction transactional. Need something from them? Get it and move on. No emotional involvement, no unnecessary exposure. Think of it as using them without letting them use you.

Step 5: Protect Your Energy

Your energy is not an infinite resource, and toxic people are like black holes—they'll suck you dry if you let them. Distance isn't just physical—it's mental. Stop letting their nonsense take up space in your head rent-free.

- **Don't Engage in Their Drama**: It's not your circus, and they're not your monkeys. Let them spiral on their own.
- **Focus on Your Priorities**: The less time you spend thinking about them, the better. Pour your energy into people and things that actually matter.

The Bottom Line

Maintaining healthy distance is about protecting your peace without completely cutting someone off. It's about limiting their access to you, shutting down their bullshit, and keeping things surface-level and transactional. You're not their therapist, their punching bag, or their confidant, so stop acting like it. Keep them at arm's length, and let them stew in their own chaos while you live your life on your terms.

8.4.5 Thriving with Chosen Family: Build Your Own Damn Tribe

Here's the truth no one likes to admit: blood doesn't mean shit when it comes to loyalty and love. Family isn't about DNA; it's about the people who show up for you, support you, and don't try to stab you in the back when things get tough. If your "real" family is a toxic shitshow, it's time to stop forcing it and start thriving with your chosen family—the people who actually have your back because they _want_ to, not because they have to.

Step 1: Define Your Tribe

Chosen family isn't about collecting a random group of acquaintances. It's about surrounding yourself with people who make you feel safe, seen, and supported. These are the ones who clap for you when you win and pick you up when you fall. They're not in it for what they can get—they're in it because they care.

- **Who They Are**: Your ride-or-die best friend, the coworker who always covers for you, the neighbor who brings over wine when you've had a shit day.
- **Who They're Not**: The toxic coworker, the fair-weather friend, or the relative who can't wait to gossip about your personal life.

Step 2: Stop Chasing Approval

One of the best things about chosen family? You don't have to beg for their approval or bend over backward to keep the peace. They like you for who you are, not for what you can do for them. Stop wasting energy on people who treat you like an obligation and pour it into the ones who actually give a damn.

- **Let Go of Toxic Relatives**: If your blood family treats you like crap, cut them loose. You don't owe them your time, your energy, or your loyalty.
- **Focus on Mutual Respect**: Chosen family thrives on reciprocity. If they're putting in the effort, you better damn well match it.

Step 3: Build Deep Connections

Chosen family isn't about quantity; it's about quality. You don't need a hundred fake friends—you need a handful of real ones. Invest in the people who invest in you. Share your wins, your fears, and your dreams, and let those connections grow into something solid.

Step 4: Celebrate the Freedom

The best part of chosen family? You're not stuck with them. These relationships exist because you *want* them, not because of some outdated idea that family is forever. If someone in your chosen family turns toxic, guess what? You can kick them to the curb without a second thought. No guilt, no drama, just peace.

The Bottom Line

Thriving with chosen family is about surrounding yourself with people who actually deserve a place in your life. It's about creating a support system that's built on trust, respect, and genuine care—not guilt, obligation, or manipulation. Let the toxic relatives stew in their dysfunction while you build your own tribe of people who actually give a damn. You're the architect of your support system, so build it with people who make you stronger, not people who drag you down. And if anyone doesn't like it? Fuck them. You're thriving without them.

Toxic Envy: Jealous Manipulators Who Try to Take You Down"

You've drawn the line. You've cut off the two-faced family members, fake friends, and emotional leeches who thought they had a lifelong VIP pass to your time and energy. You've set boundaries so solid they might as well be surrounded by barbed wire. But guess what? That doesn't mean the manipulative bullshit is over.

Because if there's one thing more dangerous than a two-faced liar, it's a **jealous two-faced liar.**

Jealousy isn't just an emotion for these people—it's their *fuel*. It's the venom they spit when they realize they can't control you anymore. Instead of working on their own pathetic lives, they'd rather sabotage yours. They don't just want to see you fail—they *need* you to fail so they don't have to face their own shortcomings.

Chapter 9 is where we expose jealousy for what it really is—**an insecure person's tantrum in disguise.** We're diving headfirst into their toxic playbook, dissecting their envy-fueled manipulation tactics, and making sure their bullshit doesn't touch you ever again.

Let them choke on their own bitterness—because you? **You're untouchable.**

CHAPTER NINE

Jealousy and Manipulation

Jealousy isn't just an emotion for two-faced manipulators—it's their fucking lifeline. These insecure parasites wake up every morning pissed off that someone else—you—is thriving, while they're stuck marinating in their own mediocrity. Instead of fixing their mess of a life, they double down on their bitterness, turning manipulation into an art form.

They twist words, spread lies, and sabotage anything they can't control—all to drag you down to their level. This chapter dives headfirst into their toxic playbook, exposing their pathetic insecurities and breaking down every manipulative tactic they use. By the time you're done, you'll know how to spot their games from a mile away and shut them down so hard they'll wish they never tried to mess with you in the first place.

Lesson 9.1: The Root of Jealousy

9.1.1 Why They're Jealous: The Insecurity Shitstorm Behind Their Behavior

Jealousy is the toxic sludge that fuels every two-faced manipulator's engine. It's not just a passing emotion for them—it's a goddamn lifestyle. They wake up bitter, go to sleep bitter, and spend every moment in between seething about the fact that someone—*you*—has something they don't. But here's the kicker: their jealousy isn't about you. It's about them and their festering pit of insecurities that they're too lazy or cowardly to deal with.

Jealousy's Rotten Core: Insecurity

At its core, jealousy is a direct reflection of their own inadequacies. These people look at your success, happiness, or confidence and see everything they *wish* they had. Instead of clapping for you or, I don't know, *working on themselves*, they'd rather drag you down to their level. Misery loves company, and these insecure bastards are always recruiting.

- **They See Themselves as Inferior**: Every time you win, it shines a spotlight on their failures. Got a promotion? They're still stuck in a dead-end job. Found love? They're swiping aimlessly on Tinder. Whatever it is, your success reminds them of everything they're not.
- **They Crave Validation**: Jealous people need constant reassurance that they're worthy, and when they don't get it, they lash out. Seeing you thrive only amplifies their internal pity party.

It's Not About You—It's About Them

Let's be clear: their jealousy is 100% their problem. You're not responsible for their insecurities, and you sure as hell shouldn't dim your light to make them feel better. The truth is, they're too busy wallowing in self-pity to realize that their jealousy doesn't make you less—it makes you *more*. If anything, their bitterness is proof that you're doing something right.

- **They're Addicted to Comparison**: Instead of focusing on their own lane, they're constantly measuring themselves against others. Spoiler alert: they always come up short because they're comparing their bloopers to your highlight reel.
- **They Fear Your Success Means Their Failure**: In their warped little minds, life is a zero-sum game. If you win, they think it automatically means they lose.

What to Do About It

You can't fix their insecurities, so don't even try. Instead:

- **Call Out the Bullshit**: If their jealousy turns into snide comments or sabotage, shut it down. "Is that jealousy I hear? You could've just said congrats." Watch them squirm.
- **Stay in Your Lane**: Keep thriving, and don't tone yourself down to make them comfortable. Your success is *not* their problem, and their jealousy isn't yours.
- **Cut the Dead Weight**: If their jealousy becomes toxic, it's time to walk away. Life's too short to babysit someone's insecurity.

The Bottom Line

Jealousy is their insecurity spilling out for the world to see. It's not about you—it's about their inability to deal with their own shortcomings. Let them stew in their bitterness while you keep winning. You didn't work this hard to let someone else's jealousy drag you down. They can choke on their envy while you enjoy your success guilt-free.

9.1.2 The Comparison Trap: Their Endless Game of "Why Not Me?

Jealous people live in the comparison trap like it's a goddamn luxury condo. Every moment of their miserable existence is spent measuring themselves against you and coming up short. Instead of focusing on their own lives—or better yet, improving their situation—they obsess over why you have what they don't. It's like a full-time job for them, except it pays in bitterness and petty resentment.

Why They Can't Stop Comparing

Here's the deal: these people are so wrapped up in their insecurities that they think life is a competition they're losing. Your wins feel like personal attacks, and instead of clapping for you, they start keeping score like it's a game of toxic bingo.

- **"They Don't Deserve It!"**: This is their favorite line. You got the promotion, the relationship, the recognition—and in their warped little heads, it's all some cosmic mistake because *they* should've been the one to get it. Never mind that you worked your ass off. They're too busy playing the victim to acknowledge reality.
- **"Why Isn't My Life Like That?"**: Every time they see your success, they spiral into a self-pity party. Instead of asking, "What can I do to improve?" they settle for, "Why does life hate me?" Pro tip: life doesn't hate them; they just refuse to get their shit together.

The Social Media Effect: Fueling the Fire

If you think they're bad in person, just wait until they see your highlight reel on social media. Every post, every achievement, every happy photo is another dagger to their fragile ego. They can't process that your life isn't perfect—it's just better than theirs because you're actually putting in the work.

- **Your Success Feeds Their Envy**: That vacation you took? Proof you're living better. That promotion? Evidence they're falling behind. Every time you win, they lose another piece of their self-worth.
- **They Weaponize Your Wins**: Ever notice how they turn your achievements into backhanded compliments? "Must be nice to afford that" or "Wow, I guess they're handing out promotions now." That's their jealousy leaking out like a busted pipe.

Why You Shouldn't Give a Damn

Here's the brutal truth: their comparison trap isn't your problem. You're not responsible for their lack of ambition, their bad decisions, or their shitty attitude. The fact that they're keeping score doesn't mean you have to play the game. Let them drown in their own envy while you keep stacking your wins.

- **Don't Apologize for Thriving**: Stop feeling bad for outshining them. You didn't bust your ass to dim your light for someone else's comfort.
- **Call Out the Snark**: When they drop a passive-aggressive comment, hit them back. "Wow, that sounded bitter—everything okay over there?" Watch them stutter as they try to play innocent.
- **Keep Your Distance**: If their jealousy becomes toxic, it's time to cut ties. Let them compare themselves to someone else while you enjoy your peace.

The Bottom Line

The comparison trap is their self-made prison, and you don't owe them the key. Their jealousy, their bitterness, their endless "Why not me?" spiral—it's all about them and has nothing to do with you. Let them stew in their misery while you keep winning. You didn't come this far to let some jealous loser drag you down. Live your life unapologetically and let them choke on their own envy.

9.1.3 The Need to Sabotage: When Jealousy Turns Into a Goddamn Bloodsport

Let's call it like it is: jealous people don't just stew in their own bitterness—they weaponize it. The moment they realize they can't compete with you, they shift gears into full-on sabotage mode. It's not enough for them to fail; they need to see you fail, too. Your success feels like a personal attack, and their fragile little egos can't handle it. So, what do they do? They start pulling strings, dropping grenades, and fucking up your life wherever they can.

Why They Do It

Sabotage isn't just a side effect of their jealousy—it's their ultimate power play. These assholes can't stand watching you thrive while they're stuck spinning their wheels, so they do whatever it takes to drag you down.

- **They Need to Level the Playing Field**: Your success highlights their failures, and instead of using it as motivation, they'd rather torch your accomplishments to make themselves feel better. It's not about winning—it's about making sure you lose.
- **It's Their Defense Mechanism**: They know they'll never match your hustle, your talent, or your resilience, so they resort to underhanded tactics. They'd rather be sneaky little snakes than face their own mediocrity.
- **They Get Off on the Drama**: Watching you scramble after one of their sabotage moves gives them a sick sense of satisfaction. It's the closest thing to success they'll ever feel, and they're addicted to it.

How They Sabotage You

Sabotage comes in many forms, and these two-faced bastards are nothing if not creative. Watch out for these classic moves:

- **Spreading Lies**: They'll twist your words, fabricate stories, and spread bullshit rumors to make you look bad. If they can't beat you, they'll tarnish your reputation instead.
- **Undermining Your Work**: Whether it's sabotaging a project at work, stealing your ideas, or conveniently "forgetting" to pass on important information, they're always looking for ways to trip you up.
- **Playing the Victim**: They'll spin a narrative where you're the bad guy, framing themselves as the poor, misunderstood soul who's just trying to survive your supposed tyranny. Fucking ridiculous.
- **Turning Others Against You**: Divide and conquer is their go-to strategy. They'll whisper in people's ears, plant seeds of doubt, and stir up drama just to isolate you.

What to Do About It

You don't have to play their game—but you *do* need to defend yourself. Here's how to handle these jealous saboteurs like the badass you are:

1. **Expose Their Bullshit**: Call them out the second you catch wind of their shady behavior. "I know what you're trying to do, and it's not going to work. Stay in your lane." Watch them backpedal like the spineless cowards they are.
2. **Fortify Your Reputation**: Make sure the people who matter know the truth about you. Document your work, keep receipts, and let your results speak louder than their lies.
3. **Cut Off Their Access**: The less they know about your plans, the less they can fuck them up. Stop sharing details with them and keep them in the dark.
4. **Don't React to the Drama**: They thrive on chaos. The best revenge? Thriving without giving a single fuck about their nonsense.

The Bottom Line

Sabotage is the jealous person's last-ditch effort to feel relevant. It's pathetic, it's desperate, and it's proof that you're doing something right. Let them waste their energy plotting while you stay focused on winning. Their need to sabotage you says everything about their insecurities and absolutely nothing about you. Keep rising, let them choke on your success, and leave their sorry asses in the dust where they belong.

9.1.4 Social Climbing and Envy: When Jealousy Meets Their Pathetic Ambition

Some people don't just want what you have—they want to *be* you, but without putting in any of the goddamn work. These are the social climbers of the world: jealous, slimy opportunists who would sell their own grandmother for a shot at stealing your spotlight. They don't just envy your success; they're obsessed with using you—or tearing you down—to claw their way to the top. Their motto? "If I can't rise, I'll burn the whole damn ladder."

Why Social Climbers Are So Pathetic

Social climbers aren't just jealous—they're *desperate*. They don't have the skills, charisma, or actual talent to earn respect on their own, so they latch onto successful people like fucking leeches. And when they realize they can't siphon enough off your success to make themselves feel important, they start plotting your downfall.

- **They're Obsessed with Appearances**: Social climbers care more about how things *look* than how they actually *are*. They'd rather fake being successful on Instagram than put in an ounce of effort to build something real.
- **They Hate That You're the Real Deal**: You worked your ass off, and they can't stand it. Your success is a constant reminder that they're a fraud, and they'll stop at nothing to level the playing field—usually by dragging you through the mud.

Their Toxic Toolbox: How Social Climbers Weaponize Envy

These backstabbing pricks are masters at combining jealousy with ambition to create the ultimate cocktail of toxic behavior. Here's how they operate:

- **Fake Friendships**: They'll cozy up to you, pretending to be your biggest supporter, all while collecting intel to use against you. "I'm so proud of you!" they say, while secretly figuring out how to copy your moves or sabotage your success.
- **Name-Dropping and Association**: They'll milk your friendship (or even just a passing acquaintance) for all it's worth. "Oh, I know [your name]," they'll brag to anyone who'll listen, as if your success somehow validates their existence.

- **Climbing by Crushing**: When using you doesn't work, they'll start tearing you down. Gossip, lies, and subtle digs— it's all fair game in their pathetic little playbook.

Why They'll Never Win

Here's the thing about social climbers: their entire identity is built on smoke and mirrors. They spend so much time trying to mimic or destroy others that they forget to build anything real for themselves. Sure, they might fool a few people for a while, but eventually, their lack of substance catches up with them. You can't fake your way to long-term success, and these assholes will never understand that.

How to Handle These Slimy Bastards

1. **Cut Off Their Access**: Stop letting them use you as a stepping stone. Don't give them advice, don't share your plans, and for the love of God, don't let them attach their name to yours.
2. **Call Out the Fakery**: When they start dropping your name or pretending they're part of your success, shut that shit down. "We're not that close, and I'd appreciate it if you stopped using me to boost your image." Mic drop.
3. **Let Their Actions Speak for Themselves**: Social climbers always reveal their true colors eventually. Let them keep digging their own graves while you focus on thriving.
4. **Protect Your Circle**: Keep your real friends and allies close, and don't let these snakes slither into your inner circle. They'll only use it as a staging ground for their next pathetic move.

The Bottom Line

Social climbers are nothing more than jealous, insecure frauds with a bad case of ambition and no fucking talent to back it up. They'll leech off your success, drag your name through the mud, and do whatever it takes to make themselves feel relevant. Don't waste your energy fighting their petty games. Cut them off, call them out, and let them implode under the weight of their own bullshit. You're too busy building something real to worry about their sad little attempts at climbing the social ladder.

9.1.5 Recognizing the Signs: Jealousy Isn't Subtle, It's Just Pathetic

Jealousy might not come with a flashing billboard, but holy hell, it doesn't stay hidden for long. Two-faced assholes aren't exactly masters of subtlety—they can't help but let their envy drip out like a busted faucet. The problem? You've probably spent too much time giving them the benefit of the doubt. Not anymore. It's time to rip off the mask and see their jealousy for what it is: a steaming pile of insecurity wrapped in passive-aggressive bullshit.

How Their Jealousy Screams for Attention

These bitter bastards aren't as sneaky as they think. Here's what to look for:

- **Backhanded Compliments**: "Wow, I didn't think you'd actually pull that off. Good for you!" That's not praise; that's their way of reminding you they didn't believe in you to begin with.
- **Passive-Aggressive Snark**: "Must be nice to have all the free time to work out." Translation? They're pissed you're in better shape than their lazy ass.
- **Always Playing the Victim**: "It's just so unfair how things work out for some people." Yeah, unfair that you actually worked hard while they sat on their couch blaming the universe.
- **Obsessive Comparisons**: They're constantly measuring themselves against you, and guess what? They're always coming up short. Spoiler alert: that's why they're so goddamn salty.

- **Sabotage Disguised as Advice**: "Are you sure you're ready for that? It sounds like a lot of pressure." No, Karen, it sounds like *you* can't handle the fact that I'm succeeding.

Why They Can't Help Themselves

Jealousy isn't about you—it's about their pathetic inability to deal with their own shortcomings. Your wins are a reminder that they're failing, and instead of fixing their shit, they lash out at you. It's not just insecurity; it's a goddamn personality flaw.

- **They Want What You Have**: Success, happiness, respect—they crave it all but aren't willing to work for it.
- **They Think Life Is a Competition**: In their tiny, warped minds, every step you take forward pushes them further behind.
- **They Hate That You Prove Them Wrong**: Your success shatters the excuses they make for their own failures.

What to Do When You Spot the Signs

1. **Call It the Fuck Out**: Don't let their bullshit slide. "Wow, you seem a little bitter—something you want to say?" Watch them stumble over their excuses.
2. **Stop Sharing Your Wins**: If they can't celebrate with you, they don't get a front-row seat to your success. Let them stew in their envy while you keep thriving.
3. **Protect Your Energy**: These people are emotional vampires. Cut their access to your life and focus on the people who actually clap when you win.

The Bottom Line

Jealousy doesn't hide—it leaks out of every passive-aggressive comment, every fake compliment, and every snide remark. Stop pretending you don't see it. Recognize the signs, call it out, and shut it down. Their bitterness has nothing to do with you and everything to do with their own pathetic insecurities. Let them choke on their envy while you keep living your best life, unapologetically and unbothered.

Lesson 9.2: Manipulation Tactics Unveiled

9.2.1 Emotional Puppeteering: Using Your Feelings Like a Goddamn Joystick

If there's one thing manipulative assholes excel at, it's turning your emotions into their personal puppet show. Emotional puppeteering isn't just a tactic—it's their bread and butter. They'll push your buttons, twist your feelings, and pull your strings until you're dancing to their tune without even realizing it. And the best part? They'll make you think it was *your* idea all along.

How Emotional Puppeteering Works

These master manipulators know that logic rarely wins over feelings, so they go straight for your emotional jugular. It's like a psychological game of chess—except they're cheating, and you didn't even know you were playing. Here's their favorite bullshit tactics:

- **The Guilt Trip**: "After all I've done for you, this is how you treat me?" Oh, fuck off. They weaponize guilt like it's an Olympic sport, making you feel like a monster for setting boundaries or saying no.
- **The Sob Story**: They'll cry, whine, and spin their sad little tale until you're the bad guy for not swooping in to save them. It's not empathy they're after—it's control.
- **The Flattery Trap**: "You're the only one I can trust with this." Translation: "I need you to do this shit because no one else will put up with me." Don't fall for it.
- **The Fake Crisis**: "I need your help right now!" Their emergencies always seem to line up with whatever you

have going on. Coincidence? Nope, just manipulation in disguise.

Why They Do It

Manipulators aren't interested in your well-being—they're interested in what they can squeeze out of you. Your emotions are just tools in their pathetic little toolbox of control. They pull the strings because it's easier than doing the work themselves.

- **They Thrive on Power**: Emotional puppeteering gives them control over your actions, decisions, and even your goddamn sanity.
- **They Hate Responsibility**: Why do something themselves when they can guilt or manipulate you into doing it for them?
- **They Fear Losing You**: They know if you wake up to their games, their power crumbles. So, they double down on the manipulation to keep you hooked.

How to Cut the Strings

1. **Spot the Patterns**: Pay attention to how they make you feel. Are you constantly walking on eggshells, guilt-ridden, or emotionally drained? That's not an accident—it's their game plan.
2. **Say No Without Explaining**: "No" is a full sentence. You don't owe them an essay on why you're not playing their game anymore.
3. **Detach From the Drama**: When they whip out their sob stories or fake crises, don't bite. "I'm sorry you're dealing with that, but I can't help right now." Period.
4. **Call Them Out**: If you're feeling bold, throw their manipulation right back at them. "Why are you trying to guilt-trip me into this? Let's cut the crap." Watch them squirm.

The Bottom Line

Emotional puppeteering is a manipulator's favorite game, but it only works if you let them play. Once you spot the patterns, you can cut the strings and leave them holding their sad little bag of tricks. Let them stew in their own drama while you take back your time, energy, and peace of mind. You're nobody's fucking puppet—don't let them forget it.

9.2.2 The Divide-and-Conquer Strategy: _Turning Allies into Enemies_

Two-faced manipulators are like generals in their own private wars. They don't just come for you—they come for your relationships, too. Their favorite tactic? Divide and conquer. These toxic bastards thrive on chaos, and they'll do anything to pit people against each other if it means staying in control. It's not enough for them to watch you struggle—they want you isolated, confused, and questioning everyone around you.

How They Execute Their Toxic Masterpiece

Divide-and-conquer isn't just a strategy for battle; for these manipulators, it's a goddamn art form. They know exactly how to stir the pot and create division while pretending to be the innocent bystander. Here's how they pull it off:

- **Spreading Half-Truths**: They'll take a tiny piece of information and twist it into something that barely resembles the truth. "Oh, I heard she wasn't too happy about what you said last week." Boom—instant tension, courtesy of their bullshit.
- **Playing Both Sides**: They'll cozy up to you, nodding along like they're on your side, and then turn around and do the same thing with the other person. It's all about keeping both of you in the dark while they control the narrative.

- **Sowing Doubt**: "I don't know if you can trust him. He's been acting kinda shady lately." They plant seeds of mistrust and then sit back to watch the fireworks.
- **Faking Concern**: "I'm only telling you this because I care." No, Brenda, you're telling me this because you're a manipulative asshole who loves drama.

Why They Do It

Manipulators thrive on power, and nothing gives them more power than controlling how people see each other. By turning allies into enemies, they create an environment where no one trusts anyone— except them. It's not just about making you miserable; it's about making themselves the center of attention in the chaos they've created.

- **They Want Control**: The more fragmented your relationships are, the easier it is for them to pull the strings.
- **They Get Off on the Drama**: Watching people fight over their lies is like reality TV for them—they love the chaos.
- **They Fear Being Exposed**: Divide-and-conquer keeps people too distracted to notice that the manipulator is the real problem.

How to Shut Down Their Games

1. **Communicate Directly**: If someone comes to you with "so-and-so said this," don't take it at face value. Go straight to the source and ask, "Did you actually say that?" Nine times out of ten, you'll find out it's a lie or a twisted version of the truth.
2. **Call Them the Fuck Out**: When you spot their manipulation, confront them head-on. "Why are you trying to stir up drama between us? What's your angle?" Watch them panic as their little scheme unravels.
3. **Strengthen Your Relationships**: Don't let them isolate you. Keep open, honest communication with the people

who matter, and don't let the manipulator wedge their toxic bullshit between you.

4. **Cut Them Off**: If someone's entire existence revolves around creating chaos, you don't need them in your life. Let them find another group to destroy.

The Bottom Line

The divide-and-conquer strategy is for cowards and control freaks who can't handle real relationships. They want to control, isolate, and manipulate you by tearing apart the connections that keep you strong. Don't let them win. Recognize the game, call it out, and burn their little empire of lies to the ground. Then, walk away like the badass you are, leaving them to drown in the drama they created.

9.2.3 Playing the Victim: Their Crown Jewel of Bullshit

If manipulation had a greatest hits album, *playing the victim* would be the chart-topping single. Two-faced manipulators love nothing more than turning themselves into the hero of a tragedy that doesn't even exist. They'll twist every situation to make themselves look like the wounded, misunderstood martyr while you're left wondering if you've accidentally wandered into a poorly-written soap opera. Spoiler alert: you didn't. This is just their favorite tactic to dodge responsibility and guilt-trip you into submission.

How They Perfect the Victim Act

These assholes have turned playing the victim into an Olympic-level sport. They've got their sad little playbook memorized, and they'll whip it out anytime they need to deflect blame or manipulate someone into doing their dirty work. Here's how they pull it off:

- **The Sob Story Showdown**: Every conversation somehow circles back to how hard their life is. "You don't understand what I've been through!" Newsflash: everyone's been through shit, but most people don't use it as a free pass to act like a jackass.

- **The Guilt Grenade**: "I guess I'm just a terrible person, huh?" They'll throw this line at you like a live grenade, hoping the explosion will make you backpedal and soothe their fragile ego.
- **Twisting Reality**: No matter what happens, they'll frame themselves as the victim. Called them out for lying? Now you're "too harsh" and "hurt their feelings." It's emotional manipulation, plain and simple.
- **The Silent Martyr**: They sulk, sigh, and mope around, making sure you *feel* their pain without them having to say a word. They want you to ask, "What's wrong?" so they can unload their bullshit on you.

Why They Do It

Playing the victim isn't just a defense mechanism for these manipulative pricks—it's their entire personality. They can't handle accountability, so they flip the script faster than a bad reality show contestant. Here's why:

- **They Want Sympathy, Not Solutions**: They don't want to fix anything; they just want you to feel sorry for them. Sympathy equals control, and that's what they're after.
- **They Dodge Accountability Like a Pro**: If they're the victim, they're never at fault. "How could you blame me when I've been through so much?" Easy. Because you're a manipulative asshole.
- **They Crave Attention**: Being the victim makes them the center of everyone's world, even if it's for all the wrong reasons.

How to Shut Down Their Pity Party

1. **Don't Play Along**: The next time they try to unload their sob story, don't take the bait. "That sucks. What are you going

to do about it?" Watch them squirm because they weren't expecting a dose of accountability.

2. **Call Out the Pattern**: "Every time we talk, you make yourself the victim. Are you ever going to own up to anything?" They'll panic because their little game depends on you not noticing.

3. **Refuse to Be Their Fixer**: They'll try to guilt-trip you into solving their problems. Don't. "Sounds like something you need to work through." End of story.

The Bottom Line

Playing the victim is a manipulator's favorite move because it shifts the blame, dodges accountability, and puts the spotlight right where they want it: on them. But their pity party only works if you show up. Recognize the act, shut it down, and leave them to wallow in their own bullshit. You've got better things to do than play therapist to a professional martyr.

9.2.4 The False Flattery Trap: Compliments with a Fucking Agenda

Let's get one thing straight: when a manipulative asshole starts showering you with compliments, it's not because they think you're amazing. It's because they want something. False flattery isn't genuine—it's a weapon, polished up to look like kindness but designed to disarm you. They're not hyping you up; they're setting you up. And when you fall for it? They've got you right where they want you.

How the False Flattery Trap Works

These manipulative clowns have mastered the art of saying exactly what you want to hear while scheming behind your back. They know that a little ego boost makes you more likely to trust them—or at least drop your guard long enough for them to screw you over. Here's how they bait the trap:

- **Over-the-Top Compliments**: "You're so talented, I don't know how you do it!" Sounds sweet, right? Wrong. They're buttering you up because they're about to ask for something—or stab you in the back when you least expect it.
- **Comparative Praise**: "You're way better than [insert name here]." Oh, so now you're the chosen one? Congrats. They're just using you as leverage in whatever petty game they're playing.
- **Flattery with Strings Attached**: "You're the only one who can help me with this." Translation: "I'm about to dump a pile of shit in your lap, and you better thank me for it."

Why They Use It

False flattery isn't about making you feel good—it's about gaining control. These manipulators want to puff up your ego just enough to make you pliable. Here's why they pull this crap:

- **They Want Something**: Compliments are the appetizer; the main course is whatever favor, information, or access they're about to demand.
- **They Need to Disarm You**: Genuine compliments make you feel safe. False flattery makes you feel safe just long enough for them to strike.
- **They're Hiding Their Real Agenda**: If they were upfront about what they wanted, you'd tell them to fuck off. Flattery is just a sugar-coated distraction.

How to Spot the Bullshit

False flattery isn't hard to recognize if you stop drinking the Kool-Aid. Here are the dead giveaways:

- **It Feels Too Good to Be True**: If their praise sounds like it belongs in a bad Hallmark movie, it's probably fake.

- **It's Always Followed by a Favor**: Pay attention to what comes after the compliments. Nine times out of ten, it's a "small favor" that conveniently screws you over.
- **It's Recycled**: If you catch them using the same lines on other people, congratulations—they're not just a manipulator; they're a lazy one.

How to Shut It Down

1. **Call It Out**: "That's nice, but what do you really want?" Watch their fake smile drop faster than their integrity.
2. **Don't Take the Bait**: When they follow up with a favor, shut it down. "I'm not available for that, but thanks for thinking of me." Short, sharp, and leaves no room for negotiation.
3. **Flip the Script**: Compliment them right back with a dose of sarcasm. "Wow, you're so good at buttering people up—it's almost convincing!" Let them choke on their own bullshit.

The Bottom Line

False flattery is nothing more than a manipulator's bait-and-switch. They're not complimenting you because they care—they're doing it because they want to use you. Recognize the trap, refuse to bite, and let them find someone else to bullshit. You don't have time for fake compliments, ulterior motives, or their toxic little games. Keep your guard up and let them drown in their own insincerity.

9.2.5 Gaslighting Galore: When They Fuck With Your Reality

Gaslighting isn't just a tactic—it's a full-blown art form for manipulative, two-faced bastards. These assholes love nothing more than making you question your own sanity. They'll twist the truth, rewrite history, and straight-up deny shit they *know* they did, all while sitting there with a smug grin like they've just won an Oscar for Best Liar in a Toxic Drama. Their goal? To confuse you so much that you start doubting your own reality—and guess who gets to play puppet master when that happens? Them.

How Gaslighting Works

These manipulative fuckers are pros at turning your brain into a battlefield. They don't just lie—they rewrite the rules of logic so you feel like you're losing your mind. Here's how they pull it off:

- **Flat-Out Denial**: "I never said that." Oh, but they did, and you both fucking know it. They're just banking on the hope that you'll start second-guessing yourself.
- **Twisting the Narrative**: "You're remembering it wrong." No, Karen, you're just a lying sack of shit. They love to reframe situations so they're never the bad guy.
- **Minimizing Your Feelings**: "You're overreacting." Translation? "I'm trying to make you feel crazy so I don't have to take responsibility."
- **Using Your Words Against You**: They'll take something you said weeks ago, twist it out of context, and throw it back in your face. "But you *said* you didn't care about that!" Nice try, asshole.

Why They Gaslight

Gaslighting isn't random—it's calculated. These toxic pricks know exactly what they're doing, and it's all about control. Here's what they get out of it:

- **Power Over Your Mind**: If they can make you doubt your own memory or feelings, they've got you by the throat.
- **Avoiding Accountability**: Gaslighting lets them dodge blame like a goddamn ninja. "I didn't do that, you're imagining things" is their way of escaping consequences.
- **Shifting the Focus**: Instead of talking about what they did wrong, now you're stuck defending your sanity. Classic diversion tactic.

Signs You're Being Gaslit

Not sure if you're dealing with a manipulative gaslighter? Here's what to look for:

- **You're Constantly Second-Guessing Yourself**: "Wait, did I really misunderstand? Am I overreacting?" Nope, you're not. They're just fucking with your head.
- **You Apologize for Things That Aren't Your Fault**: Gaslighters love to make you feel like the villain in their twisted little soap opera.
- **You Feel Confused and Exhausted**: That's not a coincidence—it's their goal. The more off-balance you are, the easier you are to manipulate.

How to Shut Down a Gaslighter

1. **Trust Your Own Reality**: Write shit down if you have to. Keep receipts, texts, and notes so you can call them out when they try to rewrite history.
2. **Call Them the Fuck Out**: "I know what you said/did, and no amount of lying is going to change that." Say it with confidence and watch them squirm.
3. **Refuse to Engage**: The best way to deal with a gaslighter is to stop playing their game. "I'm not arguing about this" is the ultimate power move.
4. **Limit Their Access**: Once you've spotted a gaslighter, start phasing them out. They don't deserve a seat at your table— or in your life.

The Bottom Line

Gaslighting is the ultimate mindfuck, but it only works if you let it. Once you see the game, you can tear it apart piece by piece. Trust your instincts, call out their lies, and take back control. These manipulative assholes thrive on confusion—so hit them with clarity, confidence, and a big middle finger. Let them choke on their own bullshit while you walk away with your sanity intact.

Lesson 9.3: The Psychological Impact

9.3.1 The Anxiety Loop: How Their Bullshit Keeps You on Edge

Two-faced manipulators don't just piss you off—they make it their full-time job to keep you trapped in a never-ending loop of anxiety. Their entire existence is designed to fuck with your head, keep you second-guessing yourself, and make sure you're always on edge. This isn't just a coincidence—it's a strategy. The more unsettled you are, the easier you are to control. And guess what? They're fucking loving every second of it.

How the Anxiety Loop Works

These assholes don't just light the match—they fan the flames until your brain feels like it's on fire. Here's how they trap you in their manipulative vortex:

- **Constant Mixed Signals**: One day, they're your biggest supporter. The next, they're acting like you're the goddamn villain. It's emotional whiplash, and you're stuck wondering, "What the hell did I do wrong?"
- **Creating Uncertainty**: Manipulators thrive on ambiguity. They'll withhold information, give vague answers, or drop cryptic comments like, "We need to talk later." What the fuck does that even mean? Now you're anxious all day waiting for the shoe to drop.
- **Planting Seeds of Doubt**: "Are you sure that's a good idea? You've been making some weird choices lately." They make you question every decision until you don't trust your own judgment anymore.
- **Keeping You Guessing**: These pricks thrive on unpredictability. You never know what version of them you're going to get—the supportive friend, the backstabbing snake, or the passive-aggressive martyr. It's exhausting, and that's exactly the point.

Why They Do It

The anxiety loop isn't just a side effect of their behavior—it's their fucking endgame. Here's why:

- **Control**: When you're anxious, you're easier to manipulate. They keep you too busy questioning yourself to see their bullshit for what it is.
- **Power**: Watching you squirm gives them a twisted sense of superiority. They don't want you confident—they want you doubting every move.
- **Distraction**: As long as you're focused on your own anxiety, you're not focused on their toxic behavior. It's the ultimate diversion tactic.

How to Break the Loop

1. **Recognize the Game**: The first step is spotting their manipulation for what it is—a calculated strategy to keep you on edge. Once you see it, you can stop falling for it.
2. **Set Boundaries Like a Badass**: "I'm not engaging with this right now." Say it, mean it, and walk the fuck away. Don't give them the reaction they're fishing for.
3. **Ground Yourself**: When they start stirring the pot, don't let their chaos drag you down. Take a deep breath, remind yourself that their bullshit isn't your problem, and stay focused on your own peace.
4. **Call Them Out**: "You're being vague on purpose, and I'm not playing this game. Be clear or leave me alone." Watch them flounder when you refuse to take the bait.

The Bottom Line

The anxiety loop is their favorite weapon because it's invisible, relentless, and absolutely fucking exhausting. But here's the truth: their power only exists if you let it. The moment you call out the game, set boundaries, and refuse to play along, their control crumbles like the fragile ego it's built on. Let them spiral in their own chaos while you reclaim your peace—and your power.

9.3.2 Eroding Self-Confidence: How They Turn Your Mind Into a Battleground

Manipulators don't just want to control you—they want to gut your confidence and leave you questioning every fucking thing about yourself. Why? Because confident people are harder to manipulate. So, these toxic assholes work overtime to chip away at your self-esteem, turning your mind into their personal playground of insecurity. It's not just cruel—it's calculated. The weaker you feel, the stronger they get.

How They Erode Your Confidence

These manipulators are like termites in your brain, slowly eating away at the foundation of your self-worth. Here's how they do it:

- **Constant Criticism Disguised as "Help"**: "I'm just trying to be honest with you." No, Karen, you're being a passive-aggressive dickhead. They nitpick your choices, your ideas, even your fucking personality, all under the guise of "helping you improve."
- **Comparisons That Cut**: "Why can't you be more like [insert someone else's name]?" Oh, I don't know, because I'm not a carbon copy of whoever the hell you're idolizing today? They love making you feel like you'll never measure up.
- **Minimizing Your Wins**: You work your ass off to achieve something, and they hit you with, "It's not that big of a deal." Well, excuse me for trying to better myself while you sit there doing nothing.
- **Subtle Digs That Stick**: "Wow, that's brave of you to wear that." Translation? They're trying to make you second-guess your every move while pretending to compliment you.

Why They Do It

Eroding your confidence isn't just a hobby for these assholes—it's their survival tactic. Here's why:

- **Control Is Easier When You Feel Small**: Confident people stand their ground. Insecure people? They're easier to push around.
- **It Makes Them Feel Bigger**: Every jab at your confidence gives them a little ego boost. It's pathetic, but it's all they've got.
- **They Fear Your Growth**: Watching you improve scares the shit out of them because it makes their own inadequacies impossible to ignore.

How to Fight Back

1. **Spot the Patterns**: Recognize their tactics for what they are—an attempt to break you down. The moment you see the game, you can stop playing.
2. **Shut Down the Criticism**: When they start with their bullshit, hit them back: "That's funny—I don't remember asking for your opinion." Or the classic, "Wow, you must be fun at parties."
3. **Own Your Wins**: Stop waiting for their validation. Celebrate your victories, no matter how small, and let their bitterness fuel your fire.
4. **Surround Yourself with Real Ones**: Cut the toxic people and build a circle of friends who actually lift you up instead of tearing you down.

The Bottom Line

Eroding your self-confidence is just another power move for manipulative pricks who can't stand your potential. But their words? They're nothing but hot air, designed to distract you from your greatness. Stop letting their insecurities shape your reality. Build yourself back up, own your power, and let them choke on the fact that they'll never be able to break you. You're stronger than their bullshit—don't let them forget it.

9.3.3 The Isolation Effect: Why They Want You All Alone in the Dark

Manipulators aren't just assholes—they're strategic assholes. One of their favorite moves? Isolating you from everyone who actually gives a damn about you. The more alone you are, the easier you are to control. They'll wedge themselves between you and your friends, family, and anyone else who might call out their toxic bullshit. It's not just about cutting you off—it's about making you dependent on them, like they're the last lifeboat on a sinking ship. Spoiler alert: they're the ones poking holes in the damn boat to begin with.

How the Isolation Effect Works

These toxic bastards don't start by saying, "You don't need anyone but me." That'd be too obvious. No, they're smarter than that—or at least they think they are. Here's how they pull it off:

- **Sowing Seeds of Doubt**: "Are you sure so-and-so really has your back? I heard they've been talking about you." They'll whisper poison into your relationships, planting suspicion and waiting for it to grow.
- **Demanding All Your Time**: "Why are you always hanging out with them instead of me?" They guilt-trip you into spending all your time with them, leaving no room for anyone else.
- **Turning People Against You**: They'll stir up drama behind the scenes, framing you as the problem so others start to pull away.
- **Playing the "I'm All You Need" Card**: They position themselves as your savior, the only one who "really

understands" you. It's not love—it's manipulation in its purest form.

Why They Do It

Isolation isn't just a coincidence—it's a calculated power move. Here's why they go to such fucked-up lengths to cut you off:

- **Control, Control, Control**: When they're the only voice in your ear, they can shape your reality however they want.
- **They Fear Exposure**: The more people you have around you, the more likely someone is to call out their bullshit. They can't risk that.
- **They Want You Vulnerable**: Alone and isolated, you're easier to manipulate. No friends to lean on, no support system to back you up—it's their dream scenario.

Signs You're Being Isolated

Not sure if someone's pulling the isolation card on you? Here's what to watch for:

- **You Feel Cut Off**: Your relationships with friends and family are slipping, and you're not sure why. Spoiler: it's because someone's been stirring the pot.
- **You're Always Defending Them**: If you find yourself justifying someone's behavior to everyone else, that's a red flag the size of a fucking skyscraper.
- **They're Constantly the Victim**: "I just don't feel like your friends like me." Translation: "Let me isolate you by making this about my fragile ego."

How to Break Free

1. **Rebuild Your Connections**: Reach out to the people you've drifted from. Manipulators hate when you have a support system, so start rebuilding yours today.

2. **Set Hard Boundaries**: "I'm spending time with my friends/family, and that's not up for discussion." If they can't respect that, they can fuck all the way off.

3. **Call Out the Manipulation**: "You're trying to isolate me, and it's not going to work." Watch their face when you shatter their little game.

The Bottom Line

The isolation effect is nothing more than a desperate attempt to control you by cutting you off from the people who care about you. But here's the truth: you're not theirs to manipulate. Rebuild your connections, call out their games, and remind yourself that their power only works if you let them. Let them stew in their loneliness while you reclaim your relationships—and your freedom.

9.3.4 Fear as a Tool: How They Keep You in Line with Their Bullshit

Manipulators love fear. It's their sharpest weapon, their most reliable tool, and the key to keeping you under their thumb. They don't need brute force—they'll use intimidation, veiled threats, and psychological mind games to make you doubt yourself and fear the consequences of stepping out of line. It's not just cruel—it's calculated, cowardly, and exactly how these toxic assholes maintain their stranglehold on your life.

How Fear Becomes Their Weapon

Fear isn't just an accident—it's their entire strategy. Here's how they wield it like a goddamn scalpel to carve away at your sense of safety and self-worth:

- **The Veiled Threats**: "If you do that, you'll regret it." Oh, really? Is that a threat or just your pathetic attempt to sound important? They never outright say what will happen, but the implication is loud and clear: do what they want, or else.

- **Creating Consequences That Don't Exist**: "If you don't stay in line, people will turn against you." They'll invent bullshit scenarios to keep you compliant, banking on the fact that you won't call their bluff.
- **Intimidation Through Silence**: Ever notice how they'll just *stop talking* when you don't do what they want? That silent treatment isn't passive—it's aggressive as hell. They're trying to make you feel like a child waiting for punishment.
- **Exploiting Your Weak Spots**: They know exactly what you're afraid of—losing a job, a friendship, your reputation—and they'll use those fears against you every chance they get.

Why They Do It

Fear isn't just a side effect of their bullshit—it's their ultimate goal. These manipulators know that a confident, fearless person is impossible to control. So, they break you down, piece by piece, until you're too scared to fight back.

- **Control Through Intimidation**: Fear makes you predictable. They want you to think twice before standing up for yourself.
- **To Keep You Small**: Fear shrinks you. It keeps you doubting yourself, second-guessing your decisions, and playing small while they bask in their perceived superiority.
- **They're Scared, Too**: Here's the kicker—they're using fear because they're scared shitless of being exposed, outed, or left behind. Their intimidation is just a projection of their own pathetic insecurities.

Signs They're Using Fear Against You

Not sure if fear is their weapon of choice? Look for these signs:

- **You're Always Anxious Around Them**: If your stomach drops every time they text or call, congratulations—you're dealing with a manipulative shithead who thrives on making you uncomfortable.

- **You Avoid Conflict**: You've stopped speaking up or pushing back because you're terrified of their reaction.
- **You Feel Trapped**: They've boxed you into a corner, making you believe there's no way out without catastrophic consequences.

How to Fight Back

1. **Call Out the Fear Tactics**: "Are you trying to scare me into doing what you want? Because it's not working." Watch them squirm when you expose their game.
2. **Stand Your Ground**: Don't let their intimidation control you. "I'm making my own decision, and I'm not afraid of the consequences." Say it loud enough for them to choke on it.
3. **Flip the Power Dynamic**: Fear only works if you buy into it. The second you stop giving a fuck about their threats, their power evaporates.

The Bottom Line

Fear is their tool, but it doesn't have to be yours. Recognize their intimidation tactics for the weak-ass bullshit they are, and refuse to let it control you. These manipulative cowards thrive on your discomfort, so hit them where it hurts: with confidence, clarity, and a complete lack of fucks to give. Let them stew in their own insecurities while you live your life fearlessly and on your terms.

9.3.5 Breaking the Hold: Tearing Their Manipulative Claws Out of Your Life

Breaking free from a manipulator isn't just about walking away—it's about ripping their toxic claws out of your mind, your emotions, and your life for good. These assholes have spent months, maybe years, weaving their bullshit into every corner of your existence. And guess what? They're not going to give up without a fight. But here's the thing: you don't owe them shit. Not your loyalty, not your patience, and sure as hell not your freedom.

How Manipulators Keep You Hooked

Manipulators don't just let you go—they tighten their grip, dragging you into a cycle of guilt, fear, and obligation. Here's how they try to keep their hold:

- **The Guilt Trap**: "After everything I've done for you, this is how you treat me?" Oh, spare me the martyr routine. They guilt-trip you into thinking *you're* the villain for wanting out.
- **Fake Redemption**: Suddenly, they're all apologies and promises. "I can change!" they say, as if slapping a fresh coat of paint on their toxic ass will make you forget the damage they've caused.
- **Emotional Blackmail**: "If you leave, I don't know what I'll do." This isn't vulnerability—it's manipulation wrapped in a sob story.
- **Breadcrumbing**: They throw you just enough affection or validation to keep you questioning your decision to leave. Don't fall for it.

Why Breaking the Hold Feels So Hard

Let's be real: manipulators don't make it easy to walk away. They've tangled themselves into your life like a fucking parasite, feeding off your energy, confidence, and goodwill. Breaking free means untangling years of manipulation—and it's not pretty.

- **They've Eroded Your Self-Worth**: After constant criticism and gaslighting, you might feel like you don't deserve better. Newsflash: you do.
- **They've Built a Web of Dependence**: Whether it's financial, emotional, or social, they've made sure you feel like you can't survive without them. Spoiler: you absolutely can.

- **Fear of the Fallout**: They've trained you to fear the consequences of leaving. But here's the truth: the fallout will suck for a bit, but it's nothing compared to the freedom waiting on the other side.

How to Break Their Hold and Take Your Power Back

1. **Cut the Cord**: Block their number, unfollow them, and stop giving them any access to your life. Yes, it's harsh. No, you don't owe them an explanation.
2. **Reclaim Your Voice**: They've silenced you long enough. Speak up, set boundaries, and don't apologize for standing your ground.
3. **Rebuild Your Confidence**: Start focusing on what makes you strong. Surround yourself with people who actually give a damn about you. The more you build yourself up, the smaller their influence becomes.
4. **Don't Engage**: They'll try to bait you back in with guilt, drama, and empty promises. Don't take the bait. Silence is your new best friend.
5. **Remind Yourself of the Truth**: Write down all the ways they've hurt you, manipulated you, and fucked with your life. Whenever you feel tempted to go back, read that list and remind yourself why you're better off without them.

The Bottom Line

Breaking the hold isn't just about cutting them out of your life— it's about cutting them out of your mind. Their power is a lie, their control is an illusion, and the only thing keeping them in your life is your willingness to tolerate their bullshit. Stop tolerating it. Reclaim your time, your energy, and your sanity. Let them rot in the toxic mess they created while you move forward, stronger and untouchable. They'll hate it—and that's just the icing on the cake.

Lesson 9.4: Winning the Psychological Battle

9.4.1 Staying Grounded: Keeping Your Cool While They Lose Their Shit

When dealing with manipulative, two-faced assholes, staying grounded is your ultimate power move. These toxic pricks thrive on chaos, drama, and dragging you into their emotional cesspool. But here's the kicker—they can't touch you if you keep your cool. Staying grounded isn't just about staying calm; it's about making sure their bullshit bounces off you like a rubber bullet while you stand there completely unbothered.

Why They Want You Off-Balance

Manipulators know that the second you lose your shit, they've won. Emotional reactions give them the leverage they need to control you. They'll poke, prod, and push every goddamn button you have just to see you snap. Here's why:

- **They Feed on Your Reactions**: Your anger, frustration, or tears are their proof that they still have power over you.
- **They Thrive on Chaos**: The more off-balance you are, the easier it is for them to twist the narrative in their favor.
- **They Want You Distracted**: If you're busy fighting your own emotions, you won't notice how much they're screwing you over.

How to Stay Grounded Like a Fucking Pro

1. **Detach from Their Drama**: Stop letting their chaos drag you down. Treat their bullshit like background noise at a shitty coffee shop—annoying but irrelevant.
   - **What to Say**: "That's your issue, not mine." Let them stew in their own mess while you stay calm.

2. **Focus on Facts, Not Feelings**: Manipulators love to twist your emotions, so don't give them the chance. Stick to the facts and shut them down when they try to derail the conversation.
   ○ **Example**: "We're not talking about how you feel—I'm focusing on what actually happened." Watch them flounder.
3. **Breathe Through the Bullshit**: When they start pushing your buttons, take a deep breath and remind yourself that their opinion isn't worth shit. Their words only have power if you let them.
4. **Master the Art of the Poker Face**: Nothing pisses off a manipulator more than you staying calm while they're trying to light a fire. Show zero emotion. Deadpan everything. Watch them lose their fucking minds.
5. **Set Boundaries and Stick to Them**: "I'm not discussing this further," or "I've already made my decision." End of story. No explanations, no debates, no room for negotiation.

What Staying Grounded Looks Like

- **They Scream, You Stay Calm**: Their tantrum isn't your cue to lose it—it's your cue to stay unbothered.
- **They Twist the Story, You Stick to Reality**: "That's not what happened, and I'm not engaging in this conversation." Let the truth be your anchor.
- **They Play Victim, You Don't Take the Bait**: "I understand you're upset, but that doesn't change my decision." Repeat as needed.

Why Staying Grounded Drives Them Insane

Manipulators want chaos, and your calmness throws a wrench in their entire strategy. When you refuse to react, they lose the ability to control you. It's like watching them try to punch a brick wall—you're untouchable, and they're left flailing like the pathetic cowards they are.

The Bottom Line

Staying grounded is your ultimate fuck-you to their manipulative games. It's the power move that keeps you in control while they unravel. Refuse to let their drama become your problem. Stay calm, stay sharp, and let them drown in their own bullshit while you rise above it all. Remember, nothing is more satisfying than watching a manipulative asshole realize they've lost control—and that's exactly what happens when you stay grounded.

9.4.2 Rebuilding Your Confidence: Taking Back What Those Manipulative Fuckers Stole

Let's get one thing straight: those two-faced manipulators didn't just mess with your life—they came for your confidence, too. Every snide remark, every calculated dig, every manipulative mindfuck was designed to make you question your worth. And maybe, for a while, they succeeded. But now? It's time to rip your confidence out of their greedy little hands and rebuild it into something so unshakable they'll choke on their own bitterness the next time they see you.

Why They Target Your Confidence

Manipulators don't come for your confidence because they're strong—they do it because they're weak. Tearing you down makes them feel bigger, stronger, and more in control. Here's why they work so hard to break you:

- **Confidence Equals Independence**: The more self-assured you are, the less likely you are to tolerate their bullshit—and they know it.
- **Your Wins Highlight Their Failures**: Your confidence is a spotlight on everything they lack, and they'd rather dim your light than fix their own shit.
- **They Need to Feel Superior**: These insecure bastards thrive on feeling like they've got the upper hand. Breaking

your confidence is just another way they try to feed their pathetic egos.

How to Rebuild Your Confidence Like a Fucking Boss

1. **Cut the Toxic Dead Weight**
   First things first: get rid of the assholes who tore you down in the first place. Block them, unfollow them, and stop giving a single fuck about what they think. They don't deserve a front-row seat to your comeback.
2. **Remember What Makes You Awesome**
   Write a list of everything you're good at, every win you've ever had, and every time you've overcome some bullshit. Read it every damn day if you have to. Your confidence isn't gone—it's just buried under their crap. Dig it out and wear it like armor.
3. **Celebrate the Small Wins**
   Confidence isn't rebuilt in a day—it's a brick-by-brick process. Start small. Nailed a work presentation? Celebrate it. Stuck to a boundary? Hell yes. Every little win is proof that you're getting stronger.
4. **Surround Yourself with Real Ones**
   You know who's great at building confidence? People who actually support you. Ditch the fakes and keep the real ones close—the ones who clap for your wins and don't feel threatened by your success.
5. **Fake It 'Til You Own It**
   Even if you're not feeling confident, act like you are. Walk into a room like you own the place, speak like your words matter (because they do), and watch as your confidence starts catching up with your actions.

What Rebuilt Confidence Looks Like

- **You Set Boundaries Without Guilt**: "No" becomes your favorite word, and you don't feel bad about saying it.

- **You Stop Apologizing for Existing**: No more "Sorry, but…" or "I hope this isn't a problem." You own your space unapologetically.
- **You Let Their Opinions Rot**: What they think of you is none of your business, and you couldn't give less of a shit if you tried.

The Bottom Line

Rebuilding your confidence isn't just about undoing the damage— they'll always be assholes, but you'll always be stronger. It's about reminding yourself that their manipulative bullshit doesn't define you. You're not broken, you're not weak, and you're damn sure not theirs to control. Take back your power, stand tall, and let them choke on the sight of you thriving. You're a badass, and it's time the world—and those manipulative fucks—remember it.

9.4.3 The Logic Shield: Using Facts to Slice Through Their Bullshit

When it comes to manipulators, emotions are their playground, and logic is their kryptonite. These toxic assholes thrive on twisting your feelings, bending reality, and pulling you into a vortex of doubt and confusion. But facts? Facts are the buzzkill they can't argue with. The *Logic Shield* is your ultimate weapon, and when you wield it, their manipulative games crumble like the pathetic house of cards they are.

Why Logic Shreds Their Manipulation

Manipulators hate logic because it's the one thing they can't twist to their advantage. They rely on emotional chaos to keep you spinning, but logic? Logic is cold, hard, and unyielding. Here's why it works:

- **It Exposes Their Lies**: "You said X last week, but now you're saying Y. Which is it?" Manipulators hate receipts, and logic is basically a fucking binder full of them.

- **It Stops Emotional Spirals**: When you stick to facts, their guilt trips and sob stories fall flat. "I'm not discussing feelings right now; let's stick to the facts." Boom—emotional manipulation neutralized.
- **It Shifts the Power Dynamic**: Logic puts you in control. You're no longer reacting to their bullshit—you're driving the conversation, and they're scrambling to keep up.

How to Build Your Logic Shield

1. **Keep Receipts Like a Boss**
   Manipulators hate evidence because it takes away their ability to rewrite history. Save texts, emails, and anything else that proves what actually happened. When they start gaslighting you, pull out your receipts like the ultimate mic drop.
2. **Stick to the Facts**
   Cut the emotional fluff and focus on what's real. "You said XYZ, and here's proof. I'm not interested in debating this." They'll try to derail the conversation, but facts don't lie.
3. **Refuse to Engage with Their Drama**
   When they start dragging feelings into the mix, shut it down. "This isn't about how you feel; it's about what actually happened." Don't let them pull you into their pity party.
4. **Ask Direct Questions**
   Put them on the spot with questions they can't squirm out of. "Why did you say one thing to me and another to them?" Their bullshit doesn't hold up under scrutiny, and they know it.

How They'll Try to Dismantle Your Logic Shield

These manipulative pricks won't go down without a fight. Here's how they'll try to weasel their way around your facts—and how to counter them:

- **Deflection**: "Why are you bringing this up now?" Counter with: "Because it's relevant, and I want answers."

- ○ **Playing Dumb**: "I don't remember saying that." Response: "Good thing I saved the text. Let me refresh your memory."
- **Turning It Back on You**: "You're always so confrontational." Response: "I'm not confrontational—I'm holding you accountable. Big difference."

Why Logic Drives Them Insane

Manipulators live for chaos, and logic is the exact opposite of what they want. When you refuse to get emotional and stick to the facts, you're stripping away their power. They can't guilt-trip you, twist your words, or control the narrative when you're armed with cold, hard truth.

The Bottom Line

The Logic Shield isn't just a tool—it's a goddamn superpower. It turns the tables on manipulators and forces them to face their lies, their contradictions, and their own pathetic attempts to control you. Stick to the facts, refuse to engage with their drama, and watch as their entire strategy falls apart. You're smarter, sharper, and way too grounded for their bullshit. Let them choke on their own lies while you walk away victorious.

9.4.4 Turning Their Tactics Against Them: *Beating the Bastards at Their Own Game*

Manipulators think they're untouchable. They think they've mastered the art of psychological warfare, and that you're just another pawn on their toxic chessboard. Well, guess what? It's time to flip the board, rewrite the rules, and use their own slimy tactics against them. These assholes have been running the show for too long, and now you're about to show them what it feels like to get played.

Why Fighting Fire with Fire Works

Let's be real: manipulative people don't respond to kindness or logic. They see those things as weaknesses to exploit. But when you throw their own bullshit back in their face? Oh, they can't handle that. Here's why it works:

- **It Exposes Their Hypocrisy**: They're so used to dishing it out, they never expect to be on the receiving end.
- **It Disarms Them**: When you flip their tactics, you take away their power. They don't know how to fight someone who's playing their game better than they do.
- **It Shuts Them Down**: Manipulators thrive on control, and nothing pisses them off more than losing it.

Their Tactics, Your Power Moves

Here's how to take their favorite manipulative games and turn them into weapons of your own:

1. **The Mirror Game**
   When they try to gaslight you, flip it right back.
   - **Them**: "You're overreacting."
   - **You**: "No, *you're* overreacting. Why are you so defensive?" Watch their brain short-circuit as they try to process their own bullshit.
2. **Weaponize Their Words**
   Save their lies, contradictions, and shady comments, then throw them back in their face at the perfect moment.
   - **Them**: "I never said that!"
   - **You**: "Actually, you did. Here's the text. Care to explain?" Boom. Game over.
3. **The Silent Treatment Slam**
   They love using the silent treatment to manipulate you? Return the favor. Except this time, it's not a game—it's you refusing to waste another second on their nonsense. Let them stew in their own silence.

4. **Flip the Victim Card**
   They're always playing the victim? Beat them to it. "Wow, I didn't realize how much you've been hurting me with your behavior. It's been so hard dealing with this." Watch their head explode as they try to play catch-up.

Why This Drives Them Insane

Manipulators hate being out-manipulated. They're not equipped to handle someone who can outsmart their games, and when you turn the tables, they lose their fucking minds. Here's what happens when you beat them at their own game:

- **They Get Defensive**: The moment you expose their hypocrisy, they'll start scrambling for excuses.
- **They Spiral**: Losing control is their worst nightmare, and you just turned it into a reality.
- **They Back Off**: Once they realize you're not an easy target, they'll start looking for someone else to screw over.

The Rules of Engagement

1. **Stay Calm, Stay Sharp**: The key to flipping their tactics is staying level-headed. Don't let them bait you into an emotional reaction.
2. **Strike When It Counts**: Don't waste time fighting every little game they play. Wait for the right moment to flip the script and hit them where it hurts.
3. **Know When to Walk Away**: Turning their tactics against them is satisfying, but don't let it consume you. Once you've made your point, move the fuck on.

The Bottom Line

Turning their tactics against them isn't about stooping to their level— it's about showing them that their manipulative bullshit doesn't work on you. You're not their victim, their pawn, or their emotional punching bag. You're the one flipping the script, taking control, and leaving them to choke on their own pathetic games. Play their game better, win, and then walk away like the badass you are.

9.4.5 Thriving Beyond Their Reach: Building a Life They Can't Fuck With

Here's the ultimate power move: thriving so hard that the manipulative assholes who tried to control you can't even touch your orbit. This isn't just about getting over them—it's about leveling up so high that their bullshit can't even cast a shadow on your shine. They wanted to break you, but instead, you're going to build a life so strong, so unapologetically yours, that they'll have no choice but to choke on their jealousy from the cheap seats.

Why Thriving is the Ultimate Revenge

Let's be clear: you're not thriving to prove anything to them. You're thriving because you fucking deserve it. But the fact that it burns their pathetic little souls in the process? Well, that's just a bonus. Here's why living your best life is the ultimate fuck-you:

- **It Shows Their Power is Gone**: The moment you stop caring about their manipulative games is the moment they lose all control.
- **It Exposes Their Weakness**: While they're still wallowing in their toxic drama, you're out here succeeding, proving they were always the problem, not you.
- **It Leaves Them in the Dust**: Manipulators can't handle being irrelevant, and nothing makes them more irrelevant than watching you thrive without them.

How to Build a Life They Can't Touch

1. **Redesign Your Circle**
   Surround yourself with people who actually lift you up. Cut the toxic assholes loose and replace them with genuine

friends, allies, and mentors. Your support system should feel like a fortress, not a battlefield.

2. **Double Down on Your Goals**
Focus on what sets your soul on fire—career, hobbies, personal growth, whatever. Throw yourself into your passions and build a life so fulfilling that their bullshit doesn't even register on your radar.

3. **Set Boundaries Like a Fortress**
If they try to sneak back in with their fake apologies and sob stories, shut that shit down. "We're done here. Take care." End of story.

4. **Celebrate the Wins**
Big or small, every victory matters. Thriving is a series of tiny wins that stack up until you're standing on a mountain of success, flipping the bird to anyone who doubted you.

5. **Live Unapologetically**
Stop toning yourself down to make other people comfortable. Be bold, be loud, and be fucking proud of who you are. Their discomfort with your success is *their* problem, not yours.

Signs You're Thriving Beyond Their Reach

- **You Don't Give a Shit About Their Opinions**: Their approval used to matter, but now? You wouldn't piss on their opinion if it was on fire.
- **They're Watching, But You're Unbothered**: You know they're stalking your social media, but instead of feeling anxious, you post your wins just to let them know they lost.
- **Their Drama Feels Irrelevant**: Whatever chaos they're stirring doesn't even register anymore because you've got better things to focus on—like your amazing life.

Why Thriving Drives Them Insane

Manipulators can't handle irrelevance, and your thriving is the ultimate proof that they don't matter anymore. They wanted to control you, but now they're stuck on the sidelines watching you live a life they'll never touch. And the best part? They know they can't come crawling back, because you've outgrown their pathetic games.

The Bottom Line

Thriving beyond their reach isn't just about moving on—it's about building a life so solid, so fucking amazing, that their bullshit doesn't even cast a shadow. You're not just surviving—you're winning, growing, and leveling up in ways they'll never understand. Let them stew in their irrelevance while you live your best, unbothered life. Success isn't just the best revenge—it's the only revenge you'll ever need.

Mind Games & Manipulation: Fighting Back in the Psychological War

You've seen it all—manipulators, liars, and insecure assholes who thrive on twisting reality to suit their pathetic little narratives. You've called them out, shut them down, and left them drowning in their own toxic waste. But don't think for a second that the war is over. Some of these two-faced bastards don't just play games—they play **mind games**.

Welcome to **psychological warfare**, where manipulators don't just lie—they invade your head, gaslight you into questioning your own reality, and push buttons you didn't even know you had. This isn't just about manipulation anymore. It's about **mental combat**, and if you don't know how to fight back, you'll find yourself tangled in their bullshit before you even realize what's happening.

Chapter 10 is your battle plan. We're breaking down the tactics these toxic masterminds use to get inside your head, how to see through their mindfuckery, and most importantly—how to **beat them at their own game**. You've come this far. Now it's time to **go to war**.

CHAPTER TEN

Psychological Warfare Strategies

Two-faced people don't just piss you off—they declare all-out war on your sanity. These manipulative assholes aren't satisfied with a little drama or a few lies; no, they want to get inside your head, rearrange the furniture, and make you think you're the problem. They play dirty, launching sneak attacks disguised as "concern," guilt-tripping you into submission, and planting landmines in your relationships just to watch the fallout.

This chapter is your battle plan—a full breakdown of the mental fuckery they rely on and exactly how to dismantle their tactics. Because here's the truth: their bullshit only works if you let it. By the end of this chapter, you'll know how to outsmart, outmaneuver, and flat-out destroy their attempts to control you.

Lesson 10.1: Understanding the Battlefield

10.1.1 The Mind Games: How They Undermine You One Mental Screw-Job at a Time

Two-faced manipulators don't just mess with your emotions—they launch full-scale assaults on your brain. Their mind games aren't casual; they're calculated as hell, designed to make you question your reality, your worth, and your sanity. It's not just toxic—it's psychological warfare. These assholes aren't content with being jerks; they want to crawl inside your head and rearrange the furniture. Let's unpack how they pull off this mental fuckery so you can shut it down.

Game 1: The Gaslight Gauntlet

Gaslighting is their bread and butter. They'll make you question things you *know* to be true until you're staring at the ceiling at 2 a.m. wondering if you're the crazy one.

- **Their Move**: "That's not what happened," or, "You're remembering it wrong." Meanwhile, you have the goddamn receipts.
- **The Goal**: To make you doubt your own memory, so they can control the narrative. If they rewrite history, they get to play the hero (or, more often, the victim).

How to Shut It Down: Hit them with the facts. "Funny, because here's the text where you said exactly that. Care to explain?" Watch their face twitch as they scramble for an excuse.

Game 2: The Comparison Con

This one's a classic. They pit you against other people, subtly or blatantly, to make you feel like you'll never measure up.

- **Their Move**: "Why can't you be more like [insert random person here]?" or, "I heard so-and-so did it better."
- **The Goal**: To erode your confidence and keep you chasing their approval like a dog after a bone.

How to Shut It Down: "If you like them so much, maybe go bother them instead of me." One sentence, game over.

Game 3: The Silent Treatment Standoff

Oh, the silent treatment—the manipulator's equivalent of flipping the board when they start losing. They disappear, withdraw, or go cold, leaving you desperate to figure out what you did "wrong."

- **Their Move**: They'll stop answering texts, avoid eye contact, or give you one-word responses. It's a power play disguised as a tantrum.
- **The Goal**: To make you so uncomfortable that you break first, begging for their attention or forgiveness.

How to Shut It Down: Don't chase them. Let them sulk in their silent corner while you go live your damn life. Their power depends on your reaction—so don't give them one.

Game 4: The Perpetual Victim Card

They'll spin every situation to make themselves look like the poor, downtrodden soul who just can't catch a break. And somehow, you're always the villain in their story.

- **Their Move**: "I can't believe you'd do this to me after everything I've been through."
- **The Goal**: To guilt-trip you into compliance.

How to Shut It Down: "Your pity party isn't my problem. Let me know when you're ready to talk like an adult." Then walk away and let them stew in their own bullshit.

The Bottom Line

These mind games aren't clever—they're just manipulative garbage designed to keep you spinning your wheels while they sit back and enjoy the chaos. Recognize the tactics, refuse to play along, and call out their bullshit at every turn. The best way to win their game? Flip the script, set your boundaries, and let them drown in the mess they created. You're smarter than their tricks, sharper than their bullshit, and way too badass to let their games mess with your mind.

10.1.2 Identifying Their Endgame: What These Manipulative Bastards Are Really After

Two-faced manipulators don't play games just for fun (though they probably get off on the drama). No, these assholes always have an endgame—a prize they're chasing while you're too busy dodging their bullshit to see it coming. Whether it's power, control, or the twisted satisfaction of watching you squirm, their goals are as selfish as they are pathetic. Let's tear apart their playbook and expose what they're really after.

Endgame 1: Control Over You

This is the holy grail for manipulators—total control. They don't just want to influence your decisions; they want to own them. If they can make you question your thoughts, your choices, and even your reality, they've won.

- **How They Get It**: Gaslighting, guilt-tripping, and wearing you down with their endless emotional bullshit. They're not just chipping away at your independence—they're bulldozing it.
- **What It Looks Like**: You start asking for their opinion on everything because you're terrified of making the "wrong" choice. Congrats, they've successfully turned you into their puppet.

How to Stop It: Take back the wheel. "Thanks for your input, but I've got this covered." End of discussion.

Endgame 2: Keeping the Spotlight on Them

Manipulators are attention junkies. They need to be the center of every story, the star of every tragedy, and the hero of every narrative. If you're outshining them, they'll sabotage you just to grab the spotlight.

- **How They Get It**: By playing the victim, stirring up drama, or hijacking your wins.
- **What It Looks Like**: You achieve something amazing, and somehow the conversation turns into how hard *they* have it. "Wow, you got promoted? Must be nice. I'm still stuck at this shitty job."

How to Stop It: "This isn't about you, Karen. Let me enjoy my moment." Watch their face crumble as they lose the spotlight.

Endgame 3: Making You Dependent on Them

These toxic pricks love nothing more than making you feel like you *need* them. They'll position themselves as the only one who "really understands" you, all while chipping away at your other relationships.

- **How They Get It**: By isolating you, tearing down your support system, and making you doubt anyone else's intentions.
- **What It Looks Like**: Suddenly, you're spending all your time with them and wondering why your friends and family seem distant. Spoiler: it's because they've been sabotaging those relationships behind the scenes.

How to Stop It: Rebuild your support system and remind yourself that you were fine before they came along—and you'll be even better after they're gone.

Endgame 4: Feeding Their Ego

Let's not forget the simplest motivation: their massive, fragile ego. Manipulators need to feel superior, and they'll use you as their emotional punching bag to get there.

- **How They Get It**: By tearing you down, one passive-aggressive comment at a time.

- **What It Looks Like**: "I'm just trying to help," they say, as they pick apart everything you do.

How to Stop It: Stop feeding their ego. "Thanks, but I didn't ask for your advice." Keep it short and watch them deflate.

The Bottom Line

Every manipulative move they make is about achieving their endgame—power, attention, dependence, or feeding their bloated ego. But the moment you see through their tactics, their whole strategy falls apart. Refuse to play their game, call out their bullshit, and focus on your own goals. Their endgame is irrelevant when you're busy winning at life.

10.1.3 The Power of Subtle Manipulation: Their Silent, Sneaky Mindfuckery

Subtle manipulation is the manipulator's favorite weapon. It's sneaky, quiet, and designed to screw with your head without you even noticing. These assholes don't come at you with blatant lies—they chip away at you piece by piece, planting seeds of doubt and steering you wherever the hell they want. It's not just shady; it's psychological warfare in its purest form. If you don't see it coming, it can wreck you before you even realize what's happening.

How Subtle Manipulation Creeps In

Subtle manipulators are like termites—they sneak in, work quietly, and by the time you notice, your mental foundation is already rotting. Here's how they pull it off:

- **The "Innocent" Suggestion**: "Are you sure that's the best idea?" They're not giving advice; they're planting doubt. By the end of the conversation, you're questioning your own fucking instincts.

- **The Strategic Compliment**: "You're so good at handling this kind of stuff; I could never do it." Translation? They're buttering you up so you'll take on more while they sit back and reap the benefits.
- **The Selective Truth**: They'll tell you part of the story, leaving out the details that might make you question them. What you don't know is exactly what screws you over later.
- **The Subtle Dig**: "Wow, you're really brave for wearing that." Sounds like a compliment, but it's designed to make you second-guess yourself.

Why Subtle Manipulation is So Effective

Subtle manipulation works because it doesn't set off alarms. It's like a slow-acting poison—you don't notice it until it's already messed with your head. Here's why it's their go-to tactic:

- **It's Hard to Pinpoint**: You can't call them out because nothing they've said is *technically* wrong. It's not what they said—it's how they said it.
- **It's Easy to Deny**: Confront them, and they'll hit you with, "I was just trying to help," or, "Wow, you're so sensitive." They twist it back on you, making you the bad guy for even noticing.
- **It Gets in Your Head**: Subtle manipulation doesn't just confuse you—it makes you doubt yourself. And once they've got you questioning your reality, they've got you right where they want you.

How to Recognize the Game

Subtle manipulation isn't always obvious, but the signs are there if you know where to look:

- **You Feel Off Without Knowing Why**: If you leave conversations feeling unsure or uneasy, that's a red flag.

- **They Never Say Anything Directly**: Everything they do is wrapped in plausible deniability. They're never "mean," but somehow you feel like shit anyway.
- **They Always "Know Better"**: Their suggestions always sound reasonable—until you realize they're steering you in a direction that benefits them, not you.

How to Shut It Down

1. **Call Out the Subtle Digs**: "Was that a compliment or an insult? Hard to tell." Watch them backpedal as you expose their little game.
2. **Trust Your Gut**: If something feels off, don't ignore it. Your instincts are louder than their bullshit.
3. **Ask for Clarity**: Force them to say what they mean. "What exactly are you trying to say?" Their vague manipulation doesn't hold up under direct questioning.
4. **Refuse to Play Along**: When they suggest something that doesn't sit right, shut it down. "Thanks, but I'm good." No explanation required.

The Bottom Line

Subtle manipulation is their stealth weapon, but it only works if you're not paying attention. Once you spot their tricks, you can dismantle them before they take hold. Don't let their sneaky bullshit get in your head. Call it out, shut it down, and leave them floundering while you keep living your life, unbothered and untouchable.

10.1.4 The Fear Factor: Using Intimidation to Gain the Upper Hand

Fear. It's the oldest trick in the manipulator's playbook, and these toxic bastards wield it like a sledgehammer to your psyche. They don't just want your respect—they want your submission. They want you too scared to question them, too anxious to stand up for yourself, and too busy tiptoeing around their bullshit to realize they're not nearly as powerful as they pretend to be. Their entire game hinges on making you believe they're the Big Bad Wolf when, in reality, they're just blowing hot air.

How They Weaponize Fear

These assholes aren't coming for you with pitchforks and torches—they're far more subtle (and pathetic) than that. Here's how they use fear to keep you in line:

- **Veiled Threats**: "If you do that, I'm not sure how it'll work out for you." Oh, really? Is that supposed to scare me, or are you just auditioning for a shitty mob movie?
- **Intimidation Through Anger**: They'll blow up over the smallest thing to keep you walking on eggshells. "You know how I get!" Yeah, unhinged and manipulative.
- **Creating a False Sense of Doom**: "If you make that decision, it's all going to fall apart." Spoiler alert: it won't. They're just terrified of losing control.
- **The Silent Treatment Power Play**: They'll freeze you out, making you wonder what you did "wrong." It's a scare tactic designed to make you crawl back, apologizing for shit you didn't even do.

Why Fear Works

Fear works because it paralyzes you. When you're too busy worrying about their reaction or the consequences they've conjured up in their twisted little heads, you're not focusing on what's actually real. Here's why they love using it:

- **It Keeps You Small**: Fear makes you second-guess yourself, your decisions, and your worth. When you're stuck doubting everything, they're free to manipulate you however they want.
- **It Keeps Them in Power**: If you're afraid of rocking the boat, they get to steer the ship.

- **It Distracts You from Their Weakness**: They're not actually as powerful as they want you to believe, but as long as you're scared, you'll never notice.

How to Dismantle the Fear Tactics

1. **Call Out Their Intimidation**: "Is that supposed to scare me? Because it's not working." Say it calmly, and watch their fake power crumble.
2. **Stop Reacting**: Their anger, threats, and silence are only effective if you let them be. Refuse to engage. "Okay, let me know when you're ready to talk rationally." Then walk the fuck away.
3. **Reality-Check Their Bullshit**: When they try to scare you with catastrophic outcomes, ask yourself: "Is this actually true, or are they just pulling this out of their ass?" Nine times out of ten, it's the latter.
4. **Stand Your Ground**: Fear only works if you bend to it. The next time they pull their intimidation tactics, plant your feet and say, "No." Watch them scramble to adjust to this terrifying new concept: your backbone.

The Bottom Line

Fear is their go-to weapon because it's easy, effective, and lets them feel powerful without actually having to do anything. But here's the truth: their power is fake, their threats are hollow, and their intimidation is just a sad reflection of their own insecurities. Stop feeding their fear machine. Stand tall, call out their games, and let them stew in the realization that you're not scared of their bullshit anymore. You're untouchable, and they fucking hate it.

10.1.5 Emotional Sabotage: Turning Your Feelings into Their Favorite Weapon

Manipulators are emotional terrorists. They don't just mess with your head—they weaponize your feelings against you, turning every ounce of empathy, love, or guilt you have into ammunition for their games. They don't care about your emotions unless they can twist them into tools for their own gain. It's not just sabotage—it's a calculated mindfuck designed to leave you doubting yourself, second-guessing your instincts, and apologizing for shit that isn't even your fault.

How They Pull Off Emotional Sabotage

These assholes don't come at you with obvious attacks. No, they sneak in under the radar, twisting your emotions in ways so subtle you don't notice until you're already knee-deep in their bullshit. Here's how they operate:

- **The Guilt Trip Olympics**: "After everything I've done for you, this is how you repay me?" Oh, cry me a fucking river. They make you feel guilty for having boundaries, saying no, or, God forbid, prioritizing yourself.
- **The Fake Empathy Card**: They'll pretend to care about your feelings just long enough to extract what they need. "I understand how you feel, but you're being a little dramatic." Translation: *Shut up and do what I want.*
- **The Out-of-Proportion Blow-Up**: They take a minor issue and turn it into a full-blown emotional disaster. Suddenly, you're apologizing for something that barely qualifies as a problem.
- **Weaponizing Your Vulnerabilities**: Everything you've ever confided in them becomes ammo for their manipulative games. "You always overreact like this—it's why people don't take you seriously." Fuck them for even going there.

Why Emotional Sabotage Works

Emotional sabotage works because it targets your core—the part of you that wants to be understood, valued, and accepted. They exploit your humanity while showing none of their own.

- **They Exploit Your Guilt**: If you're a decent person, you don't want to hurt others. They twist that instinct until you're hurting yourself to keep them happy.
- **They Overwhelm You**: By creating emotional chaos, they make it hard to think clearly. Confusion is their currency, and you're paying the price.
- **They Make You Doubt Yourself**: When your emotions are all over the place, it's easy to question your instincts and decisions—and that's exactly what they want.

How to Shut Down Their Emotional Bullshit

1. **Own Your Emotions**: Your feelings are yours, and no one gets to twist them into a weapon. "I'm allowed to feel this way, and I'm not apologizing for it." Full stop.
2. **Refuse the Guilt Trip**: "I'm not going to feel guilty for setting boundaries." Say it, mean it, and don't let their crocodile tears sway you.
3. **Stay Calm While They Spiral**: When they blow up, stay as cool as ice. Nothing deflates their emotional power trip faster than your calm, unbothered demeanor.
4. **Shut Down the Manipulation**: "I see what you're trying to do, and it's not going to work." Call it out, and they'll scramble like a cockroach under a spotlight.

The Bottom Line

Emotional sabotage is their desperate attempt to control you by turning your feelings into weapons. But once you see the game, it's over. Refuse to play along, own your emotions, and let them choke on the realization that their tactics don't work anymore. You're stronger than their manipulative bullshit, and the second they figure that out? They'll have no choice but to find a new target—or rot in their own toxic mess.

Lesson 10.2: Countering Their Tactics

10.2.1 The Shield of Awareness: Spotting Their Bullshit Before It Starts

Awareness is your first line of defense against manipulative assholes. Without it, you're just wandering around blindfolded while they rearrange your life for their benefit. But when you build the *Shield of Awareness*, you're untouchable. You see their games before they even make their first move, and nothing pisses them off more than realizing their manipulative tricks won't work on you. This isn't just self-defense—it's psychological warfare, and you're about to win.

Why Awareness is Their Kryptonite

Manipulators rely on you being oblivious. If you don't notice their bullshit, they can keep pulling strings behind the scenes while you dance to their tune. Awareness breaks their entire game plan into pieces. Here's why:

- **It Exposes Their Moves**: When you know their tactics, they lose the element of surprise. No more "How did this happen?" You'll already know exactly what they're doing.
- **It Puts You in Control**: Awareness flips the script. Instead of reacting to their bullshit, you're anticipating it—and that scares the hell out of them.
- **It Makes You Unfuckwithable**: The more aware you are, the less power they have. They can't manipulate someone who sees right through their games.

How to Build Your Shield of Awareness

1. **Know the Red Flags**
   Manipulators aren't subtle, no matter how much they think they are. Look for the warning signs:

     ○   Over-the-top compliments that feel fake as hell.
     ○   Passive-aggressive comments disguised as "jokes."
     ○   A constant need to play the victim.
     ○   Subtle digs that make you question yourself.

2. **Trust Your Gut**
   Your instincts are louder than their manipulation. If something feels off, it probably is. Don't let them talk you out of what you know to be true.

3. **Pay Attention to Patterns**
   Manipulators aren't creative—they recycle the same tactics over and over. Once you spot their pattern, it's game over. "Oh, look, another guilt trip. How original."

4. **Stay Emotionally Detached**
   Awareness isn't just about seeing their moves—it's about refusing to let those moves get under your skin. Their drama doesn't deserve a front-row seat in your head.

How They'll Try to Bypass Your Shield

These toxic bastards don't give up easily. The moment they realize you're onto them, they'll double down. Here's how they'll try to sneak past your awareness—and how to shut them down:

- **Playing Dumb**: "What? I didn't mean it like that!" Sure, Jan. They'll try to gaslight you into thinking you're overreacting. Don't fall for it.
  - **Your Response**: "I know exactly what you meant. Let's not play games."
- **Love-Bombing**: They'll smother you with fake kindness to lower your defenses.
  - **Your Response**: "This sudden attention is suspicious. What's your angle?"
- **Escalating the Drama**: If subtlety doesn't work, they'll try to create chaos to distract you.
  - **Your Response**: "I'm not engaging in this. Let me know when you're ready to talk like an adult."

The Bottom Line

The Shield of Awareness isn't just about spotting their manipulative bullshit—it's about refusing to let it affect you. Once you see their moves, you can shut them down before they even start. They can't control, manipulate, or gaslight someone who's ten steps ahead. Build your shield, stay sharp, and let them burn themselves out trying to play a game you've already won.

10.2.2 The Confidence Counterattack: The Weapon They Can't Handle

Manipulators hate confidence. It's like kryptonite to their manipulative bullshit. A confident person is harder to control, impossible to gaslight, and straight-up immune to their guilt trips and mind games. When you bring confidence into the mix, their entire strategy crumbles like a house of cards in a hurricane. That's why the best counterattack isn't just standing your ground—it's doing it with unshakable confidence that makes them choke on their own insecurities.

Why Confidence Screws with Them

Manipulators thrive on finding your weak spots, but confidence blindsides them. They rely on you doubting yourself, second-guessing your choices, and seeking their approval. Confidence shuts all that shit down. Here's why it works:

- **It Makes You Unfuckwithable**: When you're confident, their snide comments and passive-aggressive digs bounce off you like cheap bullets off Kevlar.
- **It Exposes Their Insecurities**: Your confidence highlights everything they hate about themselves, and they'll squirm under the pressure.
- **It Strips Them of Control**: Confidence means you don't need their approval or validation, and that scares the hell out of them.

How to Launch a Confidence Counterattack

1. **Stand Tall, Literally and Figuratively**
   Confidence isn't just about how you feel—it's about how you carry yourself. Walk into the room like you own the place, even if you don't.
   - **What They Expect**: You to shrink under their gaze.
   - **What You Do**: Meet their eye, hold your head high, and smile like you're daring them to try their bullshit.

2. **Speak with Authority**
   Manipulators rely on you tiptoeing around their feelings. Stop softening your words or adding question marks to your sentences.
   - **Instead of**: "I think this might work…"
   - **Say**: "This will work. Let's move forward." Period.

3. **Reject Their Guilt-Tripping**
   The moment they try to guilt you, shut it down with confidence.
   - **Them**: "After everything I've done for you, this is how you treat me?"
   - **You**: "That's not how this works. I'm making decisions that are best for me."

4. **Own Your Wins**
   Manipulators will try to downplay your achievements to keep you doubting yourself. Don't let them.
   - **What to Say**: "Yeah, I worked my ass off for that, and I'm proud of it." Watch them squirm as their little dig falls flat.

How They'll Try to Counter Your Confidence

Manipulators don't go down without a fight. The moment they sense your confidence growing, they'll ramp up their tactics. Here's what they'll do—and how to handle it:

- **Turning Up the Criticism**: They'll double down on nitpicking your every move.

- o **Your Response**: "Your opinion is noted and irrelevant."
- **Playing the Victim**: "Your confidence is making me feel small."
  - o **Your Response**: "That sounds like a you problem."
- **Spreading Doubt to Others**: "They've changed. They're so full of themselves now."
  - o **Your Response**: Let them talk. Your confidence will speak louder than their bullshit.

The Bottom Line

Confidence isn't just your best defense—it's your ultimate weapon. It shuts down their games, strips them of power, and sends a clear message: you're not someone they can fuck with. Build your confidence, wear it like armor, and watch as they crumble under the weight of their own insecurities. You're in control now, and there's nothing they can do to stop you.

10.2.3 Turning the Tables: Flipping the Script on Manipulative Assholes

Manipulators think they're running the show. They've spent their entire toxic lives perfecting the art of control, playing games, and screwing with people's heads. But here's the twist—they're not as clever as they think they are. The second you flip the script and turn their own tactics against them, they're fucked. Turning the tables isn't just a power move; it's a goddamn art form, and you're about to become a master.

Why Turning the Tables Works

Manipulative assholes are predictable. They rely on the same tired tactics—gaslighting, guilt-tripping, playing the victim—because they work on people who don't see them coming. But when you flip those tactics back on them, their entire world falls apart. Here's why it's so effective:

- **It Catches Them Off Guard**: They've spent so long perfecting their bullshit, they don't know how to handle someone who fights fire with fire.
- **It Exposes Their Game**: When you use their tactics against them, it forces them to see how transparent and pathetic they really are.
- **It Shifts the Power Dynamic**: Suddenly, they're not in control anymore—and nothing terrifies a manipulator more than losing control.

How to Turn the Tables Like a Pro

1. **Hit Them with Their Own Gaslighting**
   Gaslighting works because it makes you question your reality. Flip it back on them.
   - **Them**: "You're overreacting."
   - **You**: "No, *you're* overreacting. Why are you so defensive?" Watch them stumble over their own hypocrisy.
2. **Guilt-Trip Them Into a Corner**
   They love guilt-tripping you? Turn that shit around.
   - **Them**: "After everything I've done for you…"
   - **You**: "Funny, I was just thinking the same thing about all the times I've had your back. What are *you* doing for me right now?" Cue awkward silence.
3. **Flip Their Victim Card**
   Manipulators love playing the victim, but two can play at that game.
   - **Them**: "I feel like you're being unfair."
   - **You**: "You're right—I've been way too patient with your behavior. Thanks for pointing that out." Game. Set. Match.
4. **Expose Their Drama to the World**
   They thrive in the shadows, spreading lies and stirring up drama. Drag their shit into the light.

○ **What to Say**: "Let's clear this up in front of everyone. Care to explain yourself?" Watch them squirm as their web of lies unravels in real time.

What Happens When You Turn the Tables

Turning the tables is like flipping a switch in their toxic little world. Here's what happens:

- **They Panic**: Manipulators rely on control, and when they lose it, they spiral.
- **They Get Defensive**: Suddenly, they're the ones scrambling to explain themselves.
- **They Back Off**: Once they realize you're not an easy target, they'll either try harder (and fail) or move on to someone else.

How to Keep the Upper Hand

1. **Stay Calm**: Manipulators thrive on emotional chaos. Keep your cool, and you'll always have the upper hand.
2. **Stick to the Facts**: Don't let them derail the conversation with drama or deflection. Facts are their kryptonite.
3. **Know When to Walk Away**: Sometimes the best way to win is to disengage entirely. Let them stew in their own toxicity while you move the fuck on.

The Bottom Line

Turning the tables isn't about playing dirty—it's about showing them you're not the one to mess with. Manipulators can dish it out, but they sure as hell can't take it. Flip their tactics back on them, expose their games, and watch as they crumble under the weight of their own bullshit. You're smarter, sharper, and way more in control than they ever expected—and that scares the hell out of them.

10.2.4 Building a Fortress of Trust: Guarding Your Inner Circle Against Toxic Invaders

Trust is like a goddamn fortress—it takes time, effort, and intention to build. But manipulators? They're like termites, crawling in when you're not looking and gnawing away at the foundations until your support system crumbles. If you want to keep your life free of their toxic bullshit, you need to reinforce your inner circle. This isn't about letting just anyone waltz into your life—it's about building a fortress of trust so impenetrable that manipulators can't even get near it.

Why Trust is Your Ultimate Defense

A solid inner circle is the one thing manipulators can't destroy—if you protect it. Here's why trust is their kryptonite:

- **It Gives You a Support System**: Manipulators thrive on isolating you. A trusted circle keeps you grounded, supported, and far less susceptible to their bullshit.
- **It Exposes Their Games**: When your circle is tight, manipulators can't stir up drama or plant seeds of doubt. They're left floundering in their own mess.
- **It Shuts Them Out**: Trust creates boundaries, and boundaries are walls they can't climb.

How to Build and Fortify Your Fortress of Trust

1. **Vet the Hell Out of People**
   Not everyone deserves access to your inner circle. Be ruthless about who gets in.
   - **Red Flags**: Gossipers, people who thrive on drama, and anyone who makes you second-guess yourself.
   - **Green Flags**: Supportive, consistent, and honest people who clap for your wins and call you out (respectfully) when needed.

2. **Set Clear Boundaries**
   Even within your circle, boundaries are non-negotiable.
   Trust doesn't mean unlimited access.
   - **Example**: "I'm not comfortable discussing that," or, "That's not something I want to share right now." Period.
3. **Foster Open Communication**
   Your inner circle thrives on honesty. If something feels off, address it before it turns into a toxic spiral.
   - **What to Say**: "I noticed [X], and I wanted to talk about it. Let's clear the air."
4. **Don't Let Manipulators Sneak In**
   These sneaky bastards will try to weasel their way into your trust fortress. Watch for fake flattery, guilt-tripping, or sudden "support" when they have something to gain. Shut them down before they can even unpack their toxic suitcase.

Signs Your Fortress is Solid

- **You Feel Safe**: You're not constantly watching your back or questioning people's motives.
- **Drama is Nonexistent**: Your circle isn't perfect, but it's not a soap opera, either.
- **You're Supported and Challenged**: Your people cheer you on and keep you accountable, not tear you down.

How Manipulators React to a Strong Circle

Manipulators hate a tight, trusted group because it leaves them out in the cold. Here's how they'll try to sabotage your fortress—and how to handle it:

- **They'll Gossip About You**: "They've changed. They think they're too good for us now." Let them talk. Their bitterness doesn't touch your fortress.

- **They'll Try to Divide and Conquer**: "You know [insert name] was talking about you, right?" Response: "Nice try, but I know my circle better than you do."
- **They'll Pretend to Be Your Ally**: "I just want to be there for you." Yeah, no thanks. You've got all the support you need.

The Bottom Line

Building a fortress of trust is about protecting your peace, your energy, and your sanity. It's not about quantity—it's about quality. Surround yourself with people who've earned their place in your life, and don't let a single manipulative bastard breach the walls. Let them stand outside, choking on their own bitterness, while you thrive in a circle of people who actually deserve you.

10.2.5 Thriving With Boundaries: Drawing the Line and Daring Them to Cross It

Boundaries aren't just rules—they're survival. They're the lines that keep manipulative assholes out of your business, your head, and your peace. But let's be clear: boundaries aren't worth shit if you don't enforce them. Thriving with boundaries means not just setting them, but guarding them like your life depends on it—because when it comes to toxic people, it does.

Why Boundaries Are a Game-Changer

Manipulators can't stand boundaries. They see them as challenges, obstacles to bulldoze so they can keep feeding off your energy. But strong, unbreakable boundaries? Those are their worst nightmare. Here's why:

- **They End the Power Struggle**: Boundaries take control away from the manipulator and put it squarely in your hands.
- **They Protect Your Peace**: Every boundary is a brick in the wall that keeps their toxic bullshit out of your life.

- **They Make Them Irrelevant**: Manipulators lose their grip the moment you stop giving a fuck about their reactions.

How to Set Boundaries That Actually Work

1. **Be Brutally Clear**
   Manipulators love ambiguity, so don't give them any. Your boundaries need to be as straightforward as a sledgehammer to the face.
   - **Example**: "I'm not discussing this with you," or, "If you keep pushing, this conversation is over." No room for debate.
2. **Don't Over-Explain**
   Boundaries aren't up for discussion. You don't need to justify them, and you sure as hell don't owe anyone a detailed explanation.
   - **What to Say**: "That's my decision," or, "This is what works for me." Period.
3. **Enforce Like a Bouncer**
   Setting boundaries is step one. Enforcing them is where the real power lies. The second someone crosses the line, shut it down.
   - **Example**: "We've already talked about this. If you bring it up again, I'm leaving." Then follow through.
4. **Anticipate the Pushback**
   Manipulative people hate boundaries because they cut off their access to you. Expect guilt trips, anger, and every other trick in their toxic playbook.
   - **Your Response**: "I understand you don't like this, but it's not changing." Let them throw their tantrum—you're not moving.

How Thriving With Boundaries Looks

When you've mastered the art of boundaries, life gets a hell of a lot better. Here's what thriving with boundaries looks like:

- **You're in Control**: No one dictates your time, energy, or decisions but you.
- **Drama is Nonexistent**: Toxic people bounce off your boundaries like bugs hitting a windshield.
- **You Feel Free**: No more guilt, no more second-guessing. Just peace, clarity, and the satisfaction of knowing you're untouchable.

How Manipulators React to Strong Boundaries

Let's be honest: they're going to lose their shit. Boundaries are like kryptonite to manipulators, and they'll do everything they can to tear them down. Here's what to expect:

- **They'll Test the Waters**: "Oh, I didn't think you meant *this time.*"
    - **Your Response**: "I meant every time. Don't do it again."
- **They'll Play the Victim**: "I can't believe you'd do this to me!"
    - **Your Response**: "This isn't about you—it's about protecting my peace."
- **They'll Try to Guilt You**: "You've changed. You used to care."
    - **Your Response**: "You're right—I've changed. I care more about myself now."

The Bottom Line

Thriving with boundaries means taking back your power, protecting your peace, and refusing to let anyone's toxic bullshit derail your life. Manipulators hate boundaries because they force them to face a terrifying truth: they don't control you anymore. Set your lines, enforce them like a badass, and let them scream into the void while you live your life, untouchable and unbothered.

Lesson 10.3: Staying Mentally Strong

10.3.1 Recognizing True Support: Spotting the Real Ones in a Sea of Fake Assholes

In a world full of two-faced manipulators, backstabbers, and drama-hungry shit-stirrers, finding true support is like finding a diamond in a pile of crap. Let's get real: not everyone clapping for you actually wants you to win. Half of them are just waiting for you to trip so they can say, "I told you so." The other half? They're just clapping to distract you while they sharpen their knives. Recognizing true support means separating the real ones from the fake ones and making damn sure your inner circle is filled with people who actually give a shit.

What True Support Actually Looks Like

Here's the thing about real supporters: they don't need a spotlight or a fucking agenda. They're just there, showing up for you because they genuinely care. No strings, no bullshit, just real, unfiltered support. Here's how to spot them:

- **They Clap for You When You Win**: True supporters don't feel threatened by your success. They're the ones cheering the loudest, not quietly sulking in the corner because they didn't get their turn.
- **They Call You Out with Respect**: Real ones aren't afraid to check you when you're wrong, but they do it in a way that builds you up instead of tearing you down. "Hey, you messed up here, but I know you can fix it." That's support.
- **They Show Up When It Counts**: Talk is cheap, but actions? That's where the real ones shine. They're there when shit hits the fan, not just when it's convenient.
- **They Don't Keep Score**: True supporters don't keep a running tally of what they've done for you. They help

because they want to, not because they're planning to cash in favors later.

What Fake Support Looks Like

Now, let's talk about the impostors. These assholes are everywhere, pretending to be on your side while secretly rooting for your downfall. Here's how to spot the fakes:

- **Backhanded Compliments**: "Wow, I didn't think you'd pull that off. Good for you!" That's not support—that's their jealousy peeking out from behind a fake smile.
- **Conditional Loyalty**: They're all in when things are going well, but the second you hit a rough patch? Crickets.
- **Gossip and Drama**: If someone's constantly talking shit about others, guess what? You're not the exception—you're just not around when they do it.
- **The "All About Me" Syndrome**: Every time you try to share something, they hijack the conversation and make it about them. "Oh, you got promoted? That's cool, but let me tell you about my week."

How to Protect Yourself

1. **Audit Your Inner Circle**
   Take a hard look at the people around you. Who's genuinely rooting for you, and who's just hanging around to see what they can get? Be ruthless.
2. **Test Their Support**
   Share a small win or struggle and see how they react. The real ones will celebrate or offer a helping hand. The fakes? They'll downplay it, ignore it, or make it about themselves.
3. **Cut the Dead Weight**
   If someone's support feels fake, it probably is. Don't waste your energy trying to "fix" them. Cut them loose and focus on the people who actually give a damn.

4. **Value Actions Over Words**
    Anyone can say they're there for you, but the real ones prove it. Watch what they do, not what they say.

The Bottom Line

True support is rare, and fake support is everywhere. The key is learning to tell the difference—and once you do, stop giving your time to the fakes. The real ones are the people who lift you up, call you out (with love), and celebrate your wins without a hint of jealousy. Keep those people close and let the rest choke on their own toxic bullshit. You don't need fake cheerleaders in your corner when you've got a solid team of real ones.

10.3.2 Building Your Inner Circle: Keeping Real Ones Close and Tossing the Rest

Your inner circle isn't just some casual group of acquaintances—it's your fortress, your backbone, your ride-or-die squad that keeps you grounded when shit hits the fan. But here's the thing: not everyone deserves a spot in that circle. Some people are just there to drain your energy, stir up drama, or bask in your wins without lifting a finger when you're down. Building your inner circle means being ruthless about who gets in—and who needs to be shown the door.

Who Belongs in Your Inner Circle

Let's cut the crap: only the real ones get a seat at your table. These are the people who actually give a damn, show up, and don't bring an ounce of toxic bullshit into your life. Here's how to spot them:

- **They're Consistent**: No fair-weather friends allowed. True supporters are there for the highs, the lows, and everything in between.
- **They Speak the Truth**: They'll call you out when you're wrong, but it's never to tear you down—it's to help you level

up. "You're better than this" hits different when it comes from someone who actually believes in you.

- **They're Drama-Free**: Your inner circle should feel like a safe haven, not a goddamn soap opera. If someone thrives on chaos, kick their ass to the curb.
- **They Celebrate Your Wins Without Jealousy**: When you succeed, they're genuinely happy for you—no backhanded compliments, no passive-aggressive digs, just real pride in your achievements.

Who Does NOT Belong

Some people will try to sneak into your circle under the guise of "support." Spoiler alert: they're full of shit. Watch out for these toxic freeloaders:

- **The Energy Vampire**: They suck the life out of every interaction, leaving you drained and questioning why you even picked up the phone.
- **The Drama Dealer**: They bring gossip, chaos, and a tornado of unnecessary bullshit wherever they go.
- **The Jealous Shadow**: Instead of cheering for you, they quietly resent your success and throw subtle shade whenever they can.
- **The Opportunist**: They're only around when it benefits them. The second you're not useful? They're gone.

How to Build Your Circle Like a Boss

1. **Be Selective as Fuck**
   Your circle isn't a charity—it's an exclusive club, and not everyone gets an invite. Look for people who bring value, positivity, and honesty to your life.
2. **Test Their Loyalty**
   Share something small—good news, bad news, whatever—and watch their reaction. True supporters will cheer for you

or offer help. Fakes will downplay, dismiss, or make it about them.

3. **Set Boundaries Like a Fortress**
   Just because someone's in your circle doesn't mean they get unlimited access to your time and energy. Real ones respect boundaries; the rest will try to bulldoze them.

4. **Cut the Dead Weight**
   If someone's not pulling their weight or bringing positive energy, cut them loose. You're not running a daycare for toxic adults.

5. **Prioritize Quality Over Quantity**
   You don't need a crowd—you need a core. A tight-knit group of real ones beats a hundred fake friends every single time.

How Manipulators React to Being Shut Out

Let's be clear: the second you start building a strong inner circle, the manipulators will lose their shit. Here's how they'll react—and how to handle it:

- **They'll Play the Victim**: "I can't believe you're shutting me out!"
  - **Your Response**: "I'm prioritizing my peace. If you can't handle that, it's not my problem."
- **They'll Stir Up Drama**: "Did you hear what they said about you?"
  - **Your Response**: Ignore it. Their gossip says more about them than it does about you.
- **They'll Try to Sneak Back In**: "I've changed! I really care about you!"
  - **Your Response**: "Good luck with that, but I'm not interested."

The Bottom Line

Building your inner circle is about protecting your peace, amplifying your wins, and surrounding yourself with people who actually have your back. Be ruthless about who gets in and unapologetic about kicking out the dead weight. Let the manipulators cry, gossip, and throw tantrums while you thrive with your circle of real ones. You're not here to babysit their insecurities—you're here to build a life that's untouchable.

10.3.3 Celebrating Real Connections: Appreciating the People Who Actually Give a Damn

Let's take a moment to talk about the *real ones*. You know, the people who actually show up for you without any hidden agenda, backhanded compliments, or strings attached. In a world crawling with fake friends and manipulative assholes, these connections are rare as hell—and they deserve to be celebrated. The real ones are your lifeline, your grounding force, and the people who keep your sanity intact while the rest of the world loses its mind.

What Makes Real Connections So Damn Special

True connections aren't built on convenience or obligation—they're built on trust, respect, and genuine care. These are the people who don't just talk the talk; they back it up with action. Here's what sets them apart:

- **They're There Through It All**: Wins, losses, and everything in between—real ones show up, no matter what. They're not just there for the party; they're there for the cleanup, too.
- **They Don't Play Games**: No manipulation, no mind games, no bullshit. What you see is what you get, and what you get is someone who actually cares.
- **They Celebrate Your Wins**: When you succeed, they don't feel threatened—they feel proud. No jealousy, no passive-aggressive digs, just genuine happiness for you.
- **They Call You Out When Needed**: Real friends won't let you drown in your own mistakes. They'll check you with love, even if it's uncomfortable, because they want the best for you.

How to Celebrate and Protect Real Connections

1. **Say Thank You**
   It sounds simple, but when's the last time you actually thanked the people who've had your back? A little appreciation goes a long way.
   - **What to Say**: "I see how much you do for me, and I don't take it for granted. Thank you." Boom—connection strengthened.

2. **Reciprocate Like a Boss**
   Relationships are a two-way street. If someone's pouring into you, make sure you're doing the same for them.
   - **What to Do**: Show up, listen, and be there when they need you—just like they are for you.

3. **Protect Them from Drama**
   Don't let manipulators or toxic people poison your real connections. If someone's stirring shit, shut it down.
   - **Your Line**: "This isn't up for discussion. [Insert name] is my person, and I've got their back."

4. **Celebrate Their Wins**
   Make their wins feel as big as yours. When they succeed, you should be their loudest cheerleader.
   - **What to Say**: "You crushed it! I'm so proud of you." No fake enthusiasm—mean it.

5. **Invest in the Connection**
   Spend time with the people who matter. Call them, text them, make plans. Show them they're a priority, not an afterthought.

Why Manipulators Hate Real Connections

Manipulators can't stand real relationships. They see genuine connections as threats because they can't compete with something built on trust and authenticity. Here's how they'll try to sabotage your real connections:

- **They'll Gossip**: "Did you know what so-and-so said about you?"

- ○ **Your Response**: "If they had something to say, I trust they'd say it to my face. Nice try."
- **They'll Cause Drama**: "Why do you spend so much time with them and not me?"
  - ○ **Your Response**: "Because they add value to my life. Do you?"

The Bottom Line

Real connections are your most valuable resource, and they deserve to be celebrated and protected. They're rare as hell, so when you find them, hold on tight. Thank the people who've been there for you, show up for them in return, and never let a manipulative asshole come between you. Real connections are your shield, your strength, and your proof that not everyone in the world is a piece of shit. Appreciate them, and let the fakes choke on their jealousy.

10.3.4 Building Resilience: Becoming the Badass They Can't Break

Let's be honest: life is full of manipulators, backstabbers, and drama-loving assholes who'd love nothing more than to knock you down and keep you there. But here's the thing—they only win if you let them. Building resilience isn't just about bouncing back from their bullshit; it's about becoming so unshakable that their petty little games don't even make a dent. Resilience is your ultimate fuck-you to every person who ever doubted you, manipulated you, or tried to make you feel small.

Why Resilience Scares the Shit Out of Them

Manipulators hate resilience because it means they can't control you. They thrive on weakness, insecurity, and emotional chaos—all the things resilience destroys. Here's why it terrifies them:

- **They Lose Their Grip**: Resilient people don't crumble under pressure, which means manipulators can't use your emotions as their personal puppet strings.
- **You're Unpredictable**: Resilience gives you the power to adapt, pivot, and thrive no matter what they throw at you—and they can't stand not being able to predict your reactions.
- **It Highlights Their Fragility**: Let's face it, manipulators are weak as hell. Your resilience is a reminder that they could never handle the shit you've been through.

How to Build Resilience Like a Boss

1. **Own Your Shit**
   Resilience starts with owning your story—the good, the bad, and the batshit crazy. Everything you've been through has made you stronger, so stop apologizing for it.
   - **What to Do**: Write down the hardest things you've survived and remind yourself: if you handled that, you can handle anything.
2. **Stop Seeking Validation**
   Manipulators love to make you crave their approval. Building resilience means giving zero fucks about what they think.
   - **Your Mantra**: "Their opinion doesn't pay my bills or dictate my worth." Repeat as needed.
3. **Embrace the Bounce-Back**
   Resilience isn't about never falling—it's about getting up every damn time. When shit goes sideways, treat it like a lesson, not a life sentence.
   - **What to Ask**: "What can I learn from this?" Then use that lesson to come back stronger.
4. **Cut the Toxic Dead Weight**
   You can't build resilience when you're surrounded by people who thrive on tearing you down. Ditch the manipulators, the drama queens, and the emotional vampires.
   - **What to Say**: "This isn't working for me, and I'm done." Then walk away and don't look back.

5. **Find Your Inner Badass**
   Resilience isn't just about survival—it's about thriving. Tap into your confidence, celebrate your wins, and remind yourself that you're a force to be reckoned with.
   - ○ **Your Vibe**: "I've been through hell, and I'm still here. What's next?"

What Resilience Looks Like

- **You Don't Sweat the Small Shit**: Manipulators try to rattle you, and you respond with a shrug and a, "Nice try."
- **You Set Boundaries Without Flinching**: "No" becomes your favorite word, and you don't feel the need to explain it.
- **You Keep Moving Forward**: No matter what they throw at you, you adapt, adjust, and keep winning.

Why They Hate Your Resilience

Let's be real: manipulators can't stand a resilient person because they can't control them. Your ability to bounce back pisses them off, and your refusal to crumble under their bullshit makes them feel powerless. Here's how they'll react:

- **They'll Try Harder**: Expect a last-ditch effort to knock you off your game.
  - ○ **Your Response**: "Is that all you've got? Pathetic."
- **They'll Play the Victim**: "You've become so cold!"
  - ○ **Your Response**: "No, I've become strong. There's a difference."
- **They'll Fade Away**: When they realize they can't break you, they'll eventually slither off to find an easier target.

The Bottom Line

Building resilience isn't just about surviving manipulators—it's about thriving in spite of them. It's about becoming so strong, so grounded, and so fucking unstoppable that their games don't even scratch the surface. Let them throw their tantrums, play their victim cards, and stew in their own toxicity. You've got bigger things to do—like living your best life, completely unbothered by their bullshit.

10.3.5 Celebrating Freedom: Flipping Off the Chains of Manipulation

Freedom from manipulators isn't just a relief—it's a goddamn revolution. When you finally break free from their toxic grip, it's like ripping off a suffocating mask and taking your first deep breath in years. But here's the thing: this isn't just about surviving. It's about thriving so hard that their pathetic games seem like a distant joke. Celebrating your freedom means owning your power, rebuilding your life, and flipping a giant middle finger to every manipulative asshole who thought they could control you.

Why Freedom Feels So Damn Good

Breaking free from manipulators isn't just about peace of mind—it's about taking your entire life back. Here's why it's the ultimate high:

- **You're No Longer Their Puppet**: No more guilt trips, gaslighting, or mind games. You're finally the one pulling the strings in your life.
- **You're in Control**: Your decisions, your time, your energy—it's all yours now, and they don't get a single piece of it.
- **Their Opinions Don't Matter**: That constant background noise of their bullshit? Gone. You don't need their approval, and you sure as hell don't care about their judgment.

How to Celebrate Your Freedom Like a Boss

1. **Cut Every Tie**
   Don't just distance yourself—burn the bridge, block their number, and delete every trace of them from your life. Freedom means zero access for toxic people.

      ○   **What to Do**: Unfollow them on social media, block their emails, and ignore their attempts to weasel back in.

2. **Reclaim Your Time**
Think about all the hours you wasted dealing with their drama. Now take that time and invest it in something that actually matters—to you.
      ○   **What to Try**: Pick up a hobby, start a project, or just binge-watch something without someone breathing down your neck.

3. **Own Your Narrative**
Manipulators love to control the story, but now it's your turn. Rewrite your life on your terms, and don't let their version of events taint your truth.
      ○   **What to Say**: "That's not how it happened, but it's cute that you think so."

4. **Celebrate the Wins**
Every moment of peace, every decision you make without their interference, every time you feel genuinely happy—it's a win. Celebrate the hell out of it.
      ○   **What to Do**: Treat yourself, brag to your real friends, and let yourself feel proud for getting free.

5. **Live Loud and Proud**
Freedom isn't just about cutting them out—it's about thriving in ways they never thought you could. Shine so bright that their bitter little hearts can't handle it.

How to Handle Their Inevitable Tantrums

Let's be real: manipulators don't take rejection well. The second they realize you're free, they'll pull every trick in the book to drag you back. Here's how to shut them down:

- **The Guilt Trip**: "I can't believe you'd just cut me off like this!"
  - **Your Response**: "Believe it. Bye."
- **The Apology Trap**: "I've changed! I promise I'll do better."
  - **Your Response**: "That's great. For someone else."

- **The Drama Bomb**: "You'll regret this!"
  - **Your Response**: "Doubt it."

The Bottom Line

Celebrating freedom isn't just about escaping manipulators—it's about thriving without them. It's about reclaiming your life, your time, and your energy while they're left spinning in their own toxic mess. They wanted you to stay small, but now you're bigger, stronger, and happier than ever. So, raise a glass, take a deep breath, and toast to the fact that you're free—and they can't do a damn thing about it.

Lesson 10.4: Winning the War

10.4.1 Empowering Yourself: Owning Your Life and Giving Zero Fucks

Empowerment isn't just some fluffy self-help buzzword—it's your ticket out of the toxic shitstorm manipulative people have tried to trap you in. Empowering yourself means grabbing the reins, ditching the drama, and making it painfully clear to the assholes of the world that they no longer have a single ounce of control over you. It's not just about surviving their bullshit—it's about thriving in a way that makes them choke on their own insecurities.

Why Empowering Yourself Scares Manipulators

Manipulators thrive on control. Your empowerment shatters their entire playbook and leaves them scrambling for relevance. Here's why they can't handle it:

- **They Lose Their Leverage**: Empowered people don't fall for guilt trips, sob stories, or fake-ass apologies.
- **It Exposes Their Weakness**: Your strength highlights just how pathetic their tactics really are.

- **They Can't Handle Being Irrelevant**: Once you take back control, they're left on the sidelines, powerless and pissed off.

How to Empower Yourself Like a Goddamn Legend

1. **Stop Asking for Permission**
   Newsflash: You don't need anyone's approval to live your life. Empowerment starts when you stop seeking validation and start making decisions like the badass you are.
   - **What to Say**: "I've made my decision, and I'm good with it." Period.
2. **Set Boundaries and Enforce Them Like a Bouncer**
   Boundaries aren't suggestions—they're laws. And if someone crosses them? Show them the door.
   - **What to Say**: "That doesn't work for me, and it's not up for discussion."
3. **Reclaim Your Energy**
   Every minute you spend dealing with their drama is a minute you're not spending on yourself. Take your energy back and invest it where it matters.
   - **What to Do**: Cut off the energy vampires and focus on things that actually bring you joy.
4. **Own Your Story**
   Manipulators love rewriting your narrative to suit their bullshit. Take it back. Your story is yours, and theirs doesn't matter.
   - **What to Say**: "That's not how it happened, and I'm not letting you twist it."
5. **Celebrate Every Win**
   Big or small, every victory matters. Did you set a boundary? Celebrate it. Did you say no without apologizing? Celebrate it. Empowerment is built one win at a time.

How Manipulators Will React to Your Empowerment

Spoiler alert: they're going to lose their goddamn minds. Empowerment takes away their favorite toy—control—and they'll throw a tantrum the size of Texas to get it back. Here's what to expect:

- **The Guilt Trip**: "You've changed. You used to care about me."
  - **Your Response**: "You're right—I've changed, and I'm not going back."
- **The Fake Apology**: "I've been thinking, and I want to make things right."
  - **Your Response**: "That's great—for you. I've moved on."
- **The Escalation**: "You're going to regret this!"
  - **Your Response**: "The only thing I regret is not doing this sooner."

What Empowerment Looks Like

- **You Say No Without Guilt**: "No" is your favorite word, and you don't feel the need to explain it.
- **You Stop Giving a Shit About Their Opinions**: Their approval is irrelevant, and their criticism bounces off you like a rubber bullet.
- **You Prioritize Yourself**: Your peace, your goals, your happiness—those are your priorities now.

The Bottom Line

Empowering yourself is the ultimate act of defiance against manipulative assholes who thought they could control you. It's about reclaiming your time, your energy, and your life while they're left flailing in their own irrelevance. Stand tall, speak loud, and make it clear that you're the one in charge now. Let them stew in their bitterness while you thrive like the unstoppable badass you are.

10.4.2 Breaking Free Completely: Severing the Chains of Toxic Bullshit

Breaking free from manipulative assholes isn't just about taking a step back—it's about cutting every single chain they've wrapped around you and walking the hell away like the unstoppable badass you are. These toxic fuckers will try everything to keep you tethered to their chaos, but here's the deal: once you're free, they're nothing but a sad, irrelevant footnote in your story. Breaking free isn't just an escape—it's a declaration of independence, and it's about time you made it.

Why Breaking Free Completely is Non-Negotiable

Half-measures don't work with manipulators. These people thrive on any access to your time, energy, or emotions. If you leave the door cracked open, they'll kick it down. Breaking free completely is the only way to ensure they can't weasel their way back into your life.

- **They'll Exploit Any Weakness**: A "maybe" or "we can still be friends" is like crack to these people. Don't give them an inch—they'll take a mile.
- **They Need You More Than You Need Them**: They're not trying to "fix things"—they're trying to keep you as their emotional punching bag.
- **It's About Reclaiming Control**: Walking away isn't just about leaving them behind—it's about taking back every ounce of power they stole from you.

How to Break Free Like a Total Badass

1. **Cut Off All Contact**
   Block their number, unfollow them on every platform, and delete any messages, emails, or reminders of their existence. Don't just shut the door—fucking bolt it.

      ○ **What to Say (If You Even Bother)**: "This isn't working for me anymore. I'm moving on." Short, sharp, and final.

2. **Resist the "Closure" Trap**
   Closure is a luxury you don't need. Manipulators will use it as an excuse to pull you back in.
         ○ **Your Mantra**: "I don't need closure—I need freedom."

3. **Lean on Your Real Support System**
   Surround yourself with people who actually care about you. Real friends and family will help you stay strong when the manipulator inevitably tries to worm their way back in.

4. **Reclaim Your Time and Energy**
   Take all the time you used to waste on their drama and invest it in yourself. Whether it's hobbies, work, or just binge-watching your favorite show, make your life about *you*, not them.

5. **Stick to Your Decision**
   Manipulators are masters of guilt-tripping and gaslighting, and they'll pull out every trick in the book to make you doubt yourself. Don't fall for it.
         ○ **What to Say**: "I've made my decision, and it's final."

What to Expect When You Break Free

Manipulators don't take rejection well, so be prepared for some fireworks. Here's how they'll react—and how to handle it:

- **The Guilt Bombs**: "I can't believe you're doing this to me!"
  - **Your Response**: "This isn't about you—it's about what's best for me."
- **The Sob Stories**: "I'm really struggling without you."
  - **Your Response**: "I hope you figure it out. I'm not the solution."
- **The Rage Tantrums**: "You'll regret this!"
  - **Your Response**: "Doubt it."

Why Breaking Free Feels So Damn Good

Once you're out, you'll realize how much of your energy they were draining. You'll breathe easier, sleep better, and finally have the space to focus on the things that actually matter. Freedom isn't just a feeling—it's a fucking superpower.

- **You Stop Questioning Yourself**: No more second-guessing every move you make.
- **You Reclaim Your Identity**: Without their toxic influence, you rediscover who you are and what you want.
- **You Thrive Like Never Before**: With their bullshit out of the way, you finally have room to grow, succeed, and live unapologetically.

The Bottom Line

Breaking free completely is the only way to escape their manipulative grip for good. Cut the ties, burn the bridge, and don't look back. They'll throw tantrums, sling guilt, and try every trick in their toxic playbook, but none of it matters because you're done. You're free, you're thriving, and they're just a distant memory of the bullshit you'll never tolerate again. Let them choke on their irrelevance while you soar.

10.4.3 The Long Game of Growth: Outlasting Their Bullshit and Thriving Like a Legend

Growth isn't an overnight transformation—it's a long game, and the manipulators in your rearview mirror? They can't handle it. They wanted you stuck, doubting yourself, and spinning your wheels in their toxic little web. But the second you focus on growth, you're playing a game they can't compete in. The long game of growth isn't just about leaving their bullshit behind—it's about building a life so strong, so unshakable, that they're left choking on your dust.

Why Growth is the Ultimate Flex

Growth doesn't just piss off manipulators—it makes them irrelevant. While you're leveling up, they're stuck playing the same tired games, wondering why they can't get a reaction out of you anymore. Here's why it's the best revenge:

- **It Exposes Their Stagnation**: Growth highlights the fact that they haven't changed—and probably never will.
- **It Makes You Untouchable**: The more you grow, the harder it is for anyone to pull you back into their toxic drama.
- **It Puts You in Control**: Growth is all about taking ownership of your life. They can't manipulate someone who's steering their own ship.

How to Commit to the Long Game of Growth

1. **Set Bigger Goals**
   Manipulators wanted you to think small, but now? You're aiming higher than ever. Set goals that scare the shit out of you—and then crush them.
   - **What to Do**: Break your goals into smaller steps and tackle them one by one. Every little win adds up.
2. **Focus on Learning**
   Growth means evolving, and that starts with learning new skills, exploring new ideas, and stepping out of your comfort zone.
   - **What to Try**: Take a class, read a book, or dive into a passion you've been putting off.
3. **Surround Yourself with Growth-Minded People**
   Ditch the toxic crew and fill your life with people who inspire, challenge, and support you.
   - **What to Look For**: People who celebrate your wins, push you to be better, and actually practice what they preach.
4. **Measure Progress, Not Perfection**
   Growth isn't a straight line. There will be setbacks,

mistakes, and detours. The key is to keep moving forward, no matter what.

- ○ **Your Mantra**: "Progress is better than standing still."

5. **Celebrate Every Step**
Growth is a journey, and every milestone—no matter how small—is worth celebrating.
- ○ **What to Do**: Treat yourself, share your wins with your circle, and let yourself feel proud.

How Manipulators React to Your Growth

Spoiler alert: they're going to hate it. Growth makes their manipulative games obsolete, and they'll try everything to pull you back. Here's what to expect:

- **They'll Downplay Your Progress**: "Oh, that's nice, but it's not that big of a deal."
  - ○ **Your Response**: "It's a big deal to me, and that's all that matters."
- **They'll Try to Sabotage You**: "Are you sure you're ready for this? It seems like a lot."
  - ○ **Your Response**: "I'm more than ready, thanks."
- **They'll Play the Jealous Card**: "You think you're better than everyone now, huh?"
  - ○ **Your Response**: "I don't think it—I know it."

What Growth Feels Like

- **You Feel Lighter**: Without their bullshit weighing you down, everything feels a little easier.
- **You're Focused**: Your energy goes into building your life, not cleaning up their messes.
- **You're Proud of Yourself**: For the first time in forever, you look in the mirror and see someone who's thriving—and you don't need anyone else to tell you that.

The Bottom Line

The long game of growth isn't just about outlasting their bullshit—it's about creating a life so full, so vibrant, and so unapologetically yours that their manipulative games seem laughable in comparison. You're leveling up, building your empire, and becoming the person they always hoped you wouldn't be: someone who doesn't give a single fuck about their opinions. Let them wallow in their stagnation while you soar.

10.4.4 The Power of Reinvention: Becoming the Person They Never Saw Coming

Reinvention isn't just a makeover—it's a declaration of war against the version of you that manipulators thought they could control. It's about flipping the script, burning the old playbook, and becoming someone so powerful, confident, and untouchable that their pathetic little games seem laughable. Reinvention is your way of saying, "Thanks for the lessons, now watch me thrive while you drown in your own toxicity."

Why Reinvention is the Ultimate Flex

Manipulators rely on the idea that you'll stay the same, stuck in the version of yourself they think they know. Reinvention flips that expectation on its head. Here's why it pisses them off:

- **They Can't Predict You Anymore**: The person they thought they could manipulate is gone, replaced by someone they can't even comprehend.
- **It Shatters Their Ego**: Your growth highlights their stagnation, and it burns them to their core.
- **It Makes You Unreachable**: You've leveled up, and they're stuck trying to play the same tired games on a whole new you.

How to Reinvent Yourself Like a Goddamn Legend

1. **Burn the Old Script**
   The version of you that put up with their bullshit? That person's gone. It's time to rewrite your narrative, starting now.
   - **What to Say**: "That's who I was, not who I am. Get used to it."
2. **Redefine Your Identity**
   Stop letting other people's opinions shape who you are. Decide who you want to be, and step into that identity like it's custom-tailored for you.
   - **Your Mantra**: "I'm not defined by their expectations—I'm defined by my vision."
3. **Try New Things**
   Reinvention isn't just about ditching the old—it's about exploring the new. Take risks, try things that scare you, and discover parts of yourself you didn't know existed.
   - **What to Try**: A new hobby, a career pivot, or even a complete lifestyle overhaul.
4. **Surround Yourself with New Energy**
   You can't reinvent yourself while clinging to toxic people. Surround yourself with growth-minded, positive individuals who actually give a damn.
   - **What to Do**: Audit your circle. If someone isn't adding value, cut them loose.
5. **Own Your Reinvention**
   Don't downplay your transformation to make others comfortable. Be loud, proud, and unapologetic about who you're becoming.
   - **What to Say**: "This is the new me. Take it or leave it—I don't care either way."

What Reinvention Feels Like

- **Freedom**: You're no longer shackled by their opinions, expectations, or manipulative games.

- **Confidence**: You know exactly who you are, and you don't need anyone else's validation.
- **Excitement**: Every day feels like an opportunity to discover more about yourself and what you're capable of.

How Manipulators React to Your Reinvention

Spoiler alert: they're not going to like it. Here's how they'll try to drag you back—and how to handle it:

- **They'll Say You've Changed**: "You're not the same person anymore."
  - **Your Response**: "You're damn right I've changed. Thanks for noticing."
- **They'll Try to Guilt You**: "The old you would've cared more about me."
  - **Your Response**: "The old me was a doormat. The new me isn't."
- **They'll Play Nostalgia Games**: "Remember when we used to…"
  - **Your Response**: "Yeah, and I'm glad those days are over."

The Bottom Line

Reinvention isn't just about leaving the past behind—it's about creating a future so incredible that their manipulative bullshit doesn't even register anymore. It's about stepping into your power, owning your transformation, and becoming the person they never thought you could be. Let them wallow in their bitterness while you reinvent, evolve, and thrive like the unstoppable badass you are.

10.4.5 Building a Legacy: Living a Life They'll Never Forget (or Get Over)

Let's talk about the ultimate flex: building a legacy so strong, so untouchable, that it leaves every manipulative asshole in your past choking on their own irrelevance. Building a legacy isn't just about succeeding—it's about creating something so impactful, so undeniably *yours*, that their petty games look like dust in the wind. You're not just thriving; you're cementing your place as a goddamn legend, and there's nothing they can do to stop you.

Why Legacy Is the Ultimate Power Move

Manipulators wanted you stuck, small, and dependent on them. A legacy proves they failed. It's the exclamation point on your story— the proof that you not only escaped their bullshit, but you turned it into fuel for greatness. Here's why building a legacy is the ultimate fuck-you:

- **It Outlives Their Drama**: Their toxic games are temporary; your legacy isn't. Long after they're forgotten, what you've built will still stand.
- **It Redefines Your Story**: They thought they were the main character in your life. Your legacy makes it clear that they were just a footnote.
- **It's Unapologetically Yours**: A legacy is built on your terms, not theirs. It's the final rejection of their control.

How to Build a Legacy That Shuts Them Up Forever

1. **Define Your Vision**
   What do you want to leave behind? Whether it's a business, a movement, or simply a life well-lived, get clear on what you're building.
   - **What to Ask**: "What do I want people to remember about me?"
2. **Focus on Impact, Not Approval**
   Manipulators crave attention, but a legacy is about making a difference. Forget what people think and focus on what actually matters.
   - **Your Mantra**: "I'm here to make an impact, not friends."

3. **Turn Pain Into Power**
   Every piece of bullshit they threw your way? Use it as fuel. The more they tried to tear you down, the higher you'll rise.
   - ○ **What to Do**: Channel your experiences into something meaningful—a book, a cause, a lesson for others.

4. **Play the Long Game**
   A legacy isn't built overnight. It's about consistency, persistence, and showing up every damn day to create something bigger than yourself.
   - ○ **What to Remember**: Progress over perfection. Just keep building.

5. **Celebrate Your Wins**
   Big or small, every step toward your legacy is worth celebrating. Let yourself feel proud, even if you're still a work in progress.

What Legacy Looks Like

- **Your Success Speaks for Itself**: You don't have to explain your growth, your wins, or your goals—they're loud enough on their own.
- **You Inspire Others**: Your journey becomes proof that people can rise above even the worst bullshit.
- **You Feel Unstoppable**: With every milestone, you get closer to the version of yourself you've always wanted to be.

How Manipulators React to Your Legacy

Let's be real—they're going to hate it. Watching you succeed on such a massive scale is their worst nightmare. Here's what they'll do—and how to handle it:

- **They'll Downplay Your Impact**: "It's not that big of a deal."
   - ○ **Your Response**: "Big enough for you to notice, apparently."

- **They'll Try to Claim Credit**: "You wouldn't have gotten here without me."
  - **Your Response**: "Funny, I got here in spite of you, not because of you."
- **They'll Stew in Their Irrelevance**: And honestly? That's their problem, not yours.

The Bottom Line

Building a legacy isn't just about leaving something behind—it's about living so fully, so unapologetically, that your existence alone is a middle finger to every manipulative asshole who ever doubted you. Your legacy is proof that you're bigger than their bullshit, stronger than their games, and untouchable in ways they can't even comprehend. Build it, own it, and let them rot in the shadow of your greatness.

Thriving in Chaos – Outsmarting Manipulators at Their Own Game

You've seen the mind games, you've dodged the manipulation, and you've mastered the art of shutting down their psychological warfare. But here's the thing—manipulators don't just disappear because you've exposed them. The real pros? They thrive in chaos. They adapt, escalate, and try to shift the battlefield when they realize their usual tactics aren't working. And if you don't learn to **thrive in the madness**, you'll find yourself right back in their web.

Chapter 11 is about outsmarting these scheming bastards at every turn. You're not just playing defense anymore—you're predicting their next move, countering before they strike, and flipping their entire game upside down. This is about **staying five steps ahead, maintaining control, and leaving manipulators scrambling to keep up.** They think they're running the show? Not anymore.

It's time to **turn the tables and dominate the chaos.**

CHAPTER ELEVEN

Thriving in Chaos: Outsmarting Manipulators

Let's be real: manipulators don't operate on a higher plane of intelligence—they're just assholes with a game plan. They know how to poke, prod, and twist your emotions until you're tied up in knots, wondering if you're the problem (spoiler: you're not).]

This chapter is your crash course in beating these manipulative pricks at their own game. We're diving into the psychology behind their bullshit, teaching you how to read their moves, manage your own emotions like a goddamn pro, and flip the script with precision. With the power of emotional intelligence on your side, you'll see through their tricks, outplay their every move, and come out on top while they choke on their own manipulative nonsense.

Lesson 11.1: The Psychology of Manipulation

11.1.1 The Manipulator's Mindset: What Drives Their Behavior

Let's get one thing straight—manipulators aren't masterminds. They're insecure, power-hungry assholes who treat life like a chessboard, except they're not as smart as they think. These people are driven by one thing: control. They don't care about your feelings, your boundaries, or your sanity. They care about winning, no matter the cost. Their mindset is a twisted cocktail of arrogance, insecurity, and a desperate need to stay on top, even if it means screwing over everyone around them.

Why They Do It

- **They're Insecure as Hell**: Behind all their games and bravado is a fragile little ego that couldn't handle being seen as anything less than perfect. Manipulation is their way of hiding the fact that they're scared shitless of being exposed.

- **They Crave Power**: Manipulators thrive on control like a junkie thrives on their next fix. The more they can dominate your emotions and decisions, the bigger their ego gets. It's not about connection; it's about ownership.
- **They Get Off on Chaos**: Stirring the pot isn't just a hobby for these people—it's their life's mission. They love creating drama because it keeps them in the spotlight, where they feel most powerful.

Their Playbook

- **They Exploit Weaknesses**: Manipulators are like vultures—they circle until they find something to pick apart. Whether it's your guilt, your fear, or your desire to please, they'll zero in and use it against you.
- **They Weaponize Emotions**: Guilt trips? Check. Playing the victim? Double check. These assholes use your emotions as tools to bend you to their will.
- **They Plan Ahead**: Don't think for a second they're acting on impulse. Manipulators are always a step ahead, laying traps and setting you up to fail before you even realize what's happening.

What Makes Them Tick

- **Fear of Losing Control**: Nothing terrifies a manipulator more than the thought of someone else holding the reins. That's why they work overtime to keep you under their thumb.
- **Ego Inflation**: Manipulation feeds their narcissism. Every time they get someone to do their bidding, they feel like the king or queen of their twisted little kingdom.
- **Addiction to Validation**: They need to feel important, and manipulation is their shortcut to getting attention, respect, or whatever it is they think they deserve.

The Bottom Line

Manipulators aren't complicated—they're predictable, pathetic, and desperate for control. Their mindset is built on fear, insecurity, and a need to feel superior. Once you understand what drives them, their tactics lose their power. You see them for what they really are: scared little puppeteers who crumble the second you cut their strings.

11.1.2 The Power Of Control: Why They Thrive On Dominance

Here's the thing about manipulators: they're control freaks on steroids. Every move they make, every word they say, and every fake-ass smile they flash is part of their unrelenting quest for dominance. Why? Because control is their drug of choice, and they're addicted to the high of bending people to their will. It's not just about getting what they want—it's about knowing they're the puppet master, pulling the strings while you dance around like a clueless marionette.

Why Control Is Their Obsession

- **It Makes Them Feel Superior**: Deep down, these assholes know they're not actually better than anyone else. But if they can control you, it feeds their delusion that they're smarter, stronger, and more capable.
- **They're Terrified of Vulnerability**: Control is their armor, their way of avoiding the terrifying reality that they're just as fragile and flawed as everyone else. By dominating others, they don't have to face their own shit.
- **It's All About Power**: Let's be clear—manipulators don't just want a seat at the table; they want to own the damn table and make everyone else beg for a spot.

How They Wield Control

1. **The Emotional Puppet Strings**
    - Guilt, fear, and shame are their favorite tools. They'll make you feel like the worst person in the

world for setting boundaries or saying no.

  - *Example*: "I can't believe you'd do this to me after everything I've done for you." Translation: "Let me guilt you into submission so I can keep getting my way."

2. **The Illusion of Helplessness**
  - Some manipulators play the helpless card, acting like they can't survive without you. Spoiler alert: they can—they just don't want to.
  - *Example*: "I don't know what I'd do without you." Translation: "You're my emotional crutch, and I'm not letting go anytime soon."

3. **Divide and Conquer**
  - They thrive on sowing division. By pitting people against each other, they keep everyone too distracted to realize who's really pulling the strings.
  - *Example*: "You know, so-and-so said something interesting about you." Translation: "Let me start some shit and watch the chaos unfold while I sit back and enjoy."

4. **The Micromanager Mindfuck**
  - They micromanage every detail, from how you think to how you act, because the idea of you making decisions on your own makes their skin crawl.
  - *Example*: "Are you sure that's the best choice?" Translation: "Let me make you second-guess yourself so I can swoop in and take over."

What Happens When They Lose Control

- **They Lose Their Shit**: Manipulators without control are like toddlers without a nap—irrational, volatile, and utterly exhausting.
- **They Double Down**: If you start slipping out of their grasp, they'll escalate their tactics, pulling out all the stops to reel you back in.

- **They Play the Victim**: "Look what you're doing to me!" They'll turn on the waterworks, flip the script, and try to guilt-trip you into submission.

The Bottom Line

Control isn't just a tactic for manipulators—it's their lifeline. Without it, they're nothing but scared, insecure shells of people scrambling to stay relevant. Once you see through their bullshit, their power crumbles, and they're left exactly where they belong: out of control and out of your life.

11.1.3 Exploiting Weaknesses: How They Identify And Target Vulnerabilities

Manipulators are like bloodhounds sniffing out insecurities—they don't just stumble onto your weaknesses; they hunt for them with laser precision. Every interaction with them is like an audition, where they're mentally cataloging your fears, doubts, and soft spots. The second they find a crack in your armor, they exploit it so ruthlessly you'll wonder if they've been taking notes on your therapy sessions. Spoiler: they have—metaphorically, anyway.

How They Sniff Out Weaknesses

1. **They Test the Waters**
   - Manipulators are experts at subtle probes. They'll drop little comments, ask innocent-seeming questions, or push boundaries just enough to gauge your reaction.
   - *Example*: "Oh, you don't mind doing that extra work, right? You're such a team player." Translation: "Let me see if you're a pushover I can take advantage of."
2. **They Watch Your Reactions**
   - Every time you flinch, hesitate, or over-explain, they log it. They're not listening to your words—they're studying your body language, tone, and emotional cues.

- ○ *Example*: You stammer when defending yourself, and they think, *Perfect—this one's easy to rattle.*

3. **They Play the Long Game**
   - ○ Manipulators don't rush. They'll spend weeks or months building trust, pretending to care, and gathering intel on what makes you tick before launching their attack.
   - ○ *Example*: The "best friend" who waits until you confide in them about a personal struggle, then uses it against you when it benefits them.

Common Weaknesses They Exploit

- **Guilt**: If you have a tendency to feel bad about saying no, congratulations—you're a prime target. Manipulators will milk your guilt like a damn cash cow.
- **Fear of Conflict**: Hate confrontation? They'll bulldoze you while you're too busy avoiding a scene to stand up for yourself.
- **Need for Approval**: If you're a people-pleaser, they'll dangle validation in front of you like a carrot on a stick, keeping you jumping through hoops for their amusement.
- **Empathy**: Your compassion is their golden ticket. They'll play the victim so convincingly you'll feel obligated to fix their messes.

How They Exploit Your Weaknesses

1. **The Emotional Manipulation Game**
   - ○ They'll pull on your heartstrings like a sadistic violinist. Tears, sob stories, and guilt trips are all fair game.
   - ○ *Example*: "I just don't know how I'm going to manage without your help." Translation: "I'm going to make you feel like a monster if you say no."
2. **The Blame Shifting Olympics**
   - ○ Manipulators are gold medalists at flipping the script. If you catch them in a lie, suddenly *you're* the one who's "too sensitive" or "overreacting."

> ○ *Example*: "Wow, I can't believe you'd think that about me. I thought we were closer than that."

3. **Gaslighting 101**
   - ○ They'll convince you that your perspective is wrong, your feelings are invalid, and your memories are faulty—all so they can maintain control.
   - ○ *Example*: "I never said that. You must be imagining things."

Why It Works

- **They Make You Doubt Yourself**: Once they've planted seeds of insecurity, you start second-guessing your instincts and decisions, giving them all the power.
- **They Keep You on Defense**: By constantly targeting your vulnerabilities, they keep you too busy defending yourself to realize what they're really doing.
- **They Turn Your Strengths Against You**: Empathy, kindness, and loyalty—things you value—become weapons in their hands.

The Bottom Line

Manipulators exploit weaknesses because it's the easiest way to stay in control. They're predators, plain and simple, feeding on insecurity and doubt. But once you recognize how they operate, you can slam the door on their bullshit. Your vulnerabilities are not a weakness—they're just tools in their playbook. Take those tools away, and watch them scramble to figure out their next move.

11.1.4 The Role Of Fear And Guilt: Using Emotions To Trap Their Victims

Fear and guilt are a manipulator's bread and butter—the dynamic duo they wield like a pair of sledgehammers to keep you trapped, confused, and dancing to their toxic little tune. They don't need logic or reason; all they need is a well-placed guilt trip or a dash of fear to turn you into their personal puppet. These bastards don't play fair, but that's the point—fear and guilt are their weapons of mass manipulation, and they wield them with precision.

How They Use Fear to Control You

1. **The Fear of Consequences**
   - Manipulators love making you believe that standing up to them will unleash hellfire. They'll paint a picture of doom so terrifying you'll cave before you even try.
   - *Example*: "If you don't do this for me, you're going to ruin everything!" Translation: "I want you too scared to say no, so I'll exaggerate the fallout until you fold."
2. **The Fear of Rejection**
   - They make you think that if you don't bend to their will, you'll end up isolated, unloved, and abandoned.
   - *Example*: "I thought you cared about me. Guess I was wrong." Translation: "Let me make you fear losing me so I can keep getting my way."
3. **The Fear of the Unknown**
   - Manipulators thrive on uncertainty. They'll use it to make you cling to them for guidance, even when you know damn well they're the problem.
   - *Example*: "You'll never find someone else who understands you like I do." Translation: "I'm sabotaging your confidence so you won't leave my toxic ass."

How They Weaponize Guilt

1. **The Martyr Act**
   - Manipulators love playing the sacrificial lamb, reminding you of everything they've "done for you" to make you feel like you owe them your soul.

- ○ *Example*: "After all I've sacrificed, this is how you treat me?" Translation: "Let me guilt-trip you into submission by pretending my actions were selfless."

2. **The Victim Card**
   - ○ They'll cry, whine, and paint themselves as the poor, misunderstood hero just trying to survive in this cruel, cruel world.
   - ○ *Example*: "Everyone's always against me—can't you just be on my side for once?" Translation: "I'm making you feel like the villain so I can stay the victim."

3. **The Guilt Grenade**
   - ○ They drop explosive accusations out of nowhere, leaving you scrambling to prove you're not the monster they're making you out to be.
   - ○ *Example*: "If you really loved me, you'd do this for me." Translation: "I'm equating love with obedience so I can manipulate you."

Why Fear and Guilt Work

- **They Hijack Your Emotions**: Fear and guilt bypass logic, putting you in fight-or-flight mode where you're too overwhelmed to think straight.
- **They Create Dependency**: The more you fall for their tactics, the more you rely on them to avoid the very emotions they're causing.
- **They Paralyze You**: When you're scared or guilt-ridden, you're less likely to challenge their bullshit—and that's exactly what they want.

The Bottom Line

Fear and guilt are cheap shots, but manipulators use them because they work. They're experts at making you feel like the world will collapse if you stand your ground or prioritize yourself. But here's the kicker: their power isn't real—it's a smoke screen they've built to control you. The second you call their bluff, their whole game falls apart. So, stop letting their guilt grenades and fear tactics dictate your life. See through the manipulation, stand your ground, and watch them scramble when you refuse to play their game.

11.1.5 The Long Game: Why Manipulators Plan Their Moves Carefully

Manipulators don't play checkers—they play chess. These scheming assholes think three steps ahead, plotting every word, every action, and every guilt trip with surgical precision. The long game isn't just a tactic for them—it's their lifestyle. They don't just want a quick win; they want the whole damn board under their control. And the worst part? Half the time, you don't even realize you're a piece in their twisted game until they're already yelling "checkmate."

Why Manipulators Love the Long Game

1. **It Gives Them Power Over Time**
   - Manipulators know that a slow, steady approach is way more effective than an all-out assault. The longer they stick around, the more trust they build—and the more leverage they gain.
   - *Example*: "I've always been there for you, haven't I?" Translation: "I've spent months setting up this manipulation, and now I'm cashing in."
2. **It Builds Your Dependence on Them**
   - Over time, manipulators make themselves indispensable. They offer help, support, or advice, only to weaponize it later.
   - *Example*: "I don't know what you'd do without me." Translation: "I've made sure you feel like you can't function without me."
3. **It's Harder to Catch Them**
   - By moving slowly and subtly, manipulators make their schemes harder to spot. You don't realize what they're doing until the trap has already snapped shut.

- *Example*: "I didn't mean to upset you—I was just trying to help." Translation: "I've been chipping away at your confidence for weeks, and now you're questioning yourself."

How They Play the Long Game

1. **They Plant Seeds**
   - Manipulators drop little comments or ideas that seem harmless at first but grow into full-blown control over time.
   - *Example*: "Have you ever noticed how X always ignores you?" Translation: "I'm setting up doubt so I can control how you see others."
2. **They Build Trust, Then Exploit It**
   - They'll play the role of your confidant, soaking up your secrets like a sponge, only to wring them out later when it benefits them.
   - *Example*: "You know you can tell me anything." Translation: "Give me ammo I can use against you later."
3. **They Keep You Guessing**
   - Manipulators don't strike all at once—they keep their moves unpredictable to make you second-guess yourself constantly.
   - *Example*: "Why are you being so paranoid? I've always had your back." Translation: "I've spent months gaslighting you into thinking I'm trustworthy."

Why the Long Game Works

- **It Wears You Down**: By stretching out their manipulation, they exhaust your emotional energy until you're too drained to fight back.
- **It Normalizes Their Behavior**: The slower they escalate, the less likely you are to notice how toxic they've become.

- **It Builds Credibility**: The longer they stay in your life, the more they convince you that they're trustworthy—no matter how many red flags they wave.

How to Beat Them at Their Own Game

1. **Stay Vigilant**
   - Don't ignore subtle patterns or brush off small red flags. If their behavior feels off, it probably is.
   - *What to do*: Keep mental notes or even physical records if necessary. Their long game thrives on your forgetfulness.
2. **Set Boundaries Early**
   - Cut off their ability to worm their way into your life by establishing firm limits from the start.
   - *What to say*: "I appreciate the offer, but I've got this handled."
3. **Trust Actions, Not Words**
   - Don't let their charm or empty promises cloud your judgment. Pay attention to what they do, not what they say.
   - *What to remember*: Words are cheap; actions don't lie.

The Bottom Line

Manipulators are patient predators, playing the long game to secure total control over your life. But once you know their tactics, their carefully laid plans fall apart. The key is to stay one step ahead—recognize the seeds they're planting, refuse to give them power, and call out their bullshit the moment it surfaces. When you stop playing along, their long game collapses like a house of cards. Let them scramble to rebuild it while you walk away, completely unfazed and totally in control.

Lesson 11.2: Building Emotional Intelligence

11.2.1 Self-Awareness: Recognizing Your Own Triggers And Responses

Here's the harsh truth: manipulators thrive because most people are completely clueless about their own emotions. If you don't know your triggers, they will. If you're not aware of how you react under pressure, they'll use it against you like a goddamn playbook. Self-awareness isn't some fluffy, feel-good buzzword—it's your first line of defense. Without it, you're walking around with a giant target on your back, practically begging for someone to manipulate you.

Why Self-Awareness Is Non-Negotiable

1. **It Stops You from Being Predictable**
   - Manipulators love predictable people. If they know exactly what sets you off, they'll press that button until you break.
   - *Example*: If guilt is your kryptonite, they'll load you up with sob stories until you're doing their bidding just to "make things right."
2. **It Helps You Stay in Control**
   - Knowing your emotional triggers lets you stay calm when they try to push you over the edge.
   - *Example*: Instead of flipping out when they "accidentally" criticize you, you can step back and see it for what it really is—a cheap power play.
3. **It Makes You a Harder Target**
   - When you're self-aware, manipulators can't twist your emotions because you're already one step ahead of their bullshit.

How Manipulators Exploit Your Blind Spots

- **Emotional Reactions**: They poke, prod, and provoke until you explode—and then use your reaction to make you look like the problem.

- o *Example*: "Wow, you're so sensitive. I was just joking!" Translation: "I wanted to piss you off, and now I'm blaming you for reacting."

- **Insecurities**: They latch onto your self-doubt like a leech and drain you until you're questioning your own worth.
  - o *Example*: "Are you sure you're ready for this? I mean, I'd hate to see you fail." Translation: "I'm planting seeds of doubt so you stay small and dependent on me."
- **Need for Validation**: If you crave approval, they'll dangle it like a carrot, keeping you chasing their approval while they sit back and enjoy the power trip.

Steps to Mastering Self-Awareness

1. **Identify Your Triggers**
   - o What makes you snap, feel insecure, or doubt yourself? Write that shit down. Knowing your triggers means manipulators can't blindside you.
   - o *Example*: "I tend to react when someone questions my competence." Boom—now you're aware and ready to manage it.
2. **Track Your Emotional Reactions**
   - o Pay attention to how you respond in tense situations. Are you calm, defensive, or ready to throw a chair? Knowing your patterns lets you take control.
   - o *Tip*: After a tough interaction, ask yourself: "What set me off, and how could I have handled it better?"
3. **Own Your Flaws**
   - o Everyone's got weaknesses—welcome to being human. When you own them, manipulators can't use them against you.

    ○ *What to remember*: "Yeah, I have insecurities, but they don't define me—and they sure as hell don't give you power over me."

4. **Learn to Pause**
    ○ Manipulators rely on impulsive reactions. Train yourself to pause, take a breath, and think before responding. It's the ultimate power move.
    ○ *What to do*: Instead of snapping back, say, "I need a minute to think about that." Watch them squirm while you regain control.

The Bottom Line

Self-awareness isn't just about "knowing yourself"—it's about weaponizing that knowledge to make yourself untouchable. When you know your triggers and control your reactions, manipulators lose their grip. They can't exploit what you've already mastered. So get to know yourself better than they ever could, and let them choke on their own failed attempts to push your buttons. Being self-aware isn't just empowering—it's your ultimate fuck-you to their entire playbook.

11.2.2 Empathy As A Weapon: Understanding Their Emotions To Predict Their Moves

Empathy is often sold as this wholesome, saintly quality—something you use to connect with others and make the world a better place. Screw that. In the game of outsmarting manipulators, empathy isn't about holding hands and singing kumbaya; it's about weaponizing your ability to read their emotions and predict their next shady-ass move. Manipulators thrive on exploiting people's feelings, but when you turn the tables and start dissecting their emotional bullshit, they don't stand a chance.

Why Empathy Is Your Secret Weapon

1. **It Lets You See Through Their Act**
    ○ Manipulators are masters of pretending— pretending to care, pretending to be hurt,

pretending to be the victim. When you tap into their emotional tells, you can spot the cracks in their facade.

- *Example*: They act devastated because you set a boundary? Check the tone. Are they really upset, or just pissed their manipulation didn't work?

2. **It Helps You Stay a Step Ahead**
   - Understanding their emotions gives you insight into their motives. Are they insecure? Hungry for control? Jealous? Once you know what's driving them, you can predict their next move before they even make it.

3. **It Puts You in the Driver's Seat**
   - When you're tuned into their emotions, you control the dynamic. You stop reacting and start playing offense, steering the interaction where you want it to go.

How to Use Empathy Like a Mind-Reader

1. **Read Between the Lines**
   - Manipulators rarely say what they actually mean. Pay attention to their tone, body language, and what they're *not* saying.
   - *Example*: They say, "I'm just worried about you." Translation: "I'm trying to undermine your confidence while looking like I care."

2. **Spot Their Emotional Triggers**
   - Everyone has emotional weak points, even manipulators. Figure out what pisses them off, scares them, or makes them feel insecure. That's their Achilles' heel.
   - *Example*: If they crave control, any sign that you're slipping out of their grasp will send them into a spiral. Use that to your advantage.

3. **Mirror Their Energy**
   - People instinctively trust those who reflect their emotions. Use this to lull manipulators into a false

sense of security, then flip the script when they least expect it.

- ○ *Example*: If they're acting calm and concerned, match their tone to keep them at ease. Then, when the time is right, drop the hammer.

What Manipulators Fear About Empathy

- **You Can See Their True Motives**: Once you understand their emotions, you'll see through their manipulative games.
- **You'll Use Their Tactics Against Them**: They fear someone who can play their game better than they can—and empathy gives you that edge.
- **You're Immune to Their Victim Act**: Their crocodile tears and guilt trips lose all power when you know they're just tools to manipulate you.

How to Practice Weaponized Empathy

1. **Listen More Than You Speak**
   - ○ Let them talk. The more they reveal, the easier it is to understand what they're really after.
   - ○ *Pro Tip*: Silence makes people uncomfortable—especially manipulators. Use it to make them over-explain and expose themselves.
2. **Ask Strategic Questions**
   - ○ Get them to open up without realizing they're giving you intel.
   - ○ *Example*: "That's interesting. Why do you feel that way?" Watch as they accidentally reveal their insecurities.
3. **Don't Let Empathy Turn Into Sympathy**
   - ○ Feel their emotions, but don't get sucked into them. Sympathy is the trap; empathy is the tool. Keep your distance while you gather information.

The Bottom Line

Empathy isn't just a feel-good quality—it's a scalpel you use to cut through a manipulator's bullshit. By understanding their emotions, you take away their element of surprise and flip the power dynamic in your favor. So stop letting manipulators weaponize your empathy and start using it against them. When you can predict their next move, they lose the game before it even starts.

11.2.3 Emotional Regulation: Staying Calm Under Pressure

Manipulators thrive on chaos—they want you rattled, emotional, and completely off your game because that's when you're easiest to control. Emotional regulation? That's their kryptonite. When you stay calm under pressure, you're not just resisting their tactics; you're driving them absolutely fucking insane. Nothing pisses off a manipulator more than watching you sit there, cool as ice, while their carefully planned bullshit falls apart.

Why Emotional Regulation Is a Power Move

1. **It Stops Them in Their Tracks**
   - Manipulators feed off your reactions. If you don't give them one, their whole game crumbles.
   - *Example*: They try to provoke you into an argument, and instead of taking the bait, you respond with, "Interesting. Are you done?" Watch them short-circuit.
2. **It Puts You in Control**
   - Staying calm means you're the one calling the shots. You're not reacting to their chaos; you're controlling the narrative.
   - *Example*: They accuse you of being "difficult," and instead of defending yourself, you calmly say, "That's your opinion." Boom. No ammo for them.
3. **It Keeps Your Head Clear**
   - Emotional outbursts cloud your judgment. Staying

composed allows you to think strategically and stay a step ahead.

How Manipulators Try to Break Your Cool

1. **The Provocation Tactic**
   - They'll poke, prod, and push your buttons, hoping you'll explode so they can play the victim.
   - *Example*: "Why are you so sensitive? I was just joking." Translation: "I'm trying to piss you off so I can blame you for the fallout."
2. **The Guilt Bomb**
   - They'll guilt-trip you into an emotional response, making you feel like the bad guy for setting boundaries.
   - *Example*: "I can't believe you'd treat me like this after everything I've done for you."
3. **The Blame Game**
   - They'll accuse you of things you didn't do to make you defend yourself and lose your composure.
   - *Example*: "You're so selfish—it's always about you!"

How to Stay Calm and Unshakable

1. **Master the Pause**
   - When they push your buttons, pause. Take a deep breath, count to five, and let the initial wave of emotion pass.
   - *What to say*: "I'll respond to that when I've had time to think."
2. **Detach from Their Drama**
   - Remember: their chaos isn't your responsibility. You don't have to fix it, respond to it, or even acknowledge it.
   - *Mantra*: "Their problem isn't my problem."
3. **Focus on Facts, Not Feelings**
   - Manipulators twist emotions to suit their narrative. Counter it with cold, hard facts.

      ○ *Example*: "Actually, that's not what happened. Let's stick to the truth."
4. **Practice Poker Face Mastery**
      ○ Even if they're getting under your skin, don't let it show. A blank expression is their worst nightmare.
      ○ *What to do*: Make eye contact, stay silent, and let them dig their own grave.

The Manipulator's Meltdown

Here's the fun part: manipulators hate it when you stay calm. They'll try harder to provoke you, escalate their tactics, and eventually, they'll self-destruct when nothing works. Watching them unravel while you remain composed? Priceless.

The Bottom Line

Emotional regulation isn't just about staying calm—it's about taking control. When you refuse to let manipulators rattle you, you strip them of their power and put yourself firmly in the driver's seat. So the next time they try to drag you into their chaos, stay cool, stay steady, and let their own bullshit blow up in their face. They'll lose their shit, and you'll walk away unbothered.

11.2.4 Social Awareness: Reading The Room And Understanding Group Dynamics

Manipulators don't just work one-on-one; they love stirring up chaos in groups. Whether it's your workplace, your friend circle, or your family dinner table, these bastards know how to work a room like a toxic politician campaigning for mayor of Dysfunctionville. That's where social awareness comes in. When you can read the room and understand group dynamics, you can spot their bullshit, neutralize it, and keep yourself above the fray while they flail around trying to regain control.

Why Social Awareness Is a Game-Changer

1. **You See the Manipulation in Real-Time**
   - Manipulators rely on people being too distracted to notice their games. Social awareness lets you catch their tactics as they happen.
   - *Example*: They're whispering to one person while throwing shade at another? You've already clocked it before anyone else catches on.
2. **You Control the Narrative**
   - Understanding group dynamics means you can steer conversations, redirect drama, and shut down manipulative power plays before they escalate.
   - *Example*: They try to sow doubt about you? You casually call it out in front of the group, leaving them exposed and scrambling.
3. **You Stay Two Steps Ahead**
   - Knowing how people interact allows you to anticipate moves and position yourself as the calm, collected one in the room.

How Manipulators Exploit Group Dynamics

1. **Divide and Conquer**
   - They pit people against each other to keep everyone too busy fighting to notice the real problem.
   - *Example*: "I don't want to stir the pot, but you wouldn't believe what so-and-so said about you."
2. **Play the Hero**
   - They position themselves as the savior, solving problems they secretly caused to gain trust and admiration.
   - *Example*: "I talked to them for you. Don't worry, I smoothed things over." Translation: "I stirred the drama, and now I'm acting like the fixer."

3. **Control the Spotlight**
   - o They dominate conversations, steering attention away from their flaws and onto someone else's mistakes.

How to Use Social Awareness to Outplay Them

1. **Read the Room Like a Hawk**
   - o Pay attention to tone, body language, and interactions. Who's dominating? Who's uncomfortable? Who's suspiciously quiet? Every detail matters.
   - o *What to do*: Notice shifts in energy. If someone suddenly acts defensive or shuts down, a manipulator is probably at work.
2. **Identify Alliances and Power Players**
   - o Figure out who holds influence in the group and where the manipulator fits in. Are they trying to win over a leader? Divide the team? Knowing their angle is half the battle.
3. **Diffuse Drama Without Escalating It**
   - o When manipulators try to ignite chaos, calmly redirect the conversation or expose their tactics subtly.
   - o *What to say*: "That's an interesting perspective. Let's get back to the main point." Translation: "Stop stirring shit."
4. **Use Their Tactics Against Them**
   - o If they're dividing the group, play peacemaker and bring people together. If they're hogging the spotlight, gently shift focus onto someone else.
   - o *Example*: "Actually, I think [name] had a great idea earlier—let's hear more from them."

The Manipulator's Kryptonite

Manipulators hate social awareness because it robs them of their cover. They rely on confusion, division, and subtlety to work their magic. When you see through their act and call it out—directly or indirectly—they lose their grip on the group and are left scrambling to save face.

The Bottom Line

Social awareness is your radar, your shield, and your sword. It lets you spot manipulative bullshit before it spreads, keeps you in control of group dynamics, and makes you the one person they can't outplay. So read the room, know the players, and don't let these toxic puppeteers turn your group into their personal drama factory. Let them try—they'll fail every damn time.

11.2.5 Relationship Management: Using Emotional Intelligence To Maintain Control

Let's face it—managing relationships isn't just about "getting along" when you're dealing with manipulators. It's about controlling the dynamic so you're not the one getting screwed over. Relationship management, when done right, isn't about compromise or playing nice—it's about making sure you're the one holding the reins while they trip over their own toxic bullshit. Think of it as playing chess while they're fumbling with checkers.

Why Relationship Management Matters

1. **It Keeps Manipulators in Check**
   - When you're in control of the relationship dynamic, they can't steamroll you or turn you into their emotional punching bag.
   - *Example*: "Sure, we can talk, but let's keep it short—I've got things to do." Translation: "You're not hijacking my time, asshole."
2. **It Puts You in the Driver's Seat**
   - Emotional intelligence lets you navigate their tactics, anticipate their moves, and steer interactions toward outcomes that work for *you*.

3. **It Protects Your Peace**
   - Let's be real: not every relationship can be cut off completely, but that doesn't mean you have to let them walk all over you. Managing the relationship means setting the terms and keeping their chaos at arm's length.

How Manipulators Try to Control Relationships

1. **The Overwhelming Tactic**
   - They bombard you with problems, drama, or attention-seeking behavior, leaving you too drained to focus on yourself.
   - *Example*: "I just need you to listen to me—again." Translation: "I'm going to dump all my shit on you because I don't respect your boundaries."
2. **The Obligation Game**
   - They frame everything as your responsibility, making you feel like you owe them your time, energy, or loyalty.
   - *Example*: "But I've always been there for you." Translation: "Now you have to put up with my nonsense forever."
3. **The Fake Ally Act**
   - They pretend to be supportive while subtly undermining you, keeping you dependent on their "help."

How to Use Emotional Intelligence to Manage Relationships

1. **Set the Rules Early and Often**
   - Make it clear what you will and won't tolerate, and enforce those boundaries like a damn dictator.
   - *What to say*: "I'm happy to help when I can, but I can't always drop everything for you." Translation: "I'm not your emotional dumping ground."

2. **Stay Detached, Not Defensive**
   - Manipulators want you to react emotionally—it's how they keep control. When you stay calm and detached, they lose their grip.
   - *Example*: They say, "You're being so selfish." You respond with, "That's your opinion." End of story.
3. **Redirect the Power Dynamic**
   - If they're trying to dominate the conversation or situation, subtly take back control.
   - *What to do*: Change the subject, ask a direct question, or simply say, "We're not discussing that right now."
4. **Use Strategic Transparency**
   - Share just enough to keep things smooth but never enough for them to use against you.
   - *Example*: "I've got a lot going on, but I'm managing." Translation: "You're not getting details you can twist into ammo."
5. **Know When to Walk Away**
   - Sometimes the best relationship management tool is the door. If the dynamic is too toxic to fix, cut your losses and move the hell on.
   - *What to say*: "This isn't working for me anymore. Good luck."

The Manipulator's Nightmare

Relationship management with emotional intelligence is their worst-case scenario. You're calm, composed, and in complete control while they flail around trying to regain the upper hand. Their usual tricks—guilt, drama, manipulation—fall flat, leaving them exposed and powerless.

The Bottom Line

Relationship management isn't about making manipulators happy—it's about maintaining control and protecting your peace. By setting boundaries, staying calm, and refusing to play their games, you make it impossible for them to exploit you. Let them try their hardest; you're not just surviving their bullshit—you're thriving in spite of it.

Lesson 11.3: Using Emotional Intelligence to Outsmart Manipulators

11.3.1 The Power Of Observation: Spotting Subtle Cues And Hidden Agendas

Manipulators don't just announce their bullshit upfront—they're sneaky little bastards who thrive on flying under the radar. They hide their toxic agendas behind fake smiles, smooth words, and crocodile tears, all while pulling the strings in the background. That's why the power of observation is your ultimate weapon. When you learn to spot their subtle cues, you'll see their game for what it is and blow it to pieces before they even realize you're onto them.

Why Observation Is a Game-Changer

1. **You See the Bullshit Before It Hits You**
   - Manipulators rely on you being distracted or oblivious. When you start paying attention, their "subtle" tactics look about as subtle as a car crash.
   - *Example*: They're overly friendly all of a sudden? Yeah, they're buttering you up for something.
2. **You Spot Patterns, Not Excuses**
   - Forget their words—watch what they do. Manipulators are creatures of habit, and their actions will always reveal their true intentions.
   - *Example*: "Oh, I forgot to tell you about that decision. My bad!" No, Karen, it wasn't a mistake— it's a pattern.

3. **It Puts You Back in Control**
    - ○ When you know their game, you can outmaneuver them at every turn. They can't manipulate what you've already seen coming.

How Manipulators Operate in Plain Sight

1. **The Overly Charming Act**
    - ○ They pour on the charm like syrup on pancakes, hoping you won't notice the poison underneath.
    - ○ *Example*: "You're so good at this—I don't know what I'd do without you!" Translation: "I'm about to dump a shitload of work on you."
2. **The Inconsistent Behavior**
    - ○ One day they're your best friend; the next, they're distant or cold. That's not mood swings—that's a manipulator testing your boundaries.
    - ○ *Example*: "Oh, sorry, I've been busy." Translation: "I'm seeing how far I can push you before you snap."
3. **The Strategic Victimhood**
    - ○ They'll play the victim whenever it suits them, spinning sob stories to distract you from their actual agenda.
    - ○ *Example*: "I've just been under so much stress lately." Translation: "Feel bad for me so I can get away with more shit."

How to Hone Your Observation Skills

1. **Watch, Don't Just Listen**
    - ○ Words are cheap. Pay attention to tone, body language, and what they're doing when they think no one's watching.
    - ○ *What to look for*: Are they fidgeting, avoiding eye contact, or overly rehearsed? Those are red flags.

2. **Connect the Dots**
   - Don't treat each interaction as isolated. Look at the bigger picture and find the patterns in their behavior.
   - *What to ask yourself*: "Is this a one-time slip-up, or is this part of a larger game they're playing?"
3. **Play Dumb, Stay Sharp**
   - Sometimes the best way to catch a manipulator is to let them think they're outsmarting you. Act clueless while taking mental notes.
   - *What to say*: "Oh, I didn't realize that. Tell me more." Translation: "I'm letting you dig your own grave."
4. **Trust Your Gut**
   - If something feels off, it probably is. Manipulators rely on you second-guessing yourself. Don't.
   - *What to remember*: Your instincts are smarter than their fake-ass charm.

The Manipulator's Worst Nightmare

Manipulators count on you being blind to their tactics, but when you start observing, their entire strategy falls apart. They can't hide behind their charm or excuses when you're dissecting their every move. And the best part? They won't even realize you're onto them until it's too late.

The Bottom Line

Observation isn't passive—it's power. By watching their actions, connecting the dots, and trusting your instincts, you strip manipulators of their cover and take control of the narrative. They think they're playing you, but really, you're the one running the game. So open your eyes, sharpen your focus, and let their manipulative bullshit crumble under the weight of your newfound clarity.

11.3.2 Strategic Communication: Using Words To Diffuse Their Tactics

When it comes to manipulators, words are both their weapon and their weakness. They twist, spin, and sugarcoat everything to suit their agenda. The good news? You can beat them at their own game. Strategic communication isn't about screaming louder or trying to out-argue them—it's about using your words like a scalpel to cut through their bullshit and leave them fumbling for a response. Think of it as verbal judo: you're using their own momentum to knock them flat on their ass.

Why Strategic Communication Works

1. **It Keeps You in Control**
   - Manipulators thrive on getting you emotional. When you stay calm and deliberate, they lose their grip on the conversation.
   - *Example*: "That's an interesting perspective. Let's focus on the facts." Translation: "Nice try, but your manipulation isn't working today."
2. **It Exposes Their Games**
   - By choosing your words carefully, you force them to reveal their tactics or backpedal so hard they might trip.
   - *Example*: "Can you clarify what you mean by that?" Translation: "I'm making you squirm while I dissect your bullshit."
3. **It Puts Them on the Defensive**
   - Strategic communication turns the tables, making them react to you instead of the other way around.

Tactics for Strategic Communication

1. **Keep It Short and Sharp**
   - Manipulators love it when you ramble—it gives them more material to twist. Instead, keep your responses short and to the point.

- *What to say*: "No, that doesn't work for me." Period. No explanations, no room for negotiation.

2. **Ask Direct Questions**
   - A well-placed question can unravel their entire game. It forces them to explain themselves, which they hate because it exposes their weak spots.
   - *What to ask*: "What exactly are you trying to say?" or "Why does this matter to you so much?" Watch them squirm.

3. **Use Neutral Language**
   - Staying calm and neutral drives them crazy because they want you emotional. Responding with detached logic takes the wind out of their sails.
   - *What to say*: "I understand your concern, but that's not how I see it." Translation: "Your emotional manipulation is bouncing right off me."

4. **Redirect the Conversation**
   - If they're trying to bait you into an argument, change the subject or refocus on what actually matters.
   - *What to say*: "Let's get back to the main issue." Translation: "I'm not falling for your distraction tactics."

5. **Call Out Inconsistencies**
   - Manipulators rely on you not noticing when their stories don't add up. Point out contradictions and watch them scramble.
   - *What to say*: "That's interesting—earlier, you said something different. Can you clarify?"

Examples of Strategic Communication in Action

- **When They Guilt-Trip You**:
  - *Them*: "After everything I've done for you, you can't even do this one thing?"
  - *You*: "I appreciate what you've done, but this isn't something I can take on."
- **When They Play the Victim**:
  - *Them*: "Everyone's always against me."

- *You*: "I'm sorry you feel that way. How do you think we should move forward?" Translation: "Let's skip the pity party and get to the point."
- **When They Twist Your Words**:
  - *Them*: "So you're saying I'm the problem?"
  - *You*: "I didn't say that. Let's stick to what was actually discussed."

What Drives Them Nuts About Strategic Communication

- **They Can't Manipulate You**: When you stick to facts and stay calm, their emotional tactics bounce off like rubber bullets.
- **They Lose Control**: By forcing them to answer direct questions, you take away their ability to steer the conversation.
- **You Stay Unbothered**: Manipulators hate it when you don't rise to their bait—your composure is their kryptonite.

The Bottom Line

Strategic communication isn't just about talking—it's about taking control. By staying calm, asking the right questions, and refusing to engage with their bullshit, you dismantle their tactics piece by piece. Let them try to twist your words—they'll only end up tying themselves in knots. In the end, you'll be the one walking away with your peace intact while they stew in their frustration. Game over, and you've won.

11.3.3 Leading With Logic: Countering Manipulation With Reason

Manipulators hate logic like vampires hate sunlight. Their entire game depends on emotions—yours, not theirs. They don't want you thinking clearly because the second you do, their carefully constructed house of cards comes crashing down. That's why leading with logic is their worst fucking nightmare. It's like handing them a spotlight and forcing them to explain their bullshit in front of an audience. Spoiler alert: they can't.

Why Logic Shreds Their Tactics

1. **It Drains Their Power**
   - Manipulators thrive on emotional reactions. Logic shuts that shit down by taking emotions off the table entirely.
   - *Example*: "I understand you're upset, but what's the actual issue?" Translation: "I'm ignoring your drama and forcing you to make sense for once."
2. **It Forces Them to Play Your Game**
   - When you stick to facts and reasoning, they're stuck trying to argue in your arena—and they're terrible at it.
   - *Example*: "Let's focus on what actually happened instead of how it felt." Boom. Now they're scrambling.
3. **It Makes Their Lies Obvious**
   - Logic exposes inconsistencies like a flashlight on cockroaches. The more they try to spin, the more tangled they get.

How to Lead with Logic

1. **Stick to the Facts**
   - Don't engage with their emotional bait. Keep the focus on what actually happened, not their dramatized version of it.
   - *What to say*: "That's not how I remember it. Let's clarify what actually happened."
2. **Ask for Evidence**
   - Manipulators love vague accusations and exaggerated claims. Call their bluff by asking for specifics.
   - *What to ask*: "Can you give me an example of that?" Translation: "I'm about to make you look like an idiot."
3. **Redirect Their Nonsense**
   - If they try to derail the conversation, calmly steer it back to the main point.

- *What to say*: "Let's not get sidetracked—what's your actual concern here?"

4. **Don't Match Their Energy**
   - When they get loud, dramatic, or defensive, don't rise to their level. Stay calm and composed—it drives them fucking insane.
   - *What to do*: Maintain a neutral tone no matter how hard they try to rattle you.

What Happens When You Use Logic

- **They Run Out of Excuses**: Manipulators rely on emotional manipulation to cover up their lack of reasoning. When you strip that away, they've got nothing left.
- **They Start Backpedaling**: Logic forces them to confront their inconsistencies, and the more they scramble, the more obvious their bullshit becomes.
- **They Get Frustrated as Hell**: Watching you stay calm and logical while their tactics fail will piss them off more than anything.

Examples of Logic in Action

- **When They Exaggerate**:
   - *Them*: "You're always so difficult to deal with!"
   - *You*: "Always? Can you give me a specific example?"
- **When They Try to Play the Victim**:
   - *Them*: "You're making me feel so unappreciated."
   - *You*: "That's not my intention. Let's talk about what specifically upset you." Translation: "We're not doing this pity party shit."
- **When They Twist the Facts**:
   - *Them*: "You never support me!"
   - *You*: "Never? What about the time I [insert example here]?" Translation: "Don't make me pull out receipts."

Why They Hate It

- **Logic Makes Them Accountable**: Manipulators can't handle being called out with facts—they'd rather drown you in emotional chaos.
- **They Can't Twist Reasoning**: While they're great at twisting emotions, logic gives them nowhere to hide.
- **It Takes Away Their Control**: Leading with logic puts you in charge of the conversation, forcing them to follow your rules.

The Bottom Line

Manipulators rely on chaos, confusion, and emotional sabotage to get what they want. Logic slices through all that like a hot knife through butter. The next time they try to pull their shit, meet them with cold, hard reasoning. Watch as their tactics fall apart, their frustration bubbles over, and their carefully crafted narrative crumbles. They'll hate every second of it—and you'll walk away with your power intact.

11.3.4 Turning Their Tactics Against Them: Using Their Methods To Expose Them

Manipulators think they're the smartest people in the room—hell, they think they've invented the game. Here's the fun part: you can play it better. Turning their tactics against them isn't just satisfying—it's devastating. You're not just beating them at their own game; you're exposing their manipulative bullshit for the world to see. It's a masterclass in poetic justice, and trust me, these assholes won't know what hit them.

Why This Works

1. **It Throws Them Off Their Game**
   - Manipulators don't expect you to flip the script. When you use their own tricks against them, they're

too busy scrambling to notice the tables have turned.

- o *Example*: They guilt-trip you? Guilt-trip them right back. "Oh, I thought you understood how busy I've been. Guess not."

2. **It Exposes Their Patterns**
   - o By mirroring their tactics, you shine a spotlight on their behavior, forcing them to confront how transparent their manipulation really is.
   - o *Example*: They spread rumors about you? Casually mention how "interesting" it is that they've been talking about everyone else lately.

3. **It Takes Away Their Power**
   - o When you beat them at their own game, they lose the upper hand—and manipulators without control are about as useful as a broken umbrella.

How to Flip the Script

1. **Mirror Their Behavior**
   - o Manipulators hate seeing their own tactics reflected back at them. It's like holding up a mirror to their bullshit.
   - o *Example*: They play the victim? Hit them with: "Wow, it's tough always being misunderstood, isn't it?" Watch them choke on their own medicine.

2. **Use Strategic Silence**
   - o Manipulators rely on emotional reactions. Deny them that satisfaction by staying silent and letting their own words hang in the air.
   - o *Example*: They say, "I just don't know why you'd do this to me." You stay quiet, stare, and let the awkward silence do the work.

3. **Expose Their Inconsistencies**
   - o They love twisting the truth, but when you start pointing out contradictions, they'll fall apart faster than their shitty arguments.

- *What to say*: "Wait, didn't you say something completely different last week? I'm confused."

4. **Redirect the Drama**
   - Manipulators love making you the focus of their chaos. Flip it back onto them.
   - *Example*: "I didn't realize you felt that way. Let's talk about why you're so upset." Translation: "Let me make you squirm while everyone watches."

5. **Play the Long Game**
   - Manipulators aren't the only ones who can think ahead. Anticipate their next move and set them up to fail.
   - *Example*: If they thrive on playing the victim, document everything. When they try to twist the story, you drop the receipts.

What Happens When You Use Their Tactics

- **They Get Defensive as Hell**: Manipulators hate being called out, especially when it's done using their own tricks.
- **They Lose Credibility**: Once their games are exposed, no one buys into their bullshit anymore.
- **They Spiral**: Watching their carefully crafted narrative unravel is their worst nightmare—and your sweetest victory.

Examples of Turning the Tables

- **When They Try to Gaslight You**:
  - *Them*: "You're overreacting; that's not what I said."
  - *You*: "Funny, that's not how I remember it. Should I pull up the messages?"
- **When They Play the Victim**:
  - *Them*: "I just feel like no one understands me."
  - *You*: "It must be exhausting to always feel that way. How do you think you can fix it?"

- **When They Shift the Blame**:
  - *Them*: "This wouldn't have happened if you'd just listened to me."
  - *You*: "So you're saying it's my fault? That's an interesting take."

The Manipulator's Meltdown

When you turn their tactics against them, manipulators lose their minds. They're not prepared for someone who can outplay them at their own game. They'll try harder, double down, and flail around in a desperate attempt to regain control—all while looking more ridiculous by the second.

The Bottom Line

Manipulators think they're invincible, but the truth is, their tactics are as fragile as their egos. By using their own methods against them, you expose their games for everyone to see and take back control of the narrative. They'll hate it, you'll love it, and everyone watching will finally see them for the toxic mess they truly are. Let the games begin—and let them lose.

11.3.5 Winning Without Conflict: Resolving Situations Without Escalating Them.

Manipulators are conflict junkies—they feed off drama, chaos, and the emotional fallout they create. The louder, messier, and more explosive the situation, the better for them. But here's the plot twist: you don't have to play their game. Winning without conflict isn't just possible—it's the ultimate fuck-you. It's about shutting down their bullshit so efficiently and calmly that they don't even realize they've lost until you're already walking away with your peace intact.

Why Winning Without Conflict Is the Ultimate Power Move

1. **It Starves Them of Drama**
   - Manipulators thrive on emotional reactions. When

you refuse to engage, you cut off their supply.

- ○ *Example*: They scream, "You're being so selfish!" and you calmly reply, "Thanks for sharing your opinion." End of story.

2. **It Keeps You in Control**
   - ○ Escalation gives them the upper hand. Staying calm and deliberate ensures you're always the one holding the reins.
   - ○ *Example*: "Let's focus on resolving this instead of pointing fingers." Translation: "You're not dragging me into your shitstorm."

3. **It Makes Them Look Ridiculous**
   - ○ When you stay composed while they flail around like a toddler in a tantrum, everyone else can see who the real problem is.

How to Shut Them Down Without Starting a War

1. **Master the Art of Non-Reaction**
   - ○ Manipulators want you to snap—it validates their narrative. Deny them that satisfaction by staying calm, collected, and unfazed.
   - ○ *What to do*: When they throw accusations or insults, respond with a neutral, "I hear you." Translation: "Your drama means nothing to me."

2. **Redirect the Conversation**
   - ○ If they're steering the discussion toward chaos, gently but firmly bring it back on track.
   - ○ *What to say*: "That's not really relevant right now. Let's focus on solving the issue at hand."

3. **Use Silence as a Weapon**
   - ○ Nothing makes a manipulator more uncomfortable than silence. Let their words hang in the air and force them to deal with their own bullshit.
   - ○ *What to do*: Pause. Take a breath. Stare. Let them stew.

4. **Stick to the Facts**
   - ○ Emotional arguments are their playground, so don't

go there. Keep your responses grounded in logic and reality.

- ○ *What to say*: "Here's what actually happened. Let's stick to the facts."

5. **Politely Walk Away**
   - ○ If they keep pushing, don't give them more ammo. Politely but firmly disengage.
   - ○ *What to say*: "I don't think we're getting anywhere right now. Let's revisit this later." Then leave.

Examples of Winning Without Conflict

- **When They Try to Guilt-Trip You**:
  - ○ *Them*: "I can't believe you'd do this to me after everything I've done for you!"
  - ○ *You*: "I understand you're upset, but this is the decision I'm making."
- **When They Play the Victim**:
  - ○ *Them*: "Everyone's always against me!"
  - ○ *You*: "I'm sorry you feel that way. What can we do to move forward?"
- **When They Escalate the Situation**:
  - ○ *Them*: "You're just impossible to deal with!"
  - ○ *You*: "I'm sorry you think that. Let's focus on resolving the actual issue."

Why It Drives Them Crazy

- **They Can't Get a Reaction**: When you stay calm and unbothered, they lose their favorite weapon—your emotions.
- **They Look Like the Problem**: Without a conflict to fuel their narrative, their manipulative behavior stands out like a neon sign.
- **You Stay Unbeatable**: They can't win if you refuse to play the game.

The Bottom Line

Winning without conflict isn't about being passive—it's about being smarter, calmer, and more strategic than the manipulative assholes trying to drag you into their mess. By staying composed, redirecting conversations, and refusing to engage with their drama, you strip them of their power and keep your peace intact. Let them spiral—you've already won, and they don't even know it yet.

Lesson 11.4 Thriving With Emotional Intelligence

11.4.1 Building Stronger Relationships: Creating Bonds That Manipulators Can't Infiltrate

Let's face it—manipulators are like cockroaches: they'll crawl into any relationship crack you leave open. They love weak, one-sided connections because it's easy to exploit people who don't have their shit together. That's why building stronger relationships isn't just a nice-to-have—it's your armor. When your connections are solid, honest, and drama-proof, these toxic little gremlins can't even find a way in. And the best part? Watching them seethe on the sidelines as you thrive without their bullshit.

Why Strong Relationships Piss Off Manipulators

1. **They Can't Divide and Conquer**
   - Manipulators thrive on stirring up drama between people. When your relationships are rock solid, they can't pit you against each other.
   - *Example*: "Did you hear what Sarah said about you?" And you're like, "Yeah, she told me. We laughed about it." Boom. Game over.
2. **They Can't Twist the Truth**
   - Strong bonds are built on trust, which means manipulators can't sneak in and plant their little seeds of doubt.

- ○ *Example*: They try to spread lies, and your friend says, "Nah, I know them better than that." Instant failure for the manipulator.
3. **They Hate Seeing You Supported**
   - ○ Nothing pisses off a manipulator more than seeing you surrounded by people who actually give a shit about you. It ruins their whole game.

How to Build Relationships That Are Manipulator-Proof

1. **Cut the Fake Shit**
   - ○ Be real with people and expect the same in return. Manipulators rely on surface-level connections, so don't give them one.
   - ○ *What to do*: If someone's being shady, call it out. "Hey, that didn't sit right with me. Can we talk about it?"
2. **Set Boundaries Like a Boss**
   - ○ Strong relationships have clear lines, and guess what? Manipulators hate boundaries because they can't work around them.
   - ○ *What to say*: "I don't talk about X, and I expect the same from you." Translation: "Try me, asshole."
3. **Demand Reciprocity**
   - ○ Real relationships are give-and-take. If someone's only showing up when it benefits them, kick their freeloading ass to the curb.
   - ○ *What to notice*: Are they clapping for your wins, or are they too busy clapping for themselves?
4. **Build Trust, Not Drama**
   - ○ Trust is kryptonite to manipulators. Invest in people who prove themselves reliable, not those who thrive on gossip and chaos.
   - ○ *What to do*: Look for people who back up their words with actions. The ones who show up when it counts, not just when it's convenient.

5. **Keep Communication Tight**
   - Honest, open communication strengthens bonds and leaves no room for manipulators to wiggle in.
   - *What to say*: "If something's bothering you, tell me directly. No middlemen, no games."

Signs of a Strong Relationship

- **Mutual Respect**: Both sides value each other's time, boundaries, and opinions.
- **Consistency**: They're there for you, not just when it's easy or beneficial.
- **No Backhanded Bullshit**: Compliments are genuine, not veiled insults.
- **Drama-Free Zone**: Disagreements happen, but they're resolved without turning into a goddamn soap opera.

What Manipulators Do When They Can't Get In

- **They Sulk**: Watching you thrive without their interference makes them feel irrelevant—and they are.
- **They Try Harder**: Expect a last-ditch effort to create chaos. Stay vigilant.
- **They Move On**: Eventually, they'll slither off to find an easier target. Good riddance.

The Bottom Line

Strong relationships are a manipulator's worst enemy. They rely on cracks, doubts, and chaos to worm their way in, and when you don't give them that, their entire strategy falls apart. So build your connections on trust, honesty, and mutual respect, and let the manipulators choke on their irrelevance. The stronger your circle, the harder it is for their bullshit to get anywhere near you. Let them try—they'll fail every fucking time.

11.4.2 *Mastering The Art Of Influence: Using Emotional Intelligence To Inspire Trust*

Let's get one thing straight—manipulators think they've cornered the market on influence, but their version of "inspiring trust" is just emotional extortion wrapped in a cheap suit. Fuck that. Real influence isn't about manipulation—it's about being so damn solid that people *want* to listen to you. It's about owning the room without screaming for attention, and building trust so unshakable that manipulators couldn't break it with a crowbar. This is how you become the person everyone turns to while the toxic little drama queens choke on their irrelevance.

Why Real Influence Wrecks Manipulators

1. **They Can't Fake It**
   - Manipulators survive on lies, half-truths, and fake charm. You? You've got the real deal—authenticity— and it makes their phony shit look pathetic.
   - *Example*: You show up, deliver results, and leave. Meanwhile, they're over there spinning their wheels, trying to impress people with empty promises.
2. **It Makes You Untouchable**
   - Influence built on emotional intelligence doesn't just earn trust—it makes you unshakable. Manipulators can't twist your words or derail your momentum because everyone already knows you're the real deal.
3. **It Starves Their Ego**
   - They crave attention like a vampire craves blood. When people gravitate toward you instead of them, it's like watching their entire world implode.

How to Master Influence and Leave Manipulators in the Dust

1. **Stop Giving a Fuck About Approval**
   - Real influence isn't about kissing ass—it's about

earning respect by being yourself. Stop pandering and start owning who you are.

- *What to say*: "This is how I see it, take it or leave it." Translation: "I don't need your validation, and that's why people trust me more than you."

2. **Be the Calm in Their Shitstorm**
   - Manipulators thrive on chaos, but when you stay calm and collected, you become the steady force everyone turns to.
   - *What to say*: "I hear there's a lot going on. Let's cut through the noise and get to the real issue." Translation: "I'm the adult here, and you're just a drama-addicted child."

3. **Call Out Their Fake-Ass Behavior**
   - When manipulators try to undermine you, expose their tactics with brutal clarity.
   - *What to say*: "It's interesting how you always seem to have a problem but never a solution." Translation: "I see your bullshit, and so does everyone else."

4. **Own the Fucking Room**
   - Confidence, honesty, and results speak louder than manipulative noise. When you walk into a space knowing your shit, manipulators don't stand a chance.
   - *What to do*: Speak with conviction, deliver on promises, and let your actions do the talking. Manipulators love to overpromise and underdeliver—your competence makes them look like amateurs.

5. **Use Empathy Like a Weapon**
   - Manipulators use empathy to manipulate. You use it to connect, inspire, and lead. Big difference.
   - *What to say*: "I get where you're coming from, but here's what we need to focus on." Translation: "I hear you, but I'm still in control."

What Manipulators Do When You Take Over

- **They Panic**: You're stealing the spotlight they desperately need to survive, and they don't know how to handle it.
- **They Overcompensate**: Expect them to crank up the fake charm, make bigger promises, or stir up drama to claw back attention.
- **They Crash and Burn**: Eventually, their tactics can't compete with the genuine trust and respect you've built. Watching them implode? Priceless.

Examples of Influence in Action

- **When They Try to Steal Your Thunder**:
    - *Them*: "Oh, I was going to suggest that, too!"
    - *You*: "Great minds think alike, but I've already got it covered." Translation: "Sit down. I already won."
- **When They Stir Drama**:
    - *Them*: "Don't you think they handled that badly?"
    - *You*: "It's easy to criticize from the sidelines. Let's focus on what actually needs to be done." Translation: "Your pot-stirring bullshit isn't welcome here."
- **When They Try to Undermine You**:
    - *Them*: "Are you sure this is the best approach?"
    - *You*: "Yes, I've considered all the factors. If you have a better idea, I'm all ears." Translation: "Bring something real to the table or shut the hell up."

The Bottom Line

Influence isn't about playing dirty—it's about showing up with integrity, results, and a confidence that manipulators can't touch. While they're busy scheming and twisting themselves into knots, you're earning real respect and building connections that actually matter. Let them play their petty games—you've already won the war. Their desperation to compete with you will be their undoing, and you'll be too busy thriving to even notice.

11.4.3 Becoming Unmanipulatable: Making Yourself Immune To Their Tricks.

Manipulators are like viruses—they need a weak host to survive. They thrive on self-doubt, emotional reactivity, and your need for validation. But when you become unmanipulatable, you're like a brick wall they keep slamming into over and over again. Their tricks don't work, their games fall flat, and eventually, they'll give up and crawl back into the shadows where they belong. This isn't just about surviving manipulation—it's about making yourself so damn untouchable that they don't even bother trying.

Why Being Unmanipulatable Is Their Worst Nightmare

1. **They Can't Control You**
   - Manipulators rely on pushing your buttons to steer you where they want you to go. When you stop reacting, they lose their power.
   - *Example*: They say, "You're so selfish for not helping me!" and you reply, "That's your opinion." Watch their control dissolve like sugar in hot coffee.
2. **Their Tactics Bounce Right Off**
   - Guilt trips? Nope. Gaslighting? Not today. When you know their moves, they can't get under your skin.
3. **They Lose Interest**
   - Manipulators don't waste time on people they can't manipulate. Becoming immune means they'll eventually fuck off and find a weaker target.

How to Make Yourself Unmanipulatable

1. **Stop Giving a Shit About Approval**
   - Manipulators thrive on your need to be liked, accepted, or validated. The second you stop caring

what they think, their power evaporates.

- ○ *What to tell yourself*: "I don't need anyone's approval to be confident in my choices."

2. **Own Your Boundaries Like a Boss**
   - ○ Clear, unapologetic boundaries are a manipulator's kryptonite.
   - ○ *What to say*: "I've already made my decision, and it's not up for discussion." Translation: "Fuck off with your guilt trips."

3. **Master Emotional Neutrality**
   - ○ Manipulators want you emotional—it's how they get you to react without thinking. When you stay calm, they're left floundering.
   - ○ *What to do*: Take a breath, pause, and let their words hang in the air. Silence is a power move.

4. **Learn to Say No Without Explaining**
   - ○ Every time you justify your "no," you give manipulators a chance to argue.
   - ○ *What to say*: "No, that doesn't work for me." That's it. No essays, no excuses, just a hard stop.

5. **Detach from Their Drama**
   - ○ Don't get sucked into their chaos. Remember, their mess isn't your responsibility.
   - ○ *What to think*: "Their problem isn't mine to fix. I'm not their emotional janitor."

Signs You've Achieved Unmanipulatable Status

- **They Get Frustrated**: When their tactics fail, manipulators tend to double down or throw tantrums. That's your cue that you're winning.
- **They Call You "Cold" or "Selfish"**: This is their last-ditch effort to guilt you. It's a sign you're enforcing boundaries like a pro.
- **They Eventually Back Off**: No manipulation means no reward, and manipulators don't waste energy where they can't win.

Examples of Being Unmanipulatable

- **When They Try to Guilt-Trip You**:
    - *Them*: "I can't believe you're doing this to me!"
    - *You*: "I understand you're upset, but this is my decision." Translation: "Cry me a river—I'm still not budging."
- **When They Gaslight You**:
    - *Them*: "That's not what I said!"
    - *You*: "We both know what was said, and I'm not debating it." Translation: "Nice try, but I'm not playing this game."
- **When They Push Your Boundaries**:
    - *Them*: "Just this once—please?"
    - *You*: "No. I've already made myself clear." Translation: "Go beg someone else."

The Bottom Line

Becoming unmanipulatable is about reclaiming your power and shutting down the manipulative bullshit before it even starts. When you stop giving a damn about their approval, stop reacting to their drama, and start enforcing your boundaries like your sanity depends on it, manipulators lose every shred of control. Let them try—they'll fail spectacularly, and you'll walk away unbothered, untouchable, and fully in charge.

11.4.4 Emotional Balance: Thriving Despite External Chaos.

Manipulators are chaos addicts. They love stirring shit up, creating drama, and watching the world around them burn—all while they stand there pretending they had nothing to do with it. But here's the thing: their chaos only works if you let it. Emotional balance is your ultimate defense. When you're unshakable, their antics are just noise in the background, like a crappy garage band trying to disrupt a symphony. This isn't just about keeping your cool—it's about thriving in the middle of their toxic circus and making them realize they can't touch you.

Why Emotional Balance Sends Manipulators Spinning

1. **They Can't Rattle You**
   - Manipulators want you emotional, reactive, and off your game. When you're calm, they've got nothing to latch onto.
   - *Example*: They accuse you of being "difficult," and you just shrug and say, "Noted." They won't know what to do with that.
2. **It Exposes Their Tactics**
   - Your balance highlights their chaos. While they're flailing around trying to create drama, you're sitting there, sipping your metaphorical tea and letting them self-destruct.
3. **It Puts You in Control**
   - When you're emotionally steady, you get to steer the situation. Their tricks don't work because you're not playing their game.

How to Build Emotional Balance

1. **Stop Absorbing Their Bullshit**
   - Manipulators thrive on making their chaos your problem. Don't let them.
   - *What to tell yourself*: "This isn't mine to fix." Let them drown in their own mess.
2. **Practice the Power of Pause**
   - When they push your buttons, take a breath. That pause is where you regain control and decide how to respond—or whether to respond at all.
   - *What to do*: Count to five. Watch them squirm. Then calmly reply, "I'll think about that."
3. **Detach From the Drama**
   - You're not a character in their soap opera, so stop

letting them cast you as one. View their antics like you're watching a shitty reality show: entertaining, but not worth getting invested in.

- ○ *What to think*: "Not my circus, not my monkeys."

4. **Focus on What You Can Control**
   - ○ Emotional balance is about knowing what's within your power and letting go of the rest. Their chaos? Not your problem.
   - ○ *What to do*: Redirect your energy toward what actually matters—your goals, your peace, and your own damn life.

5. **Use Silence as a Weapon**
   - ○ You don't have to respond to every jab or guilt trip. Sometimes the best response is no response.
   - ○ *What to do*: Let their words hang in the air like the awkward bullshit they are. Silence is louder than any comeback.

What Emotional Balance Looks Like in Action

- **When They Try to Provoke You**:
  - ○ *Them*: "You're just being so selfish!"
  - ○ *You*: "That's one way to look at it." Translation: "Your opinion is irrelevant."
- **When They Create Drama**:
  - ○ *Them*: "Everyone's talking about how difficult you are."
  - ○ *You*: "That's interesting. Thanks for letting me know." Translation: "I don't care, and now you look stupid."
- **When They Play the Victim**:
  - ○ *Them*: "I can't believe you'd do this to me!"
  - ○ *You*: "I'm sorry you feel that way." Translation: "Your guilt trip isn't working, but nice try."

Why Manipulators Hate Emotional Balance

- **They Can't Get a Reaction**: Your calmness is like a brick wall to their wrecking ball—it doesn't budge.

- **They Look Like the Problem**: While you're calm and composed, they're flailing around looking like a dramatic mess.
- **They Lose Their Power**: Chaos is their currency, and when you refuse to engage, they go bankrupt.

The Bottom Line

Emotional balance isn't just about staying calm—it's about showing manipulators that their chaos is powerless against you. When you stop reacting, stop absorbing their drama, and start focusing on what actually matters, their entire strategy falls apart. Let them throw tantrums, stir the pot, and flail around trying to get your attention. You'll be too busy thriving in your unbothered bubble to notice—or care.

11.4.5 Long-Term Growth: Using Emotional Intelligence To Strengthen Your Life

Here's the thing about manipulators—they want you stuck. Stuck in their drama, stuck in your own head, stuck playing the same bullshit games over and over again. Why? Because as long as you're not growing, they've got a chance to keep you under their thumb. But when you start using emotional intelligence for long-term growth? Game over. They can't manipulate someone who's too busy thriving, leveling up, and building a life so strong it's basically a fortress they can't even scratch.

Why Long-Term Growth Terrifies Manipulators

1. **You Outgrow Their Bullshit**
   - Manipulators thrive on people who stay stagnant. When you grow, you leave them behind like the emotional parasites they are.
   - *Example*: They try their same old guilt trip, and you just laugh because you've heard it all before.
2. **They Can't Keep Up**
   - Manipulators aren't equipped to deal with someone

who's constantly improving themselves. They can't play chess with a person who's moved on to 3D strategy games.

3. **You Stop Giving a Fuck About Them**
   - Growth means your priorities shift, and manipulators fall off the list entirely. Watching you care less and less? That's their personal nightmare.

How to Use Emotional Intelligence for Long-Term Growth

1. **Master the Art of Self-Reflection**
   - Growth starts with understanding where you've been and where you want to go. Look back at the times you let manipulators pull your strings and learn from it.
   - *What to think*: "That was a lesson, not a loss. I'm stronger because of it."
2. **Invest in Healthy Relationships**
   - Cut the dead weight. Surround yourself with people who actually lift you up instead of dragging you down.
   - *What to do*: Build a circle of people who challenge you, support you, and never weaponize your emotions.
3. **Prioritize Your Peace**
   - Manipulators thrive on chaos, but long-term growth is about choosing peace every damn time.
   - *What to say*: "If it costs me my peace, it's too expensive."
4. **Set Bigger Goals**
   - Manipulators want you to stay small so they can control you. Prove them wrong by dreaming big and chasing it relentlessly.
   - *What to focus on*: Career, health, relationships, personal growth—whatever fuels you, pour everything into it.

5. **Use Every Interaction as a Learning Opportunity**
   - ○ Every time a manipulator tries their tricks, it's a chance to refine your boundaries, strengthen your resilience, and level up your emotional intelligence.
   - ○ *What to think*: "You're not breaking me—you're making me smarter."

Signs You're Growing Out of Their Reach

- **You Don't React**: Their old tactics don't even phase you anymore.
- **You Feel Lighter**: Cutting ties with manipulators and choosing growth makes you feel freer than ever.
- **They Stop Trying**: Eventually, they realize you're not coming back to their level—and it kills them.

Examples of Long-Term Growth in Action

- **When They Try to Pull You Back**:
  - ○ *Them*: "You've changed—you're not the same person anymore!"
  - ○ *You*: "You're right. I grew up." Translation: "And you're still the same manipulative jerk."
- **When They Test Your Boundaries**:
  - ○ *Them*: "Can't you just do this one thing for me?"
  - ○ *You*: "No, that doesn't work for me." Translation: "I'm not your doormat, so stop asking."
- **When They Play the Victim**:
  - ○ *Them*: "I guess I don't matter to you anymore."
  - ○ *You*: "That's not my responsibility." Translation: "Nice guilt trip. Not buying it."

The Bottom Line

Long-term growth is the ultimate revenge against manipulators. While they stay stuck in their same tired games, you're out here thriving, achieving, and building a life they'll never touch.

Emotional intelligence isn't just your shield—it's your launchpad to a better future. So let them stew in their mediocrity while you soar past them, untouchable, unstoppable, and completely unbothered. Growth isn't just about getting better—it's about leaving their toxic asses in the dust.

Types of Two Faced People You Will Meet

1. The Vindictive Ex-Wife

Psych Analysis

The vindictive ex-wife isn't just bitter—she's a goddamn expert in weaponizing bitterness. To the outside world, she's the poor, innocent victim who somehow survived your "tyranny," but behind the scenes? She's playing puppet master, pulling strings to ruin your life one petty move at a time. Her bread and butter is her two-faced nature: to everyone else, she's the fragile, wronged party; to you, she's a manipulative nightmare who won't stop until you're emotionally drained, financially ruined, or, hell, both.

Her real issue? Insecurity. She can't stand the fact that she's no longer relevant in your life, and losing control of you was the ultimate blow to her fragile ego. Every manipulative act she pulls is an attempt to claw her way back into the driver's seat of your life. Her favorite tools include lies, exaggerations, guilt trips, and outright sabotage. She's the kind of person who'll write a letter to your federal judge to "recommend" the maximum sentence, not because she believes in justice, but because watching you suffer is her twisted form of closure.

What She's Trying to Accomplish

Revenge. Plain and simple. She doesn't just want you to feel bad—she wants you to feel like you're losing at life. Her ultimate goal is to punish you for moving on, for being happy without her, or for existing at all. If she can ruin your reputation, alienate you from your kids, or fuck up your career, she'll consider that a job well done. But here's the real kicker: she doesn't just want you to fail—she wants everyone else to see you fail, so she can bask in the glow of her "victory."

Her biggest fear? Becoming irrelevant. That's why she clings to the drama like a lifeline. If she can't have you, she'll settle for being the villain in your story, because at least that keeps her in the narrative.

How to Shut It Down

1. **Go No Contact (When Possible)**
   - If you don't have kids or shared responsibilities, cut her off completely. No phone calls, no texts, no "accidental" run-ins. Block her on every platform and make it clear that she no longer has a place in your life.
   - *Why It Works*: She can't manipulate what she can't access. Taking away her connection to you is like ripping the batteries out of her chaos machine.
2. **Document Every Damn Thing**
   - Keep meticulous records of every interaction. Emails, texts, voicemails, screenshots—save it all. Vindictive ex-wives love rewriting history, so having receipts is your best defense when her bullshit inevitably escalates.
   - *Why It Works*: Two-faced manipulators hate hard evidence. It's like holding up a mirror to their lies, and they can't stand the reflection.
3. **Control the Narrative**
   - Don't let her control how others see you. If she's spreading lies, get ahead of it. Be honest with your inner circle about her manipulative behavior so they know what's really going on.
   - *Example*: "Hey, just a heads-up—Roslyn's been saying some things about me that aren't true. I wanted to set the record straight so you're not blindsided."

    ○ *Why It Works*: People are less likely to fall for her sob stories if they already know the truth.

4. **Lawyer Up**
   ○ If she's meddling in legal matters—custody battles, alimony disputes, or slandering you in court—get a damn good lawyer. Don't try to reason with her; let the professionals handle it.
   ○ *Why It Works*: Judges care about evidence, not theatrics. Your lawyer will cut through her drama and keep the focus where it belongs.

5. **Don't Engage with the Crazy**
   ○ She thrives on your reactions. If she can get under your skin, she wins. Stay calm, stay quiet, and don't let her bullshit drag you into an emotional spiral.
   ○ *Why It Works*: Without your reactions to fuel her, she loses her power.

Closing Thoughts on the Vindictive Ex-Wife
The vindictive ex-wife is the ultimate two-faced manipulator, a master at playing the victim while orchestrating your destruction behind the scenes. But here's the thing—she's predictable. Once you recognize her patterns, you can dismantle her tactics piece by piece. Cut her off, document everything, and refuse to give her the emotional reactions she's desperate for. Let her stew in her own bitterness while you move on with your life. Her chaos might feel like a hurricane, but when you stop feeding it, it fizzles into nothing. The best revenge? Thriving in a life she no longer has the power to ruin.

2. The Gossiping Coworker

Psych Analysis
The gossiping coworker is the office's own self-appointed chaos coordinator. They're not just annoying—they're dangerous. These two-faced bastards thrive on spreading half-truths, exaggerations, and outright lies to anyone who'll listen. To your face, they're all smiles, nodding along as if they're your biggest supporter. But the

second you leave the room, they're whispering shit to the boss, twisting your words, and planting seeds of doubt about your competence. Why? Because they can't shine on their own, so they dim everyone else's light to make themselves look brighter.

At their core, these people are riddled with insecurity. They know they're mediocre at best, so they rely on manipulation to stay relevant. Gossip isn't just idle chatter for them—it's a weapon, a way to control the narrative and keep themselves at the center of the drama. Their biggest fear? Being irrelevant. Their second biggest fear? Being exposed for the frauds they really are.

What They're Trying to Accomplish
The gossiping coworker's primary goal is to climb the ladder by tearing you down. They don't want to be the best; they just want you to look worse. By spreading rumors and twisting facts, they create a smokescreen that hides their own incompetence while making you look like the office villain. They're sucking up to the boss, playing the victim to colleagues, and pretending to be your friend—all at the same damn time.

Their dream scenario? You take the fall for something they started while they swoop in to "save the day" and soak up the glory. Bonus points if they can make you question your own abilities in the process.

How to Shut It Down

1. **Starve Their Gossip Machine**
   - Keep conversations strictly professional. No personal stories, no office complaints, no comments about your workload. Even a harmless "This week's been tough" can turn into "They're overwhelmed and can't handle the job."
   - *Why It Works*: They can't twist your words if you don't give them anything to work with.

2. **Document Their Bullshit**
   - Gossiping coworkers rely on verbal manipulation, but documentation is their kryptonite. Keep a record of every project, decision, and task you're responsible for. When they try to spin a story about you, pull out the receipts.
   - *Why It Works*: A paper trail destroys their credibility. They can't argue with hard evidence, no matter how much they try to squirm.
3. **Call Them Out in Public**
   - When you hear they've been spreading rumors, confront them calmly but firmly—preferably in front of others.
   - *Example*: "Hey, I heard you mentioned [insert gossip here]. Can you clarify where that came from?" Watch them stumble over their excuses.
   - *Why It Works*: Two-faced manipulators hate being exposed. Public accountability is their worst nightmare.
4. **Build Relationships with Decision-Makers**
   - Don't let the gossiping coworker control the narrative. Keep your boss and key colleagues updated on your work directly. Share your wins, document your progress, and make sure the right people know what you're contributing.
   - *Why It Works*: When the truth about you is already out there, their lies won't stick.
5. **Deflect Their Drama**
   - When they try to gossip with you, shut it down immediately.
   - *Example*: "Interesting. Have you spoken to them directly about that?" or "I'd rather not get involved in office drama."
   - *Why It Works*: They'll avoid you when they realize you're not a willing audience for their bullshit.

Closing Thoughts on the Gossiping Coworker

The gossiping coworker is a parasite feeding off office chaos. They smile to your face, stab you in the back, and act like they're doing everyone a favor by "sharing the truth." But here's the thing—they're not as clever as they think they are. Once you stop giving them ammunition, document your work, and call them out strategically, their power evaporates. While they're busy spreading bullshit, you'll be outshining them at every turn. The best part? Watching their two-faced grin disappear when they realize they've lost control of the narrative. Let them choke on their own lies while you rise above their nonsense.

3. The Jealous Sibling

Psych Analysis

Ah, the jealous sibling—a walking bundle of insecurity wrapped in fake smiles and passive-aggressive digs. These two-faced bastards have been stewing in resentment ever since you beat them in a game of Monopoly when you were eight. They're not just envious of your success—they're *offended* by it. Every achievement you've ever had feels like a personal insult to them, and their life's mission is to drag you down to their miserable level.

To your face, they'll say things like, "Wow, you've really done well for yourself," while behind your back, they're telling the family, "Well, you know they only got where they are because they got lucky." They'll hijack your dad's Facebook account to post passive-aggressive bullshit, pretend to be your biggest fan at family dinners, and then twist every word you say into something toxic when you're not around. Why? Because they're terrified of being overshadowed. Their biggest fear is that no one notices them anymore, and your success is the blinding spotlight they'll do anything to dim.

What They're Trying to Accomplish

This sibling isn't interested in personal growth—they're interested in dragging you through the mud. Their ultimate goal is to level the playing field, not by working harder or achieving more but by making sure you look like a failure in front of the people who matter most.

If they can plant seeds of doubt in the family, make others question your integrity, or sabotage your reputation, they'll consider it a win. Their dream scenario? Everyone turns on you, and they get to sit back and bask in the glow of finally being the "good one" for once in their pathetic life.

How to Shut It Down

1. **Refuse to Play the Game**
   - Jealous siblings thrive on competition. They want you to feel like you have to prove yourself, to engage in their petty tit-for-tat nonsense. Don't. The best response to their bullshit is calm indifference.
   - *What to Say*: "I'm happy with where I'm at, but thanks for your concern." Watch them squirm when you refuse to take the bait.

2. **Expose Their Two-Faced Behavior**
   - When they trash you to other family members, address it head-on. Calmly, directly, and preferably in front of others.
   - *Example*: "Hey, I heard you told Mom I only got my promotion because I kissed ass. If you have a problem with me, let's talk about it here."
   - *Why It Works*: Two-faced manipulators hate being confronted. They rely on operating in the shadows, and dragging their nonsense into the light shuts them down fast.

3. **Set Boundaries Like a Boss**
   - Limit how much access they have to your life. Don't share your plans, your struggles, or your wins with them. Treat them like a nosy neighbor who doesn't need to know what's going on behind your front door.
   - *Why It Works*: If they don't know what's happening in your life, they can't twist it into a weapon against you.

4. **Don't Engage with Their Drama**
    - If they hijack your dad's Facebook to post some passive-aggressive crap about you, don't respond publicly. That's exactly what they want. Instead, address it offline.
    - *What to Say*: "If you have something to say about me, do it directly. Leave Dad out of it."
    - *Why It Works*: You're taking the high road while making them look childish and desperate.
5. **Strengthen Relationships That Matter**
    - Jealous siblings love to isolate you from the family by poisoning your relationships. Don't let them. Build strong, direct connections with the people who matter—parents, siblings, or anyone they're trying to manipulate.
    - *Why It Works*: When your family already knows the truth about you, your jealous sibling's lies won't stand a chance.

Closing Thoughts on the Jealous Sibling
The jealous sibling is the ultimate two-faced family member—pretending to root for you while secretly working overtime to bring you down. They're petty, toxic, and exhausting, but they're also predictable. Once you stop engaging with their nonsense, expose their manipulative behavior, and set ironclad boundaries, their power crumbles. The best revenge? Living your life so well that their jealousy becomes irrelevant. Let them seethe in their own insecurities while you thrive, unbothered and untouchable. Family or not, no one gets a free pass to drag you down

4. The Shady Business Partner

Psych Analysis
The shady business partner is the corporate version of a snake in a suit. They shake your hand with one goal in mind: figuring out how to screw you over while smiling in your face. They're two-faced to the core, pretending to be your ally while secretly cutting side deals,

stealing your ideas, and setting you up to take the fall when shit inevitably hits the fan.

What drives them? Insecurity and greed. They don't believe they have the talent, intelligence, or creativity to succeed on their own, so they latch onto people like you to do the hard work. Their biggest fear is being exposed as the fraud they are, which is why they bury their tracks in deception and spin. They'll act like your biggest cheerleader in meetings but spend their free time figuring out how to turn your successes into their gain.

What They're Trying to Accomplish
The shady business partner's goal is simple: profit at your expense. Whether it's financial gain, credit for your ideas, or positioning themselves as the "star" of the team, they want the rewards without putting in the work. Bonus points if they can shift any blame onto you when things go wrong.

Their dream scenario? You bust your ass to close the deal, and they walk away with the accolades, the promotion, or the money. If they can make you look incompetent or unreliable in the process, even better— they'll solidify themselves as the hero while leaving you in the dust.

How to Shut It Down

1. **Document Everything**
    ○ Treat every agreement, decision, and conversation like a potential court case. Get it in writing—emails, contracts, meeting notes, even text messages. If they try to twist the narrative, you'll have the proof to shut them down.
    ○ *Why It Works*: Shady partners rely on verbal manipulation and plausible deniability. Hard evidence destroys their ability to rewrite history.
2. **Watch for Red Flags**
    ○ Are they evasive when it comes to sharing details? Overly secretive about certain aspects of the

business? Quick to deflect blame? These are all signs they're up to something shady. Trust your gut—if it feels off, it probably is.

- *Example*: If they say, "Don't worry about it; I've got it covered," what they really mean is, "I'm hiding something, and I don't want you to ask questions."

3. **Protect Your Intellectual Property**
   - If you're bringing ideas, strategies, or innovation to the table, make damn sure you're the one who owns them. Trademark your concepts, keep personal copies of your work, and don't share more than necessary.
   - *Why It Works*: They can't steal what's locked down.

4. **Control the Narrative**
   - Build strong relationships with key stakeholders—clients, investors, or other team members. Make sure your contributions are known so your shady partner can't claim credit for your work.
   - *What to Say*: "I'm excited about the progress we've made on this project. Here's what I've been focusing on..." Subtle, but effective.

5. **Confront Them Strategically**
   - If you catch them in a lie or shady behavior, don't blow up on the spot. Gather evidence, stay calm, and confront them in a controlled environment.
   - *What to Say*: "I noticed some discrepancies with [specific issue]. Can you explain what's going on?" Watch as they scramble to justify themselves.
   - *Why It Works*: They rely on emotional reactions to derail the conversation. Staying calm forces them to deal with facts.

6. **Exit When Necessary**
   - If their behavior becomes toxic or damaging, start planning your exit. Shady partners don't change, and staying in the relationship will only drag you down. Protect yourself, protect your assets, and get the hell out.

Closing Thoughts on the Shady Business Partner

The shady business partner is a two-faced parasite, thriving on your hard work while plotting your downfall behind closed doors. They're greedy, manipulative, and utterly devoid of loyalty, but they're also predictable. Once you recognize their patterns—secrecy, blame-shifting, and credit-stealing—you can outmaneuver them at every turn. Document everything, protect what's yours, and don't be afraid to walk away when the time comes. Let them drown in their own deception while you build success they'll never be able to touch. In the end, the best revenge is thriving without them.

5. The Overbearing Parent

Psych Analysis

The overbearing parent is a master of two-faced manipulation disguised as "love." They'll say, "I'm only doing this because I care," while they bulldoze through your boundaries like a goddamn wrecking ball. Their favorite tools? Guilt trips, unsolicited advice, and a constant reminder of all the "sacrifices" they made for you—like raising you was some heroic feat and not, you know, their responsibility as a parent.

At their core, these parents are control freaks. They're terrified of becoming irrelevant in your life, and the thought of you making decisions without consulting them sends them into a tailspin. They see your independence as a threat because it means they're no longer running the show. Their need to meddle isn't about helping you—it's about keeping you tethered to them, ensuring they remain the central figure in your life.

What They're Trying to Accomplish

The overbearing parent wants to maintain control. They can't handle the idea of you making decisions on your own because it means they're no longer needed. By constantly inserting themselves into your life, they create a sense of dependence that keeps them in power. Their ideal scenario? You consult them on everything, from your career to your relationships to what kind of toothpaste to buy.

But it's not just about control—it's also about ego. They want to feel important, relevant, and indispensable. Their biggest fear? That you'll stop needing them, move on, and build a life where they're nothing more than a side character.

How to Shut It Down

1. **Set Boundaries Like a Steel Wall**
   - Be clear, firm, and consistent. If they're constantly prying into your personal life, tell them straight up: "I appreciate your concern, but I'm handling this on my own." No wiggle room, no exceptions.
   - *What to Say*: "I love you, but I need to make my own decisions. Please respect that."
   - *Why It Works*: Overbearing parents rely on blurred boundaries. Clarity makes it harder for them to overstep.

2. **Limit Their Access to Information**
   - Stop oversharing. The less they know about your plans, the less they can meddle. Treat them like you would a nosy coworker—keep it polite but surface-level.
   - *Example*: Instead of telling them about your new job before you've even signed the contract, wait until it's a done deal.
   - *Why It Works*: They can't control what they're not aware of.

3. **Anticipate the Guilt Trips**
   - Overbearing parents love to weaponize guilt: "After everything I've done for you..." or "If it weren't for me, you wouldn't be where you are." Recognize this tactic for what it is—emotional manipulation—and refuse to engage.
   - *What to Say*: "I appreciate everything you've done, but that doesn't mean I can't make my own choices now."
   - *Why It Works*: You're acknowledging their effort without letting them use it as leverage.

4. **Stick to Your Decisions**
   - Once you've set a boundary or made a choice, stand your ground. Don't let their constant nagging wear you down.
   - *Example*: If they push back on a decision, repeat yourself without getting emotional: "I've already decided. Let's move on."
   - *Why It Works*: Consistency shuts down their attempts to argue or guilt you into changing your mind.
5. **Distance Yourself If Necessary**
   - If they refuse to respect your boundaries, it's okay to take a step back. Limiting contact doesn't mean you don't love them—it means you value your peace of mind.
   - *What to Do*: Start small—skip a call or visit here and there. If they escalate, consider reducing contact even further.
   - *Why It Works*: Distance creates space for them to reflect on their behavior and gives you room to breathe.

Closing Thoughts on the Overbearing Parent

The overbearing parent is a master of two-faced manipulation, cloaking their need for control in the guise of love and concern. But here's the truth: love doesn't mean crossing boundaries, and concern doesn't justify emotional sabotage. The key to dealing with them is standing firm—set boundaries, limit their access, and don't fall for their guilt trips. Let them stew in their frustration while you focus on building a life that's yours, not theirs. At the end of the day, your independence isn't a rejection of their love; it's a testament to their success as a parent. They'll figure that out eventually—or they won't. Either way, you're in control now.

6. The Manipulative Friend

Psych Analysis

The manipulative friend is a wolf in sheep's clothing, the kind of two-faced piece of shit who smiles in your face while plotting behind your back. They're not just in your life to support you—they're there to extract as much benefit as possible while giving you the bare minimum in return. Need a shoulder to cry on? Sure, they'll listen—until they turn around and tell everyone about your "issues." They pretend to celebrate your wins but secretly root for your failure because your success is a reminder of how little they've accomplished.

What drives them? Jealousy and insecurity. They can't handle the idea of you outshining them, but instead of working on themselves, they'd rather drag you down to their level. They use manipulation—guilt-tripping, emotional blackmail, and subtle gaslighting—to keep you in their orbit while making sure you're never quite happy or confident enough to realize you deserve better.

What They're Trying to Accomplish
The manipulative friend's main goal is control. They want to be the puppet master in your life, deciding how much attention, success, and happiness you're allowed to have. They thrive on creating dependency, making you feel like you need them, even when they're the root of your problems.

Their dream scenario? You rely on them for advice, support, and validation, all while they quietly sabotage you behind the scenes. If they can make themselves look like the hero while subtly undermining your confidence, they'll consider that a win.

How to Shut It Down

1. **Test Their Loyalty**
   - Share something minor but fake and see what happens. If it comes back to you from someone else, you've got your answer: they're a snake.
   - *Example*: Tell them you're thinking about quitting your job when you're not. If your boss pulls you aside a week later, congratulations—you've caught them red-handed.

    ○ *Why It Works*: Manipulative friends can't resist the urge to gossip. Once they're exposed, their credibility takes a nosedive.

2. **Set Clear Boundaries**
    ○ Manipulative friends love to blur lines. Be direct and unapologetic when setting boundaries: "I don't feel comfortable discussing this," or "I need some space right now."
    ○ *Why It Works*: Boundaries are kryptonite to people who rely on emotional manipulation.

3. **Stop Feeding Their Ego**
    ○ Don't give them the validation they crave. If they fish for compliments or try to guilt-trip you, shut it down.
    ○ *What to Say*: "Why do you feel the need to compete with me? This isn't a contest."
    ○ *Why It Works*: Calling out their behavior forces them to confront their insecurities, which they hate.

4. **Limit Your Vulnerability**
    ○ Be careful what you share. The less they know about your struggles and plans, the less they can use against you.
    ○ *Example*: If you're going through a tough time, confide in someone you trust implicitly—not the manipulative friend who's likely to weaponize your pain.
    ○ *Why It Works*: They can't manipulate what they don't know.

5. **Call Out Their Bullshit**
    ○ When they try to guilt-trip or gaslight you, don't let it slide. Call them out calmly and directly: "That's not how it happened, and you know it."
    ○ *Why It Works*: Manipulative friends rely on subtlety. Exposing their tactics forces them into the spotlight, where they can't operate as easily.

6. **Cut Them Loose**
    ○ If they refuse to change or their manipulation becomes toxic, it's time to walk away. Manipulative friends don't deserve unlimited chances.

- *What to Do*: Gradually reduce contact or have a direct conversation about why the friendship isn't working.
- *Why It Works*: They can't control you if they're not in your life.

Closing Thoughts on the Manipulative Friend

The manipulative friend is a master of two-faced fuckery, pretending to have your back while sticking the knife in when you're not looking. They're toxic, exhausting, and ultimately not worth the energy. The best way to handle them? Expose their lies, set firm boundaries, and, when necessary, cut them out of your life completely. True friends lift you up—manipulative friends pull you down. Know the difference, and don't be afraid to walk away from anyone who doesn't add value to your life. Let them stew in their insecurity while you move forward, stronger, smarter, and free from their bullshit.

7. The Victim Player

Psych Analysis

The victim player is a professional martyr, a two-faced manipulative master of woe-is-me bullshit. To everyone else, they're a poor, misunderstood soul who "just can't catch a break." Behind the scenes, though, they're a scheming emotional vampire who thrives on guilt, pity, and attention. They'll spin every situation to make themselves look like the victim, even when they're the ones who started the damn fire.

Their biggest weapon is their sob story—endless tales of betrayal, hardship, and injustice, all conveniently designed to make you feel like you *owe* them something. And if you dare call them out? Prepare for the waterworks and the classic "I can't believe you'd say that to me" routine. At their core, they're terrified of accountability. Blaming themselves is never an option, so they project their failures, insecurities, and shortcomings onto everyone else.

What They're Trying to Accomplish

The victim player has one goal: control through guilt. They want you to feel responsible for their problems so they can manipulate you into fixing their mess, giving them sympathy, or excusing their bad behavior. Their dream scenario? You bend over backward trying to "help" them while they sit back and play the helpless, wounded hero. They'll suck the life out of you with their constant "poor me" routine, all while making you feel like the bad guy for wanting to step away.

How to Shut It Down

1. **Refuse to Feed the Guilt Machine**
   - Victim players rely on guilt to manipulate you. Don't let them twist your emotions into a weapon against you.
   - *What to Say*: "I'm sorry you're going through that, but I'm not in a position to help."
   - *Why It Works*: You're acknowledging their feelings without taking responsibility for their problems.

2. **Call Out Their Patterns**
   - When they pull the victim card repeatedly, point it out.
   - *What to Say*: "You always seem to be the victim in every situation. Have you thought about why that keeps happening?"
   - *Why It Works*: Shining a light on their behavior forces them to confront their own role in their problems.

3. **Set Boundaries Without Apology**
   - Don't let them drain your time, energy, or resources. Make it clear what you're willing to do—and what you're not.
   - *What to Say*: "I care about you, but I can't keep getting involved in these situations."
   - *Why It Works*: Boundaries cut off their ability to make you their emotional crutch.

4. **Redirect the Responsibility**
   - Victim players hate accountability, so redirect the conversation back to them.
   - *What to Say*: "That sounds tough. What do you think you can do to fix it?"

- o *Why It Works*: It puts the responsibility where it belongs—on them.
5. **Distance Yourself If Needed**
    - o If they refuse to change or keep dragging you into their pity party, it's time to step back.
    - o *What to Do*: Gradually reduce contact and make your boundaries non-negotiable.
    - o *Why It Works*: You're protecting your peace while forcing them to find a new target for their manipulative games.

Closing Thoughts on the Victim Player

The victim player is the ultimate two-faced manipulator—an emotional leech who thrives on pity while quietly pulling the strings. They're exhausting, toxic, and downright infuriating, but they're also predictable. Once you stop feeding their guilt trips and redirect responsibility back onto them, their power disappears. Don't let their sob stories suck you into their drama. True strength isn't about fixing their mess—it's about refusing to carry their baggage. Let them stew in their self-made misery while you focus on living your best, drama-free life.

8. The Opportunistic Stranger

Psych Analysis

The opportunistic stranger is the ultimate two-faced wildcard—a snake in disguise who sees every interaction as a chance to take advantage of someone naïve enough to fall for their bullshit. They're not your friend, your ally, or even a decent human being—they're a manipulative opportunist who sizes you up like a target at a carnival game. They'll flash a fake smile, pretend they're "just trying to help," and wait for the perfect moment to strike.

What drives them? Greed and self-interest. They don't care who they hurt or how much damage they cause, as long as they walk away with whatever it is they're after—your money, your time, your connections, or your trust. Their biggest fear? Being exposed for the lying, manipulative piece of shit they really are.

What They're Trying to Accomplish

The opportunistic stranger doesn't want a relationship; they want a transaction. Their goal is to get something out of you before you realize you've been played. Maybe they're angling for cash with a sob story about needing gas money, or they're trying to use your connections to boost their status. Whatever the case, they're all about taking and never giving. Their dream scenario? You fall for their act, hand over what they want, and only realize you've been screwed when they're long gone.

How to Shut It Down

1. **Question Their Intentions**
   - Opportunists rely on you not asking questions. The second you start digging deeper, their carefully constructed act starts to crumble.
   - *What to Say*: "Why do you need me to help with this? What have you tried on your own?"
   - *Why It Works*: They hate being put on the spot. The more you question them, the harder it is for them to keep up their facade.

2. **Trust Your Gut**
   - If something feels off, it probably is. Opportunistic strangers are pros at masking their intentions, but your instincts will often pick up on their bullshit before your brain does.
   - *What to Do*: If they're oversharing personal details, being overly friendly, or trying too hard to get you to say "yes," step back and assess.

3. **Don't Engage Emotionally**
   - These manipulators love to play on your emotions—sympathy, guilt, or even flattery. Refuse to bite.
   - *What to Say*: "I'm sorry, but I'm not in a position to help."
   - *Why It Works*: Shutting them down without emotion leaves them with nothing to latch onto.

4. **Protect Your Resources**
   o Don't hand over money, personal details, or favors without vetting their story first. Opportunists thrive on urgency, so slow the situation down and do your due diligence.
   o *What to Say*: "Let me think about it and get back to you." (Translation: I'm not falling for your scam.)
   o *Why It Works*: It gives you time to verify their intentions—or let them disappear when they realize you're not an easy target.
5. **Call Them Out (If Needed)**
   o If their bullshit becomes obvious, don't be afraid to confront them.
   o *What to Say*: "This feels like a scam. Care to explain yourself?"
   o *Why It Works*: Opportunists hate being exposed. A direct confrontation is often enough to send them running.

Closing Thoughts on the Opportunistic Stranger
The opportunistic stranger is a two-faced scavenger, prowling for the next person dumb enough to believe their act. They're not just manipulative—they're shameless. But here's the thing: their game only works if you let it. Question their motives, protect your resources, and refuse to play into their sob stories or flattery. Once they see you're not an easy mark, they'll move on to someone else. Let them. You've got better things to do than deal with their pathetic hustle.

9. The Passive-Aggressive Colleague

Psych Analysis
The passive-aggressive colleague is the ultimate two-faced professional, a backhanded manipulator who specializes in subtle sabotage. They're the ones who smile sweetly during meetings, nod along with your ideas, and then casually throw you under the bus with a well-timed, "I just think maybe we should revisit that

approach." They don't have the guts to confront you outright, so they let their little barbs, veiled insults, and "helpful" suggestions do the dirty work.

At their core, passive-aggressive colleagues are cowards. They thrive on control but don't have the backbone to demand it directly. Instead, they undermine you in sneaky, underhanded ways to make themselves look better. Their biggest fear? Being called out. These manipulators rely on plausible deniability, so the thought of having their behavior exposed terrifies them.

What They're Trying to Accomplish
The passive-aggressive colleague wants to make themselves look good at your expense. They're not outright competitors—they're subtle saboteurs, using fake politeness and passive digs to chip away at your confidence and credibility. Their dream scenario? They plant enough doubt about you in the minds of your boss or team that you're sidelined while they quietly take credit for your hard work.

How to Shut It Down

1. **Spot the Subtle Digs**
   - These assholes are masters of phrases like, "I thought you'd want to know..." or "I was just trying to help." Learn to recognize their trademark moves: vague critiques, backhanded compliments, or sudden "concerns" about your work.
   - *What to Do*: Write down their comments and note the context. Patterns will emerge, and you'll be ready to counter them when it counts.
2. **Confront Them Directly (But Calmly)**
   - They rely on their passive-aggressive tactics going unchallenged. Call them out—firmly, calmly, and with no room for them to wiggle away.
   - *What to Say*: "I noticed you brought up some concerns about my project in the meeting. Can you explain what you meant?"

- ○ *Why It Works*: They hate direct confrontation. It forces them to either explain their behavior or admit they were stirring the pot.

3. **Document Their Bullshit**
   - ○ Keep a record of any passive-aggressive comments or actions, especially if they happen in meetings, emails, or collaborative work.
   - ○ *Example*: When they "forget" to include you in an important email chain or make subtle jabs during a presentation, jot it down.
   - ○ *Why It Works*: If their behavior escalates, you'll have evidence to back up your claims when you address it with higher-ups.

4. **Control the Narrative**
   - ○ Passive-aggressive colleagues love whisper campaigns, so get ahead of them by being open and proactive about your work. Keep your boss and team updated on your progress so there's no room for doubt.
   - ○ *What to Do*: Send regular updates on your projects, cc'ing key stakeholders. Make your contributions impossible to ignore.
   - ○ *Why It Works*: When everyone knows exactly what you're doing, their little digs won't stick.

5. **Use Their Tactics Against Them**
   - ○ Fight fire with fire—respond to their passive-aggressive behavior with sharp, pointed sarcasm that exposes their nonsense.
   - ○ *What to Say*:
     - ■ When they say, "I just assumed you already knew that," reply with, "Thanks for assuming—next time, just let me know directly."
     - ■ If they say, "I was just trying to help," hit them with, "Great! Next time, try asking before stepping in."

- ○ *Why It Works*: It flips the script and forces them to deal with your directness.
6. **Involve Higher-Ups if Necessary**
   - ○ If their behavior becomes disruptive or toxic, don't hesitate to escalate. Present your evidence calmly and professionally to your boss or HR.
   - ○ *What to Say*: "I've noticed a pattern of undermining comments from [Colleague's Name]. Here's what I've documented, and I'd like to address it before it affects team dynamics further."
   - ○ *Why It Works*: Formal intervention sends a clear message: their bullshit won't be tolerated.

Closing Thoughts on the Passive-Aggressive Colleague
The passive-aggressive colleague is a sneaky, two-faced pain in the ass who hides their manipulation behind a mask of politeness. They rely on their tactics going unnoticed, but once you expose their behavior, their power disappears. The key is to confront them calmly, document their nonsense, and make sure your contributions are front and center. Let them choke on their fake smiles while you outshine them with competence and confidence. They'll hate it—and you'll love every second.

10. The Charismatic Liar

Psych Analysis
The charismatic liar is a two-faced manipulative showman who could charm the pants off a mannequin. They're magnetic, smooth-talking, and utterly full of shit. To your face, they're dazzling, funny, and oh-so-relatable—spinning stories so perfectly crafted you'll feel like the idiot for doubting them. But beneath the charisma? They're a pathological liar who sees honesty as optional, loyalty as negotiable, and truth as whatever serves their agenda.

Their power lies in their confidence. They don't just lie; they sell their lies like they're pitching the next billion-dollar idea on Shark Tank. People believe them because they *want* to, and that's their secret weapon. The charismatic liar thrives on your trust, exploiting it to build their image while quietly dismantling yours. Their biggest fear? Getting caught. Their charm is their armor, and once it cracks, their entire facade crumbles.

What They're Trying to Accomplish

The charismatic liar doesn't just want to win—they want to dominate. Their goal is to control how they're perceived by others while manipulating you into doubting yourself. They'll steal credit for your work, twist facts to make you look bad, and craft elaborate lies to position themselves as the hero of every story.

Their dream scenario? Everyone loves and admires them while you're left cleaning up the mess they created. If they can manipulate you into questioning your own version of events, that's just icing on the cake. They don't just lie to win—they lie to erase your credibility and keep themselves in the spotlight.

How to Shut It Down

1. **Fact-Check Their Bullshit**
   - Charismatic liars rely on people taking them at their word. The easiest way to disarm them is to verify everything they say.
   - *What to Do*: If they claim credit for an idea, ask for specifics: "That's interesting—can you explain how you came up with that?" If they dodge, you've caught them.
   - *Why It Works*: Lies unravel under scrutiny, and they hate being pinned down.
2. **Document Everything**
   - These manipulators are slippery as hell, so keep records of every conversation, agreement, and decision.
   - *Example*: After a meeting, send a follow-up email summarizing what was discussed and agreed

upon. That way, when they inevitably try to rewrite history, you have proof.

- *Why It Works*: Hard evidence destroys their ability to spin the narrative.

3. **Call Out Their Contradictions**
   - Charismatic liars thrive on consistency, so when their stories don't add up, expose the gaps.
   - *What to Say*: "Didn't you say last week that the client requested something different? Which version is accurate?"
   - *Why It Works*: It forces them to explain themselves publicly, which they're not prepared for.

4. **Build a Network of Allies**
   - Don't let their charm isolate you from the team or group. Share your concerns with trusted colleagues and keep them informed about your work and contributions.
   - *Why It Works*: When others know the truth, the liar's influence weakens.

5. **Refuse to Engage in Their Drama**
   - When they try to manipulate you with flattery, guilt, or elaborate stories, shut it down.
   - *What to Say*: "That's an interesting perspective. Let's stick to the facts and focus on what's next."
   - *Why It Works*: You're deflecting their charm and forcing the conversation back to reality.

6. **Expose Them (When Necessary)**
   - If their lies are causing harm, don't hesitate to confront them with evidence in a calm but firm manner.
   - *What to Say*: "I've noticed some discrepancies in what you've been saying about [specific topic]. Can we address this?"
   - *Why It Works*: Public exposure is their kryptonite. Their charm won't save them when the facts are staring them in the face.

Closing Thoughts on the Charismatic Liar

The charismatic liar is a dangerous two-faced manipulator who weaponizes charm to control the narrative and undermine everyone around them. But here's the secret: their charm only works if you let it. Once you start questioning their stories, documenting their lies, and refusing to play along, their facade cracks faster than cheap glass. Let them drown in their own contradictions while you stay grounded in the truth. Remember, confidence doesn't equal credibility, and charisma is no match for cold, hard facts.

11. The Sabotaging Mentor

Psych Analysis

The sabotaging mentor is the ultimate two-faced manipulator, hiding their destructive intentions behind a facade of guidance and wisdom. They position themselves as the generous teacher, the experienced guru who *just wants to help you succeed*. But in reality? They're plotting your downfall while patting you on the back. Their playbook includes withholding critical information, giving you advice designed to make you fail, and taking credit for your successes while magnifying your mistakes.

What drives them? Fear and ego. They see you as a threat, someone who might one day outshine them, and that terrifies them to their very core. Instead of lifting you up like a true mentor, they prefer to keep you under their thumb, ensuring you'll never reach their level—or worse, surpass it. Their biggest fear? Watching you succeed without them, leaving their manipulative ass in the dust.

What They're Trying to Accomplish

The sabotaging mentor wants to maintain control and protect their position at all costs. They want to be seen as the all-knowing authority, the indispensable figure whose "help" is essential to your success. If they can keep you doubting yourself, dependent on their guidance, and failing just enough to stay below their level, they've won.

Their dream scenario? You remain perpetually stuck in a cycle of seeking their approval, never quite succeeding, and always needing their "help" to move forward. Meanwhile, they sit back, basking in the glow of their supposed wisdom and watching you spin your wheels.

How to Shut It Down

1. **Trust, But Verify**
   - Don't take their advice at face value. Cross-check what they tell you with other sources, whether it's colleagues, industry best practices, or just plain common sense.
   - *What to Say*: "That's an interesting suggestion. I'll do some research to make sure I'm covering all my bases."
   - *Why It Works*: It sends a clear message: you're not blindly trusting them, and you're willing to fact-check their guidance.
2. **Keep Your Plans Close**
   - Don't give them a play-by-play of your ideas or strategies. Share only what's absolutely necessary and keep the rest to yourself.
   - *What to Do*: If they ask for details, be vague: "I'm still refining my approach, but I'll share when it's ready."
   - *Why It Works*: They can't sabotage what they don't fully understand.
3. **Document Your Work**
   - Sabotaging mentors love to take credit for your successes and blame you for failures. Keep meticulous records of your contributions, decisions, and progress.
   - *What to Do*: Follow up every conversation or meeting with a summary email: "Thanks for the input today. Here's what I'll be focusing on…"

○ *Why It Works*: It creates a paper trail that protects your work and makes it harder for them to rewrite history.

4. **Build a Support Network**
   ○ Don't rely solely on this person for guidance or feedback. Seek out advice from other mentors, peers, or trusted colleagues who aren't threatened by your success.
   ○ *Why It Works*: A diverse network of support dilutes their influence and gives you alternative perspectives.

5. **Expose Their Sabotage**
   ○ If their manipulations become obvious, confront them calmly but firmly. Call out their behavior without letting them gaslight you into doubting yourself.
   ○ *What to Say*: "I noticed the advice you gave me on [specific issue] didn't align with the best practices I've researched. Can we clarify why that was suggested?"
   ○ *Why It Works*: Exposing their inconsistencies forces them to backpedal or admit they're not as helpful as they claim to be.

6. **Outgrow Them**
   ○ Ultimately, the best way to beat a sabotaging mentor is to surpass them. Focus on developing your skills, building your reputation, and succeeding on your own terms.
   ○ *What to Do*: Use their bullshit as motivation to prove you don't need their manipulative "help" to thrive.
   ○ *Why It Works*: Watching you succeed without them is their worst nightmare—and your ultimate revenge.

Closing Thoughts on the Sabotaging Mentor
The sabotaging mentor is a wolf in mentor's clothing, pretending to

guide you while secretly rooting for your failure. They're petty, insecure, and terrified of being left behind, which is why they'll do everything they can to keep you stuck. But here's the secret: their power lies in your trust. Once you start questioning their advice, documenting your progress, and building a support network outside of their influence, their manipulation falls apart. Let them stew in their own mediocrity while you rise above their bullshit. Nothing pisses off a sabotaging mentor more than watching you succeed without them—and that's exactly what you're going to do.

12. The Gaslighting Romantic Partner

Psych Analysis
The gaslighting romantic partner is the ultimate two-faced emotional terrorist. They're the charming, supportive lover one moment and the manipulative, reality-warping mindfuck the next. This isn't your average partner—they're a master of deception, using gaslighting to make you question your memories, your instincts, and eventually, your own damn sanity. They'll lie straight to your face, deny things you know happened, and twist every conversation until you're apologizing for shit they did.

What drives them? Control. They don't just want a relationship— they want dominance. Gaslighting gives them the upper hand, turning your confusion into their power. At their core, they're deeply insecure, terrified of being exposed as weak, unworthy, or replaceable. Their manipulation isn't about love; it's about maintaining control over you at any cost.

What They're Trying to Accomplish
The gaslighting romantic partner's goal is to rewrite reality. They want to be the authority in your life, the person who dictates how you see yourself and the world around you. By undermining your confidence and making you doubt your perceptions, they ensure you stay dependent on them. Their dream scenario? You're so tangled in their web of lies and emotional manipulation that you can't imagine life without them.

How to Shut It Down

1. **Trust Your Instincts**
   - Gaslighters thrive on making you doubt your gut. When something feels off, trust that feeling—it's your brain's way of telling you that their version of events doesn't add up.
   - *What to Do*: Write down what actually happened as soon as possible. Your own documentation will serve as a reality check when they try to twist things later.
   - *Why It Works*: You're taking back control of your narrative.

2. **Call Out the Manipulation**
   - When they deny, deflect, or twist the truth, call it what it is: gaslighting.
   - *What to Say*: "I know what I heard. Trying to make me doubt myself isn't going to work."
   - *Why It Works*: Naming their behavior takes away the power of their subtlety.

3. **Keep Evidence**
   - Gaslighters rely on your confusion to stay in control, so keep receipts. Screenshots, texts, emails—anything that proves your side of the story.
   - *What to Do*: If they deny saying something, pull up the proof: "Here's the text where you said that."
   - *Why It Works*: Hard evidence is the kryptonite to their lies.

4. **Set Boundaries with Consequences**
   - Don't just tell them to stop—make it clear what will happen if they don't.
   - *What to Say*: "If you keep trying to twist my words, this conversation is over."
   - *Why It Works*: Boundaries force them to change their behavior—or risk losing access to you.

5. **Stop Explaining Yourself**
   - Gaslighters love to drag you into endless arguments where they poke holes in your reality. Don't take the bait.

- ○ *What to Say*: "I'm not going to debate this. I know what's true."
- ○ *Why It Works*: Refusing to engage denies them the satisfaction of controlling the conversation.

6. **Get Support**
   - ○ Gaslighting thrives in isolation. Share your experiences with trusted friends or a therapist to get an outside perspective.
   - ○ *What to Do*: Say, "This is what's happening. Am I crazy, or is this manipulation?" Let them validate your reality.
   - ○ *Why It Works*: A strong support system keeps you grounded and makes it harder for the gaslighter to isolate you.

7. **Leave (If Necessary)**
   - ○ If the gaslighting continues despite your efforts, it's time to walk away. This isn't just about the relationship—it's about protecting your mental health.
   - ○ *What to Do*: Cut ties, block them, and focus on rebuilding your confidence.
   - ○ *Why It Works*: You're taking control of your life and refusing to be their victim anymore.

Closing Thoughts on the Gaslighting Romantic Partner
The gaslighting romantic partner is a master of emotional warfare, manipulating you until you don't know which way is up. But here's the thing: their power only works if you let it. By trusting your instincts, setting firm boundaries, and refusing to engage in their twisted games, you can take back control

Betrayal, Lies, & Two-Faced Parasites

Life teaches you a lot of lessons, but the biggest one? **Trust is a liability.** I've dealt with my fair share of backstabbers—family, exes, and so-called business partners who all had one thing in common: **jealousy, weakness, and an inability to stand on their own without trying to take me down in the process.**

The common denominator? **Weak men, fake women, and people who crumble when standing next to someone who actually knows how to win.**

I don't dwell on this bullshit, but I **never forget.** And if there's one lesson I've learned, it's this: **When someone shows you their true colors, believe them the first time.**

My Two-Faced Sibling

My Sister operates with a carefully crafted dual persona: the outward-facing version she presents to the world and the manipulative, self-serving reality beneath the surface. She has mastered the art of playing the victim while actively engaging in behavior that contradicts the image she wants others to see. Here's how she embodies the classic definition of a **two-faced** person:

1. The "Nicest Person in the World" Facade vs. The Manipulative Reality

My sister **loves to claim** she is the nicest, most beloved person around. She projects an image of kindness, generosity, and moral superiority. However, her actions tell a completely different story:

ART OF DEALING WITH TWO FACED PEOPLE

- **She hijacked my father's Facebook account** to post derogatory messages about me framing it as though he had done it. A genuinely "nice" person wouldn't manipulate family members for personal gain.
- **She rewrites history to suit her narrative,** pretending a random woman was responsible for her getting her home when, in reality, our father paid for it.
- **She meddles in others' grief,** making her ex-boyfriend's death about herself by contacting his widow repeatedly, disregarding boundaries, and centering herself in the widow's mourning process.

Her actions are self-serving and deceptive, designed to **control perception rather than reflect genuine kindness.**

2. Preaching Loyalty While Backstabbing Family

My sister acts as if she is the **pillar of family values,** but in reality, she actively **betrays, belittles, and undermines** her own relatives:

- When our **father had a heart attack**, she showed zero compassion. Instead of supporting her niece, she questioned why she would visit him more than once, as if familial care had an expiration date.
- When her **ex-sister-in-law, my ex wife Roslyn died,** she callously remarked, *"We're going to dance on her grave."* This deeply hurt her grandson, who was close to Roslyn.
- Despite playing the **role of a loving sister,** she constantly finds ways to diminish and insult me, her younger sibling's success, claiming it's "unfair" because she *did everything right.*

She uses family when it benefits her but turns on them when it threatens her ego. **Her loyalty is a performance, not a principle.**

3. The Victim Complex vs. The Saboteur

She **loves to play the victim,** painting herself as the one who has been wronged by life, relationships, and even her own family. Yet, **she is the common denominator in her failures** and frequently sabotages others.

- She **blames others** for her inability to maintain relationships, despite a **clear pattern of driving people away** with her controlling nature and lack of accountability.
- She spent years telling people she **was waiting for her parents to die before getting married** so they wouldn't ruin her wedding. This illustrates a deep **sense of entitlement** and a **need to control** situations before they even happen.
- She **berates her sibling for his past mistakes** while simultaneously **criticizing his success**, proving she **can't stand being outshined.**

She is **only a victim when it benefits her narrative; otherwise, she is the one pulling the strings.**

4. The "Successful Overachiever" Image vs. The Reality

She prides herself on being an **overachiever**—the one who took the hardest classes, did extra work, and followed all the "right" steps. But **if she was truly successful, she wouldn't need to keep proving it.**

- She **hasn't built lasting stability** despite her academic achievements. She brags about her education but **filed for bankruptcy** after her ex-boyfriend abandoned her and left her with his debts.
- She **joined a fetish website** at the urging of a now-deceased boyfriend and even **became the moderator of a controversial group.** This is completely at odds with her

holier-than-thou, morally superior persona and displayed naked pictures of herself

- She constantly **boasts about her teaching career** as if it makes her a saint, yet **she lacks emotional intelligence and integrity,** qualities essential for a true educator.

Her life is a **house of cards** built on exaggerations and selective storytelling.

5. The Gossip Queen Who Can't Keep a Secret

My sister portrays herself as **trustworthy and well-liked**, yet she is notorious for **spilling secrets and spreading gossip.**

- She **can't hold onto information** without using it as social currency, whether it's **family drama, financial struggles, or personal failures.**
- She **weaponizes the past** to berate others, bringing up old stories to make herself look better while putting others down.
- She **twists narratives** to paint herself in a favorable light, ensuring **she's always the hero or the victim—but never the villain.**

Her **two-faced nature is most evident in her gossiping**—she'll pretend to be a confidante, only to use that trust against you later.

Conclusion: Two-Faced Nature in Action

My Sister is the textbook definition of **a two-faced person**— someone who carefully constructs an image of kindness, success, and integrity while actively engaging in behavior that contradicts those claims.

- **She preaches loyalty but betrays family.**
- **She plays the victim while manipulating others.**

- **She brags about success while struggling to keep her life together.**
- **She claims to be kind while gossiping and tearing people down.**

At the end of the day, her **biggest enemy is herself,** with desperate need to be superior forcing her into **constant contradiction, deception, and self-sabotage.** Her two-faced nature is not just a personality flaw; it's a survival mechanism designed to protect a fragile ego that can't handle the reality of her own failures.

My Ex Wife: A Study of Two-Faced Treachery

The Mask She Wore

To the outside world, Roslyn played the role of a *devoted daughter*, a *social butterfly*, and a *woman scorned* who, according to her own twisted narrative, had escaped the clutches of an abusive husband. She spun a web of lies so convincingly that even those closest to her struggled to separate fact from fiction.

- **The Dutiful Daughter** – She pretended to be caring for her mother, Janet, while secretly raiding her prescription medications for her own habit.
- **The Social Charmer** – A constant presence at bars, she presented herself as a fun-loving, free-spirited woman, all while masking the destruction she left behind.
- **The Victim** – Rather than admitting her own failures, she fabricated abuse allegations, playing the fragile woman in distress to manipulate the legal system.

The Reality Behind the Lies

Behind closed doors, the truth was far uglier. Roslyn wasn't just manipulative—she was ruthless in her pursuit of self-interest, no matter the cost to those who once loved her.

- **The Addict** – Popping pills like candy, she was deep into substance abuse, prioritizing her next high over her responsibilities as a wife and mother.
- **The Abandoner** – She walked out on her husband and eight-year-old daughter, choosing a life of drinking and speed-fueled chaos over the stability of her own family.
- **The Liar** – False abuse accusations, a bogus restraining order, and a campaign of slander were all part of her arsenal. When challenged, she doubled down instead of admitting the truth.

The Ultimate Betrayal

Not satisfied with simply destroying her own family, she tried to take it one step further.

- **Attempted Custody Coup** – She and her boyfriend schemed to steal custody of our grandson, JoJo, from his father—then had the audacity to blame the entire plan on me when it failed.
- **A Snake in the Courtroom** – Despite abandoning her own daughter, she still found the time to write a letter to the federal judge sentencing me, throwing me under the bus with false claims of undiscovered crimes and urging the court to impose the harshest sentence possible.

Final Verdict

Roslyn was the definition of a **two-faced, backstabbing opportunist**— a woman who weaponized lies, addiction, and manipulation to escape responsibility while burning down everyone around her. Whether as a mother, a wife, or a grandmother, she left only chaos in her wake, ensuring that no one ever walked away from her unscathed.

Lesson Learned

Some people aren't just toxic—they're a full-scale hazard zone. Roslyn wasn't a mistake; she was a warning sign in human form.

Two-Faced Business Partners

Throughout my life, I've had my fair share of business partners. Some were solid, stand-up people—the kind you could count on in a pinch. Others? They were jealous, backstabbing, two-faced opportunists who couldn't stomach my success after I walked out of prison and built something for myself.

They know who they are. And if they're reading this, they're probably wondering how I know about the shit they said behind my back. Well, let's just say—nothing stays hidden forever.

The Radio Show Snake

There was one guy in particular—a **leech in a microphone**—who I did a radio show with for years. To my face, he played the role of the loyal co-host, the partner-in-crime (metaphorically speaking, of course). But behind my back? Different story.

- **The Envious Wannabe** – He wanted what I had but lacked the guts or the brains to build it himself. So he did the next best thing—latched onto my success like a parasite while badmouthing me to anyone who'd listen.
- **The Backdoor Businessman** – Used the platform we built together to springboard his own business, riding my wave while quietly undermining me at every opportunity.
- **The Classic Betrayal** – Once he got what he wanted, he conveniently forgot all about loyalty, proving that some people are only in your corner when it benefits them.

Gary Paro: The Setup Artist

Then there was **Gary Paro**, a former business partner and an old partner-in-crime. I had no idea at the time, but while we were out hustling, Gary had his own skeletons rattling in the closet— specifically, **mail fraud charges** he conveniently forgot to mention.

- **The Desperate Informant** – When the feds came knocking, Gary decided he wasn't going down alone. Instead of facing the music like a man, he cooked up an elaborate setup— one that would put me directly in the crosshairs of the DEA.
- **The Cancer Con Job** – He spun a sob story about his fiancée having cancer, playing on my sense of loyalty. Said he needed money for her treatment and that if I could find narcotics, he had a buyer willing to pay a large commission. Turns out, that "buyer" was the **fucking DEA**.
- **The Ultimate Snake Move** – He wasn't just cooperating— he was manufacturing a crime, leading me straight into a sting operation just to shave time off his own sentence.

The Common Thread

What ties these two-faced bastards together? **Jealousy. Fear. Weakness.**

- Some **resented my success** and wanted to tear me down when they realized they couldn't replicate it.
- Some **needed a scapegoat** for their own failures and had no problem serving me up to save their own skin.
- Some **wanted to use me**, taking what they could before discarding me like yesterday's trash.

Lesson Learned

I don't dwell on the betrayals, but I sure as hell don't forget them. If there's one thing I've learned, it's this: **never underestimate how low people will sink when they feel small in your shadow.**

Final Words: Stay Sharp, Stay Unbreakable

If you've made it this far, congratulations—you're no longer an easy target. You've got the tools, the strategies, and the mindset to identify, expose, and dismantle the manipulative bastards who thrive on deception. You've learned how to recognize the warning signs, outmaneuver their bullshit, and cut them off before they can do any real damage.

But let's be clear: the world isn't going to suddenly become a kinder, more honest place just because you're better at spotting its snakes. Two-faced people will always exist—at work, in your social circles, in your own goddamn family. The difference now? **They won't stand a chance against you.**

Here's the final lesson: **Trust is a privilege, not a right.** Too many people hand it out like candy, only to be blindsided when it blows up in their face. You? You're not that person anymore. You know better.

You don't owe explanations, second chances, or the benefit of the doubt to anyone who's shown you their true colors. The moment someone tries to twist reality, rewrite history, or undermine you in the shadows, you cut them off at the knees—no hesitation, no guilt.

This book wasn't about making you paranoid. It was about making you **aware**. About sharpening your instincts so you don't just **survive** the two-faced game—you **win** it.

So go forward, stay sharp, and never let these manipulative pieces of shit steal another second of your peace.

—Larry Levine

www.ingramcontent.com/pod-product-compliance
Lightning Source LLC
Chambersburg PA
CBHW070016100426
42740CB00013B/2512